S P

S £30.00
9C

INTERNATIONAL DEBT AND CENTRAL BANKING IN THE 1980s

STUDIES IN BANKING AND INTERNATIONAL FINANCE

Published by Macmillan in association with the Centre for Banking and International Finance, The City University, London

General Editor: Geoffrey E. Wood

Roy A. Batchelor and Geoffrey E. Wood (*editors*)
EXCHANGE RATE POLICY

Forrest Capie and Geoffrey E. Wood (*editors*)
FINANCIAL CRISES AND THE WORLD BANKING SYSTEM

Brian Griffiths and Geoffrey E. Wood (*editors*)
MONETARY TARGETS
MONETARISM IN THE UNITED KINGDOM

Donald R. Hodgman and Geoffrey E. Wood (*editors*)
MONETARY AND EXCHANGE RATE POLICY

Zannis Res and Sima Motamen (*editors*)
INTERNATIONAL DEBT AND CENTRAL BANKING IN THE 1980s

International Debt and Central Banking in the 1980s

Edited by
Zannis Res and Sima Motamen

in association with the
CENTRE FOR BANKING AND INTERNATIONAL FINANCE
THE CITY UNIVERSITY
LONDON

**MACMILLAN
PRESS**

First published 1987

Published by
THE MACMILLAN PRESS LTD
Houndmills, Basingstoke, Hampshire RG21 2XS
and London
Companies and representatives
throughout the world

Printed in Hong Kong

British Library Cataloguing in Publication Data
International debt and central banking in
the 1980s. — (Studies in banking and
international finance)
1. Debts, External   2. Banks and
banking, Central
I. Res, Zannis   II. Series
336.3'6   HJ8015
ISBN 0-333-40218-9

Contents

Foreword   vii

Notes on the Contributors   viii

1   Introduction   1
    Zannis Res and Sima Motamen

PART I   THE 1983 CONFERENCE

2   Notes on the Problem of International Debt   21
    Allan H. Meltzer

3   A Central Banker's View about the International Debt
    Crisis   31
    Brian Quinn

4   The Lessons of the Crisis: a Developing Country View   41
    Carlos Geraldo Langoni

5   The International Debt Crisis – A Growth-oriented
    Management Approach   57
    Paulo Pereira Lira

6   The International Debt Threat: a Way to Avoid a
    Crash   69
    Minos Zombanakis

PART II   THE 1984 CONFERENCE

7   Properties of Monetary Systems   83
    Allan H. Meltzer

    Comment on 'Properties of Monetary Systems'   105
    Geoffrey E. Wood

8   The Costs and Benefits of International Banking   113
    Shelagh A. Heffernan

    Comment on 'The Costs and Benefits of International
    Banking'   136
    D. Fitzgerald

    Reply to Comments by D. Fitzgerald   139
    Shelagh A. Heffernan

9   International Lenders of Last Resort: Are Changes
    Required?   141
    Stephany Griffith-Jones and Michael Lipton

    Comment on 'International Lenders of Last Resort:
    Are Changes Required?'   164
    K. Phylaktis

10 The Theory of Last Resort Lending   167
    Michael Beenstock

    Comment on 'The Theory of Last Resort Lending'   184
    Lionel D. Price

11 Country Risk: A Model for Predicting Debt Servicing
    Problems in Developing Countries   187
    R. J. Taffler and B. Abassi

    Comment on 'Country Risk: A Model for Predicting
    Debt Servicing Problems in Developing Countries'   224
    Roy Batchelor

Index   229

Foreword

In the late 1970s and early 1980s, the world became increasingly aware of the mounting problems of international debt, and the ability of the debtor countries to repay.

This book is concerned with the international debt crisis and its solutions, particularly the role of Central Banks. The collection of papers, presented in two consecutive conferences, includes the views of central bankers, Euromarket leaders and economists spread around the globe from Europe to South America. Conflicts of interest between North and South are clearly identified and various authors propose policies which attempt to resolve such conflicts. There is no unanimity of views, only a genuine endeavour to avoid the collapse of the international financial system and learn from the mistakes of the past.

Part I of the book has a sense of urgency focusing on how central bankers can avert a financial crash. Part II is more reflective, analytical and with a longer view in questioning the merits of monetary systems and central banking; contrast A. Meltzer's contribution in each part, Langoni's concern about debt repayments and Beenstock's views on last resort lending. Such multiplicity of views presented in this volume will, we hope, contribute to a deeper understanding of the problems of international debt and the corresponding solutions.

Phyllis Brand, Debbie Gill and Pat Baker provided valuable secretarial assistance in organising the conference and preparing the manuscript.

ZANNIS RES
SIMA MOTAMEN

Notes on the Contributors

B. Abassi is the Director of Planning and Projects at the National Enterprise for Production of Passenger Cars in Algeria. He was previously the Director of Planning at the Ministry of Heavy Industry.

Roy Batchelor is Director of Research, Centre for Banking and International Finance, The City University Business School.

Professor Michael Beenstock is Esmée Fairbairn Professor of Finance and Investment, The City University Business School.

Professor D. Fitzgerald is Visiting Professor, The City University Business School.

Dr Stephany Griffiths-Jones is Lecturer in the Institute of Development Studies, University of Sussex.

Dr Shelagh A. Heffernan is Lecturer in Economics, The City University Business School.

Professor Carlos Geraldo Langoni was formerly Governor of the Central Bank of Brazil.

Michael Lipton is a Professorial Fellow at the Institute of Development Studies, University of Sussex.

Professor Paulo Pereira Lira was formerly Governor of the Central Bank of Brazil.

Professor Allan H. Meltzer teaches at Carnegie-Mellon University, Pittsburgh, USA.

K. Phylaktis is Director of Undergraduate Studies, Centre for Banking and International Finance, The City University Business School.

Lionel D. Price is Adviser, International Division, Bank of England.

Brian Quinn is Assistant Director, Bank of England.

Zannis Res is Director, Centre for Banking and International Finance, The City University Business School.

Dr R. J. Taffler is Dearden Farrow Professor of Accounting and Financial Analysis, The City University Business School.

Professor Geoffrey E. Wood teaches at the Centre for Banking and International Finance, The City University Business School.

Minos Zombanakis is Chairman, CIGNA International Holdings.

1 Introduction

Zannis Res and Sima Motamen

This volume collects the proceedings of two conferences held at The City University, in October 1983 and May 1984. Both conferences were concerned with international debt problems. The first conference examined the current problems, and solutions proposed for them, while the second was more analytical, examining the workings of the international monetary system and reflecting on how difficulties could be avoided in the future. This introduction summarises the main points of the chapters and sets out some general conclusions.

THE 1983 CONFERENCE

The 1983 conference was opened by Allan Meltzer, who disputed the view that the oil price increases of the 1970s were the main source of the debt problems of developing countries. He points out that while the oil price shock of the 1970s might have had something to do with the international debt crisis of the late 1970s and early 1980s, it would be misleading to regard the oil price shock as the sole source of the debt problem. He contrasts effects on countries such as Brazil, an oil importer, and Mexico, an oil exporter. Mexico was anticipating a rise in oil prices, perhaps to $80–$100 per barrel, and on that basis devoted a large share of its borrowed capital to investment in oil projects. Consequently, when the oil price fell, Mexico found itself unable to pay its debts. On the other hand, Brazil, which was an oil importer, undertook wasteful investments in nuclear power.

Meltzer highlights the structural differences in the debt problems of various developing countries and points out the drawbacks of the IMF's proposed economic strategies for Latin American countries such as Mexico, Argentina and Brazil. These strategies, which advocate a reduction of imports by each country, ignored the strong trade links between the Latin American countries, and hence ultimately led to an overall reduction of trade between them, with no significant balance of payments gains by any country.

Meltzer also comments on the behaviour and measures adopted by the developed countries and the creditor banks. He points out the uncertainties that such unpredictable and erratic actions bring in the world financial system. As to a solution of the debt problem, he suggests that creditor banks should reduce the book value of their loans to market value. This, he proposes, can be done by an exchange of debt for equity. Thus the creditors and debtors share the loss, the claims become marketable and the creditors acquire an interest in the efficiency of the enterprises in the debtor countries.

Meltzer believes that no single Central Bank need undertake to serve as lender of last resort to the international financial system. Nor, in his view, is an international Central Bank required. Banking panics can be prevented by normal central bank behaviour in domestic banking systems – acting as lenders of last resort to their own system.

Brian Quinn in Chapter 3 agrees that the starting point of the debt problem was not the oil price shock of 1973. His analysis commences with developments which took place in the financial system during the decade before 1973. In his review of events, he points out that during that decade commercial banks expanded their lending to LDCs quite substantially, because these countries seemed to have good growth prospects. At the same time, LDCs tended to finance their development projects mostly through borrowing from commercial banks. The oil price rise of 1973 substantially worsened the outlook for most developing countries. Nevertheless commercial banks continued to be major providers of funds to these developing countries. The banks were, essentially, recycling the OPEC surpluses to the deficit countries. In the light of information available at the time, this was by and large a sensible policy. But the proportion of short-term borrowing rose rapidly, debt service ratios increased sharply and channels for financing trade were converted to channels for deficit and development financing.

The second oil price rise of 1979–80 brought consequences similar to the first, but this time developed countries adopted policies which were less inflationary. There was less monetary accommodation. The effective exchange rate of the dollar increased sharply; this increased the costs of developing countries' debt service, as a good portion of this debt was dollar denominated, and at interest rates linked to US rates. The reaction of both the borrowing countries and the banks to these changes was slow, but serious tensions started to emerge in the international financial market. Mexico's declaration of a moratorium in August 1982 increased these tensions. Quinn believes that a crisis at that time was averted 'maintly because all the parties involved were prepared to do things which were against instinct' (p. 35), in the sense that banks continued to lend to LDCs, central banks made some commitments and borrowing countries took unpopular measures to adjust domestic programmes.

How can a long-term solution be found? Quinn suggests that it is not very helpful to ask whether the nature of the problem was a 'liquidity problem' or a 'solvency problem', since both of those views are defensible. Instead, he argues one should try to assess the period a country's debt servicing problem will last. In his view for some countries the problem is not transitional; it may persist for some time. He proposes three possible courses of action: (a) to do nothing, (b) to look for a single 'big' solution to all problems and (c) to continue with *ad hoc* management. Quinn assesses each possibility and concludes that the last option, 'continued management on something like the present line for some time to come' seems to be the best. He believes that given time the market mechanism, along with the IMF programmes and official support, can cope with the problems.

Langoni (Chapter 4) analyses the underlying causes of the Brazilian financial difficulties. He points out that when the initial signs of crisis became apparent neither the governments and central banks of developing countries nor of industrialised countries realised the extent of the crisis. They were all unprepared to take action and were hoping that market interest rates would soon fall, and thus alleviate the difficulties. Langoni explains how Brazilian ability to borrow in the markets was reduced; a circumstance which was not directly a consequence of Brazil's own financial behaviour but a spillover from the actions of others. To cope with these unexpected interruptions Brazil adopted some adjustment policies. Nevertheless, the country lost about US $2 billion of trade related lines of credit.

Langoni asserts that the main lesson is that the market mechanism did not lead to an optimum solution. He claims that overborrowing by the developing countries is necessarily associated with overlending by banks. There are faults on both sides. He believes that a self-correcting mechanism which affects the expected rate of return was not sufficient to produce the gradual slow-down in the supply of resources which would signal the need for internal adjustments in the borrowing countries.

In his view, more action by central banks and their governments is required for a gradual re-establishment of the working of the market-place. He considers the new role of IMF in this area as evidence of the need for continued action to keep the adjustment process going. Langoni states that despite this the burden of adjustment has fallen disproportionally upon the developing countries, whereas the international banks as a whole were not severely affected.

He does not believe the LDCs to be faultless. He attributes some of the difficulties of the developing countries to their slow reactions to economic change, and to their problems with establishing a suitable political process to adjust social aspirations to availability of resources. In this respect he cites examples of the misuse of resources and of wasteful investments.

Langoni believes that the industrialised countries are irresponsible in allowing rapid increases in interest rates or movements in exchange rates and by increasing protectionism. He suggests that the best solution to interest rate variability is to devise a mechanism through which the interest rate will be equalised to an agreed upon level of normal or equilibrium long-term rate of interest; a level which is possibly different by only a modest margin from the long-run expected rate of inflation. By this mechanism any higher than expected rates would be financed by the proceeds coming from lower than expected ones.

Further, he argues that while it is important to improve cooperative action between private sources of funds such as domestic sources and commercial banks, and the multilateral sources of funds such as the IMF, intense efforts should be made to substitute private sources of funds for the IMF.

Finally, Langoni stresses what he sees as the urgent need for co-ordinated action by the industrialised countries, as well as international action, to distribute the cost of adjustment more equally among the participants.

A different view of the Brazilian debt problem and a possible solution for it is given by Paulo Pereira Lira in Chapter 5. In his exposition of the background to the Brazilian engagement in external debt, Lira explains that by the late 1960s, Brazil's objective was to accelerate the rate of economic growth over and above what could have been achieved with domestic savings and make the accelerated growth sustainable over time. Such an acceleration of the rate of growth implied that resources had to go into investment. Moreover, the domestic rate of return on investment had to be higher than the international rate of interest. On this basis Brazil adopted a development and financial policy to obtain an inward transfer of resources through the International Borrowing System 'IBS' (a term which he uses to mean borrowing from multinational commercial banks). To make the accelerated growth sustainable over time, Brazil followed three policies: (a) export promotion, (b) spread of amortisation payments to different multinational commercial banks, and (c) pursuit of a policy of building up international reserves well above the IMF recommendation of 3 months imports. Thus Brazil hoped to limit her future borrowings. The above policies led to a rise in the domestic rate of interest well above the international rate of interest. Lira believes that, initially, despite all the difficulties, Brazil managed to keep its external debts in good order and pursued policies to avoid outward transfer of resources. However, after the second oil price shock of 1979 and the changes in the policy stance of the Fed, international interest rates increased sharply and adversely affected Brazil's debt management.

Lira points out some of the policy changes advocated by the IMF, and the drawbacks of the IMF stabilisation programme for developing countries and Brazil in particular. He considers the substantial decrease in the international bank loans to developing countries in the second half of 1982 to have been largely due to Mexico's declaration of a moratorium. He argues that although the IMF's stabilisation programme might have been more in accordance with Mexico's objectives of outward transfer of resources, it was not appropriate for Brazil. Accordingly, he does not consider it appropriate for Brazil to be tied to the 'IBS' and suggests that it might be better if Brazil adopted a partial temporary disengagement from the IBS, for a period of perhaps five years. During that period borrowing relationships and short-term financing facilities related to trade should continue. At the same time Brazil's Treasury should assume responsibility for loan obligations abroad of every borrower in the country. Lira proceeds to give a detailed explanation of the disengagement programme and argues that by pursuing this approach the Brazilian government may carry through its growth programme while controlling inflation.

In brief, Lira argues that the Brazilian debt problems are mainly the consequences of external shocks and mismanagement of the international financial system, rather than domestic misuse of borrowed funds.

Zombanakis (Chapter 6) also gives a brief review of the international events which led to the banking crisis of the 1970s and early 1980s. He explains how in the aftermath of the oil price rise of 1973, the major Western banks expanded loans to developing countries, but within a few years realised their critical situation.

Zombanakis traces the problem back to the roles that can be played by lenders of last resort. He asserts the importance of the IMF and argues that an increase in its quota should be promptly ratified. Also, he underlines the importance of the IMF's role as a mediator between the commercial banks and the borrowing countries, and suggests that the IMF should intervene by giving assistance to the borrowing countries to facilitate long-term adjustments. This assistance should be given through various plans and programmes that enable the countries involved to repay their debts as well as improving their economies. The IMF could then bring in the creditors and propose a realistic rescheduling of the loans to between 11–13 years. The last years of the loan can be guaranteed to be repaid by the IMF, thus signifying that the programme carried the IMF's approval. Such a programme, in Zombanakis's view, would be less restrictive than a short-term rescue, and would give the borrowing country time to adjust its economy to realistic goals over a period of years, in the expectation that as world conditions returned to normal, it will be able to repay its obligations. Arrangements under the agreed programme could be interrupted, if the IMF and the creditors were unhappy with the borrower's progress. Furthermore, in extreme cases, if the borrower failed in its commitments to the IMF programme the guarantees would be revoked. Zombanakis advances additional suggestions for reducing reliance on the Euro-dollar market, and for the terms of re-scheduling loans. Moreover, he puts forward proposals to establish a Guarantee Loan Fund (GLF), which will be administered by the IMF in conjunction with the other programmes, and which involves a group of ten countries.

THE 1984 CONFERENCE

In the first chapter of the 1984 conference, Allan Meltzer assesses the properties of various monetary standards. In this chapter he touches on four issues: (a) a survey of monetary standards, and

Keynes's views on different standards, (b) underlying reasons for government involvement in creation of money, (c) the choice between fixed and flexible exchange rates and (d) some empirical studies of the performance of the US economy under various monetary standards.

Meltzer explains that the difference between various monetary standards arises from the private and social costs and benefits associated with each monetary standard, and uses these criteria as the basis for his analysis. In his view, the principal differences in cost of each monetary arrangement to individuals or societies arise from three sources:

(1) Cost of producing and storing money.
(2) Cost of organising and administering the system.
(3) Cost of uncertainty associated with each standard.

Meltzer argues that there is no monetary system that can provide complete price, interest rate and exchange rate stability. Differences in cost and the distribution of the cost burden depend upon properties of the monetary and economic system and on the nature of shocks and disturbances. Meltzer then proceeds by giving a brief history of various monetary systems and arrangements, beginning with the gold standard.

He underlines a number of factors which led to the departure from the gold standard before the Second World War, and notes Keynes's opposition to the return to the gold standard.

Meltzer then reviews the Bretton Woods system and points out Friedman's opposition to fixed exchange rates and his support for floating exchange rates. He argues that Friedman's preference for floating exchange rates is based on his calculation of the resource cost of a commodity standard for the US, and his belief that floating exchange rates encouraged trade among countries. In Meltzer's view, Friedman neglected the costs arising from uncertainty about the future value of money. Meltzer also observes that a decade of fluctuating exchange rates has not led to countries reducing trade barriers.

Meltzer then turns to the role of government in the supply of money, and to how it affects the distribution of risks and opportunities. He argues that 'the role of government and the distribution of risks and opportunities arises from four choices: the medium of exchange, the standard of value, private or public production of money, and the international standard – fixed or floating exchange rate'. He considers the role of money as a standard of value as the major reason for the government's involvement in the creation of money. Furthermore, he argues that the cost of producing money to serve as a standard of value is less for the government than for the public. In this respect, the importance of the government's power to act as the lender of last resort is emphasised.

In the third section of his chapter, Meltzer discusses fixed and floating exchange rates and draws attention to Keynes's views on this subject. Meltzer argues that the operating characteristics of systems based on fixed or floating exchange rates depend on a number of institutional arrangements, such as the fiscal system, the types of shocks (whether due to demand or supply), the relative frequency and durability of different shocks, and a number of other factors. At the end of this section, Meltzer notes that 'an important difference between monetary arrangements determining the medium of exchange, standard of value, production of money and choice of international regime is the degree to which these arrangements reduce risk towards the minimum level inherent in nature and trade'.

The final section of Meltzer's chapter is devoted to an empirical examination of the differences between standards. Here he considers the behaviour of nominal money, GNP, and velocity, within the framework of the quantity theory identity, across the six policy regimes the US has experienced since 1890. The study shows a distinct decline in variability of nominal and real GNP growth, money growth and velocity growth under the Bretton Woods system. It also shows that the variability of real growth dominated the variability of nominal GNP throughout and that there is a positive correlation between the variability of money growth and that of velocity growth.

Finally, Meltzer concludes that the findings of his empirical study suggest that risk or uncertainty in the growth of real and nominal income 'is more likely to be reduced by arrangements that reduce the variability of money growth than by policies that attempt to offset fluctuations in the demand for money or velocity'. Further-more, contrary to Keynes's views, Meltzer argues that the empirical studies show that 'a monetary rule that held money growth constant would reduce risk below the level observed under any of the standards'.

Geoffrey Wood (Chapter 8), in his comments on Meltzer, argues that though Meltzer is right to say that Keynes opposed the return to gold standard in 1925, he under-emphasises that Keynes's oppo-sition was to the choice of parity rather than the standard itself. In this respect Wood notes some historical evidence of Keynes's view on this issue.

Wood disputes Meltzer's separation of the functions of money as a medium of exchange and as a standard of value. He argues that 'one cannot separate the medium of exchange function from the store of value function'. In Wood's view 'if private collective action introduces a medium of exchange, it can and does introduce a store of value'. Hence, 'separating the two functions can not help to bring in government'. He also rejects Meltzer's view of the role of government as a lender of last resort and argues that private banks can act like a government and produce money that is free of default risk. However, Wood agrees with Meltzer that 'government money emerges because of some externalities or enforcement costs associated with private money'.

The question of whether the establishment of an International Central Bank (ICB) is desirable, is the theme of the paper presented by Shelagh Heffernan (Chapter 8). She argues that the fragility of the present international financial system indicates the need for an International Central Bank. She lists three important functions of a national central bank, namely: (a) the stabilisation of the price level through control of the money supply, (b) minimisation of financial crises and hence the role of the central banks as lenders of last resort and (c) the placement of government debt on the most favourable terms possible. However, she argues that the International Central Bank should not necessarily have the same functions as a country's central bank. In her view an ICB should have as its primary task the maintenance of international financial stability. At a secondary level it could reduce the real resource costs associated with international banking.

Heffernan argues that all the factors which give rise to market fragility are observable in the present state of the international financial system. The intervention of a third party to act as an ICB is important for the maintenance of financial stability and prevention of an international financial crisis. However, an ICB need not act as LLR. Rather its role would be co-ordinating the LLR activities of national central banks.

In analysing the costs and benefits of an ICB, she considers the 'moral hazard' and the incentive to 'free ride' as the two serious drawbacks of ICB. These costs can be minimised by careful monitoring conducted by an ICB. It is argued that the major benefit of an ICB is that it can provide a pool of information for the lenders.

A comment on Heffernan's chapter is presented by D. Fitzgerald. He disputes Heffernan's views about the need for the establishment of an ICB due to 'increasing fragility of the International Financial System'. Fitzgerald argues that all the evidence indicates that 'banks are managing to write off problem loans slowly but surely out of high profit levels'. The case of West German banks as well as Continental Illinois are cited as two pieces of evidence that the central banks of individual countries do protect the major banks from their own follies. Fitzgerald is not convinced that the possibility of contagion is best handled by a lender of last resort in the form of an ICB.

Concerning the question of availability of information, Fitzgerald argues that instead of bringing in an ICB the problem can be solved by an organisation publishing details of variable risk-related insurance premiums that would be charged if an insurance scheme operated.

Finally, Fitzgerald comments on the way an ICB should be operated and finds Heffernan's suggestions in that respect too restrictive and involving too much bureaucracy.

In a reply to Fitzgerald's comments, Heffernan highlights some of the points which she considered were misinterpreted by Fitzgerald. Heffernan stresses that an International Central Bank is not synonymous with an international lender of last resort. Its role is preservation of international financial stability, which is partly accomplished through the co-ordination of the LLR activities of national central banks. Moreover, Heffernan notes that though it is difficult to estimate the extent of financial fragility, it is not correct to deny that the problem does exist. She also disagrees with Fitzgerald's view that the problem will be solved in a few years if bankers refrain from further 'reckless' Third World lending. In this respect she questions the description of reckless lending and argues that the rescheduling agreements merely postpone the threat to financial stability and do not necessarily eliminate it.

Finally, with respect to Fitzgerald's comments about the 'totalitarian' nature of an ICB, Heffernan argues that the ICB's function is mainly preservation of stability through the coordination of national central bank activities.

Chapter 9 urges the desirability of an International Lender of Last Resort (ILLR).

In this chapter by Griffith-Jones and Lipton it is argued that with the expansion and internationalisation of commercial banks, the existence of an appropriate ILLR facility is essential to ensure the stability of the international financial system. Such facilities, together with adequate supervision, can also ensure a growing flow of credit to borrowers. It is argued that the absence of such facilities may hurt the developing countries.

Griffith-Jones and Lipton in their analysis consider that the main task of a national LLR is to maintain the capacity of the banking system to lend and to prevent crises of confidence in the banking system. It is stressed that 'LLR is not a substitute for financial markets, but a necessary condition for their contribution to stable growth'. They then assert that the tasks of an ILLR cannot be carried out by national lenders of last resort. This is due to the possibility that there may exist conflict of interest between the parent banks, subsidiaries, depositors and borrowers of different national origins.

Griffith-Jones and Lipton discuss the insufficiencies of the current ILLR arrangements and highlight the associated uncertainties. In view of these asserted shortcomings, it is argued that an appropriate ILLR which involves better information, sustained counter-cyclical flows and diversification of lending can help in restoring financial stability.

To reduce the uncertainties associated with sovereign debt and spread the risk of default, Griffith-Jones and Lipton propose that banks should seek a greater diversity of customers among LDCs. This attempt, however, should be made by all banks and not an individual bank. In this respect, the ILLRs obligation to offer supervisory pacts and better information may be further strengthened by the ILLR providing collateral, when debt restructuring is required. Such a facility, however, may be provided only as a contingency plan, in which case it would be accompanied by some penal rate. That is to say, whenever a bank needs to call upon the ILLR, 'the ILLR would purchase some or all of the banks claim upon sovereign debt at a substantial discount. This would impose a de facto penal rate and turn large but default claims on now insecure Sovereign debt into a smaller amount of good collateral'. It is argued that, with such plans, private banks deposits and capacity to lend would survive, though the banks would suffer onerous terms for using ILLR facilities. Furthermore, it is argued that the problems of 'free ride' can be avoided if closer supervision reinforces clear-cut ILLR arrangements. In this respect, Griffith-Jones and Lipton stress that such rigorous supervision ought to become acceptable to commercial banks and big international lenders because it would eliminate free riders.

A comment on Griffith-Jones and Lipton is presented by Phylaktis. She disputes the need for an ILLR and questions the underlying assumption of Griffith-Jones and Lipton's argument. She says Griffith-Jones and Lipton's stress on the need for ILLR arises from the assumption that the debt problems of LDCs are due to lack of liquidity, whereas these debt problems are largely due to mismanagement and misallocation of borrowed funds. Moreover, she argues that the same factors which contributed to the failure of the IMF might also lead to the failure of the ILLR arrangements proposed by Griffith-Jones and Lipton.

Further analysis of the role of LLR and the circumstances under which the need for such a body arises are the theme of Chapter 10 by Michael Beenstock. In this chapter, it is argued that in a rational society where information is fully available and insurance and capital markets function efficiently, there is no need for a LLR. It is in an irrational society that 'an external rational agency is required to protect society from itself'. Nevertheless, even in this type of society, if labour and product markets behave in a perfectly competitive manner, the need for a LLR would be redundant. The other circumstances which indicate the case for LLR are certain catastrophes such as wars, or large scale economic destruction.

To explain the relation between information, rational behaviour of the market and stability, Beenstock considers a position where there is full disclosure of information about all companies and banks. Under such conditions, he argues, two types of assessments about stricken banks can be made. First, it might be thought that the problem was simply due to bad luck and the business is essentially sound; or second, the business has no prospects. In the first case the capital market will ensure that the bank will survive and its losses will be absorbed. In the second case, according to a rational decision of the capital market, the bank would go out of business. In neither of the cases, however, is government involvement necessary, since there is full disclosure of information and a rational capital market. These features of the market also ensure that collapse of one bank would not lead to the collapse of the others. Similar considerations apply to the public; full information about the financial position of banks prevents the spread of panic.

If there is inadequate disclosure of information, however, the difficulties of individual banks may lead to the fear that all banks are in trouble. In such circumstances the panic of risk averse investors and depositors is rational and bank runs are induced. Beenstock argues that, 'it is at this point that the LLR issue is raised, though it might be enough if the authorities insist on adequate disclosure of information'.

These arguments are then stated formally and the effect of one bank's default on confidence in the other banks is analysed.

Beenstock then proceeds to analyse the role of deposit insurance and argues that 'deposit insurance will make the system more robust'. In other words, in the absence of full information, deposit insurance will stabilise the system; hence the need for LLR disappears. However, a run on the banking system as a whole, as distinct from on an individual bank, is an uninsurable risk. Therefore it is argued that, in such a case government can be the only conceivable underwriter, since it can print money to satisfy the demand for cash, and hence act as a LLR. Beenstock stresses the point that Bagehot's argument about the need for a LLR is based on the assumption of incompleteness of information, inefficient capital market and irrational behaviour of society.

Beenstock then discusses various theories which attempt to explain the underlying causes of panic and the need for LLR. One of the well known theories of bank panic is that of Minsky. According to his thesis, there are several factors and stages which lead to bank panic and bankruptcy. These stages may begin by:

(a) favourable exogenous shock which results in a boom,
(b) subsequent expansion of money supply and credit extension,
(c) onset of a state of euphoria which encourages some bankers to engage in Ponzi finance (by which is meant 'payment commitments exceeding anticipated cash receipts for all periods except some terminal period'),
(d) a period of swindle and fraud caused by a desperation to keep the period of euphoria continuing and finally,
(e) a stage of revulsion during which banks go bankrupt.

On this basis Minsky suggest the need for LLR as a means to prevent revulsion.

Beenstock disputes Minsky's thesis as not being able to explain why bankers, in the first place, pursue policies that they know will lead to disaster, and why it should be assumed that every entrepreneur is engaged in Ponzi finance. The other theory which is referred to is catastrophe theory, and its application to bank runs, as presented as a model by Ho and Saunders (1980). Such models have the property that in most situations, the system will adjust smoothly in response to shocks, but in some circumstances a small change in one variable can lead to a large and irreversible collapse in the system. Beenstock rejects this as a description of the banking system and argues that the theories are mostly based on irrational assumptions about human behaviour and do not provide sufficient insights into the cause of bank runs and a theoretical argument for the need for LLR. Beenstock, however, agrees with Batchelor's (1983) explanation of bank runs, which is based on the central assumption that 'depositors do not have full information about individual banks'. Under these conditions, if one bank gets into difficulty, depositors would think that other banks may be affected by similar problems. This lack of information generates the run and creates the need for LLR.

Beenstock argues that in the case of a market failure due to unavailability of information, the absence of LLR would entail a drastic fall in the quantity of money. With perfectly flexible wages and prices, however, the aggregate price level would fall in proportion with the quantity of money and leave the quantity of money unchanged. In such circumstances the real cost to the society would be the erosion of trust in each other, but since there would be no deflation, there would be no need for LLR. On the other hand, in case of sticky wages and prices, such bank failures would be deflationary. The intervention of the authorities acting as a LLR would then be required to increase the supply of cash and keep the real quantity of money unchanged. The first best solution, he argues, is to increase price flexibility.

In brief, he concludes that disclosure of all necessary information, as well as efficient functioning of the capital market remove the need for a LLR. An LLR is a second best solution. (Beenstock also argues that an alternative to LLR is to set up a 'lifeboat' operation in which weak banks are supported by strong banks.)

Price, in his comments to Beenstock's chapter, notes that 'in an uncertain world, we cannot be sure that competitive markets will deliver a Pareto-optimum unless such markets exist in each and every one of Arrow–Debreu's state contingent commodities'. Price argues that, even if banks disclose information on their lending, there remains considerable uncertainty about the net worth of a bank at any moment. It is argued that as long as uncertainty about the future remains, even with information about the present, there is a possibility of bankruptcy and a subsequent run. In such instances, the existence of a LLR can avert the possibility of a run.

In the next chapter, Taffler and Abbassi present an econometric model to analyse country risk and to forecast sovereign debt default. The objective of the chapter is to identify in advance those countries which might fail to meet their external debt obligations. These debts are divided into two categories: sovereign debt, and non-publicly guaranteed private external debt.

The development of an operational discriminant model of country risk is explained. Next, the *ex-ante* predictive ability of the function over the period 1979–83 inclusive is examined and finally, a comparison is made between the results of the model and those provided by a consensus view of bankers' judgements as measured by *The Institutional Investor*.

The chapter comments on the four systems of country risk appraisal used by the US banks and notes the shortcomings of each method. Moreover, it assesses the two approaches advocated by the two international banking magazines, *Euromoney* and *The Institutional Investor*.

The model of debt servicing capacity is derived from fitting a discriminant function to data from two populations. Two groups were formed on the basis of whether a given country for a particular year was reported as having been obliged to seek a rescheduling of part or all its debt on a bilateral or multilateral basis. The function derived consists of four variables, two measuring debt servicing capacity directly and two others which are indicators of monetary policy.

The performance of the model was evaluated across the five year period 1979/83, which is subsequent to the development of the early warning model. Results showed that 69 per cent of the 73 rescheduling cases in this period were correctly anticipated. The model appeared quite robust to the major structural changes in the economic environment since it was developed.

The model tests the predictive ability of the approach used by *The Institutional Investor* credit rating and finds it inadequate, with high prediction errors.

Roy Batchelor in his comment to the Taffler–Abbassi chapter praises their work highly. However, Batchelor points out a shortcoming of discriminant analysis; namely, discriminant analysis is not able to identify the best alternative solution to rescheduling. Batchelor also notes that it would be useful to develop separate discriminant functions for sub-groups of the large set of economies considered. Moreover he argues that, 'although the list of variables considered in the initial factor analysis is large, it none the less covers only half of the rescheduling story'.

Finally, Batchelor comments on the interpretation of discriminant analysis. He observes that discriminant analysis at best attaches a measure of 'risk' to each actual and potential borrowing country. However, these measures reflect only the risk characteristics of the individual country which is not enough from the point of view of the practical bankers. The important consideration for the lenders is the extent to which the risk is diversifiable.

OVERVIEW

In concluding this introduction, the main issues in the chapters can be summarised as follows.

The discussions in the first conference revealed that there was a more or less common view that the oil price rise of 1973 was not the starting point of a crisis. Nor were the borrowing developing countries the only parties responsible for the problems of international debt. The erratic behaviour of the developed countries in terms of sharp rises in the interest rates, rapid fluctuations of exchange rates and increased protectionism, also played an important role. Furthermore, attention was drawn to the drawbacks of some of the IMF programmes for developing countries. As for the solution, there was a divergence of views – some believed that the market mechanism along with the IMF programmes and official support could eventually avert any crisis, whereas some others found the market mechanism unable to cope with the problem and called for some more direct action by the central banks to help the market back to its place.

Overall there was a general recognition that any course of action should be accompanied by some supportive programmes of the IMF.

In the second conference, which took a more theoretical approach to the question of bank panics and bank runs, the differences of views were more acute. Some of the participants stressed the need for the establishment of an International Central Bank (ICB) and an International Lender of Last Resort (ILLR) to stabilise the international financial system and avert the banking crisis. Others, however, rejected the need for such bodies. They argued that the system is ultimately capable of returning to stability. Nevertheless, adoption of some measures by individual countries, to reduce risk and increase information, can be helpful.

The events which followed the second conference clearly revealed that though the international debt problem is not entirely eliminated, it no longer poses a threat of total collapse of the system. Indeed, the timely actions on the part of the banking system of each lending country, have managed to isolate individual bank failures from the international banking system, and hence avert panic and crisis. Thus, the system has managed to continue its operation without the establishment of an ICB or ILLR.

References

BATCHELOR, R., 'The Avoidance of Catastrophe: Two Nineteenth Century Banking Crises', City University Business School, 1983.
HO, T. and A. SAUNDERS, 'A Catastrophe Model of Bank Failure', *Journal of Finance*, December 1980.

Part I
The 1983 Conference

2 Notes on the Problem of International Debt

Allan H. Meltzer

A typical oration on the debt problem usually starts by outlining its alleged causes. Pride of place is almost certain to be given to the oil shocks of the 1970s. These produced an increased cost of imports, for many countries, and a simultaneous increase in the volume of financial assets owned by the oil exporters. Many of these assets were held as short-term deposits at Euromarket banks. The banks bid for these deposits in the open market to finance loans to many countries including the Latin American and Eastern European countries that stand high on everyone's list of large debtors.

This explanation is not entirely wrong, but it is far from correct. The principal debtors include Mexico, an oil exporter, Argentina, a country close to energy self-sufficiency, and Brazil, a large importer of oil. The problem debtors also include several countries of Eastern Europe, notably Poland, Romania and Yugoslavia. One is an oil producing country, another a large producer of coal. No one, I believe, would try to explain the economic problems of these countries as a result of the oil shocks or the energy problems of the 1970s.

The converse is no less true. Many developing countries, including some with the best records of growth, have no problems with debt or debt service. The list of countries that pay their debt is much longer than the list of problem debtors. It includes Malaysia, Singapore, Taiwan, Thailand and many others. For non-OPEC developing countries as a group, estimated debt service is about 20 per cent of exports and not very different from the 1973 to 1979 average of 16 per cent.[1]

The difference in experience reflects mainly two factors. One is the way different countries manage resources and use domestic saving and capital imports. The other is the way in which the world community, orchestrated by the International Monetary Fund and the central banks of the creditor countries, responded to the debt problem in 1982 and 1983.

MISTAKES AND MISMANAGEMENT

It is not by accident or chance that major debt problems are in Latin America. For decades the United Nations Economic Commission for Latin America, ECLA, urged these countries to restrict imports by using tariffs and quotas of various kinds, to substitute domestic production for imports, and to promote exports of manufactured goods. These policies encourage inefficient production and penalise the use of low cost substitutes. They encourage the misuse of resources and waste. When adversity occurs, the least efficient producers have greatest difficulty adjusting and surviving. The rise in oil prices was the shock for Brazil, the fall in oil prices the shock for Mexico, political instability and gross mismanagement the shock for Argentina, the surge in interest rates a shock for all of them, but for other countries as well. The distinguishing feature is not what happened in the world, important as that was, it is what caused these particular countries to be so damaged.

In the recent period of high real interest rates and world recession, the developing countries of Asia have moved ahead, while many of the countries of Latin America have fallen behind. The ECLA programme encouraged inefficient production and, since decisions were shifted to a state bureaucracy, it encouraged state planning of investment and production. Considerably more than 50 per cent of the productive assets in Brazil and Mexico are in enterprises owned or directed by government, quasi-government or military bureaucrats. More damaging still is the concentration of planning and decision-making power in a state bureaucracy with power to regulate prices, subsidise production, control the exchange rate and, in these and other ways, distort the use of resources and promote inefficiency.

Imagine the waste of capital that occurs when loans to farmers are made at nominal rates of interest of 15 to 20 per cent while inflation ranges from 40 to 80 per cent or more. Add the waste from investment in nuclear power or the production of gasohol to reduce energy imports. Throw in low interest loans to encourage the construction of apartments for the managerial and salaried classes. These are only a few of the more obvious types of waste in Brazil in the 1970s that continued in the 1980s.

A typical discussion of the debt problem dramatises the problem by comparing the amount of debt outstanding to current GNP. This measure is virtually meaningless. It says next to nothing about a country's financial position or its ability to pay.

A comparison of Argentina and Korea illustrates the reason. In both countries, debt had about the same relation to GNP in 1980. Argentina had lower debt service – payments of current interest and repayments of principal – as a percentage of GNP. Korea used its debt mainly to finance investment in productive capital. These investments, if managed effectively, produce a stream of income and exports that pays the interest and the principal. GNP grows, and the ratio of debt to GNP falls because the country is wealthier and can repay outstanding debts. A large part of Argentina's debt financed capital flight by private individuals who protected themselves against political instability, inflation, and outrageous economic policies.

Mexico incurred a substantial part of its debt to finance investment in oil wells and related projects. Many of these investments were undertaken at a time when many alleged experts predicted that oil prices would reach $80 to $100 a barrel by the end of this decade. Instead, prices fell, and Mexico's investments declined in value.

Mistakes and mismanagement made the problem worse. The Mexican economy is centralised and inefficient. Many of the investment and production decisions are planned by the bureaucrats in Mexico City who control the economy and the government enterprises. The Mexican government chose to share its anticipated wealth before it was earned. Transfers and social benefits increased to distribute the oil profits to the voters. The promises remained after the oil revenues declined. We know from our own experience how difficult it is to reduce social benefits after they are promised. The benefits must be reduced to lower costs and shift income from personal consumption and imports to interest payments and debt service.

These are not intended to be complete accounts of the prospects or problems of Korea, Brazil, Argentina and Mexico. The short histories point out that ability to pay depends much more on the productivity of the economy and its efficiency and much less on the amount of debt relative to GNP or exports. Where economic mismanagement is the norm, output and productivity rise slowly or not at all. It is difficult to service the debt without reducing incomes. The same debt is less burdensome where resources are used productively and the debt is serviced from the earnings that it helped to produce.

Mismanagement is not confined to local bureaucracies. The policies of the International Monetary Fund spread the debt problem from one country to another by imposing rules of adjustment that make little sense when applied to many countries.

The Fund encourages countries to contract imports and expand exports while at the same time requiring lower inflation as a condition of obtaining loans. The first effect of anti-inflationary policy is on output, so output and imports fall in response to these policies.

One country's imports are someone else's exports. In the case of Argentina, Brazil and Mexico, linkage is extensive. Much of the burden of reduced imports by Mexico and Argentina, required by the IMF adjustment programme, fell on Brazil. Brazil's exports fell when Argentina and Mexico restricted imports. Brazil's ability to service its debt moved from doubtful to impossible.

The Fund required Brazil to reduce spending and imports, and expand exports. The combined effect of contraction in Mexico, Argentina and Brazil is a substantial reduction in the volume of trade. Since the three economies are related, they are harmed by each other's policies, and still other countries are harmed as well. It is not surprising to learn that many other countries in Latin America, and elsewhere, have lost the markets for their exports and are required to borrow from the Fund. Austerity is imposed, and world output and exports shrink. In 1982, twenty countries renegotiated their debts.

The Fund policy may serve a useful purpose when applied to one country at a time. It makes little sense to apply the policy multilaterally. The Fund's policy makes the problem worse by contracting world output. Few countries are immune or unharmed when contractive policies are applied simultaneously by many countries. The burden of debt service is raised by these policies. And the problem is made worse by the restrictive trade practices and rising protectionism of the developed, creditor countries.

OTHER WAYS TO MAKE THE PROBLEM WORSE

The United States, Canada, Germany, France and other developed countries make the problem worse by financing large budget deficits in the world capital markets and using the proceeds to maintain consumption and transfer payments. While they preach austerity abroad, these countries practice redistribution and promote consumption spending at home. And they add to the problem by following unstable monetary policies that increase uncertainty and sustain high interest rates.

The leading banks in the United States add to the burden by practising a type of economic flim flam that has many aspects of a Ponzi scheme. When debtors cannot pay the interest on their outstanding debts, the creditor banks, acting as a group, extend the maturity of the debt and lend more money. The debtors pay a large fee, at times hundreds of millions of dollars, to get the debt extension and more time. A large part of the proceeds of the new loan is used to pay the banks fees and the interest on the old loan. Often the entire proceeds are spent this way.[2]

The banks record the fees and interest payments as current income, but they receive in payment mainly the money which they and the International Monetary Fund have advanced. That is why the outstanding debt increases and why the creditors are so eager to increase the International Monetary Fund quotas. Without more lending by the Fund, the creditor banks would get back about what they advance in new loans.

Any merit in this scheme results from postponing the problem by extending the maturity of the debt. Delay and postponement can help, if the time is used to develop a long-term plan. Nothing of the kind has occurred or is in prospect. The debts get larger, not smaller. The payments for interest and debt service can decline only if the banks are willing to extend the maturity of the debt far enough into the future or if interest rates fall.

The policy of the Fund and the creditor countries is a policy of hope and fear. The hope is that eventually commodity prices will rise and that interest rates will decline. These is no sound basis for this hope. Commodity prices often rise in periods of expansion, but interest rates typically rise also. The excessive money growth maintained for the past year by the major creditor countries, other than Japan, contributes to higher commodity prices and interest rates. The debtors will receive more for their exports but pay more interest on their loans. There is no reason to expect a net gain to the debtors, although a gain may occur. That is the hope of the bankers.

Fear takes many forms. Will Mexico continue its austerity programme? Will Brazil carry out its agreements and reduce its consumption? Will Argentina ever achieve enough economic and political stability to be able to pay the interest on its outstanding debt? Will Poland continue as it is? Is there some reason to believe that the Polish or Argentine debts will ever be worth the amounts that the banks show on their books? Will the debtors form a cartel and default? Will the world financial system collapse?

These recurring fears show how small is the progress and how great is the uncertainty. Continued uncertainty depresses long-term investment and discourages lending and borrowing to finance productive capital. Nothing is gained by postponing the problem unless the time is used to reduce uncertainty. Much is lost by continuing the current policy which forces many countries to contract trade simultaneously.

SOLVING THE PROBLEM

A solution to the debt problem starts by recognising why the problem persists. There are two reasons. One reflects the behaviour of the creditors who have strong incentives to carry most of the debt on their balance sheets at face value. The other is the nature of the debt, much of it so-called sovereign debt guaranteed by governments. No one knows what these guarantees mean or what they are worth. The governments have promised to pay foreign exchange which they do not have and cannot obtain except by exporting more than they import.

The banks' loans are overvalued relative to the amount that they would command if sold in the market-place. But the banks benefit from pretending this is not so. They earn sizeable fees when they renegotiate, and they do not have to report losses to their stock-holders. Of course, the banks do not receive any fees except as they and others lend additional amounts to pay the fees, but they are able to report paper profits while they wait for an IMF bail-out and hope for an increase in world growth.

The late Wilson Schmidt, President Reagan's nominee to be Executive Director of the World Bank and a long-time colleague on the Shadow Open Market Committee, often pointed out that debtor countries can always pay their debts. Brazil, Mexico and Argentina have large resources, and the governments of these countries own a large part of the active, producing assets in those countries. Some of the firms are poorly managed, over-regulated or required to overman. Others remain profitable and are capable of selling their output in competitive, world markets.

If the debtors retire part of their guaranteed or sovereign debt by giving an equity claim against valuable assets in exchange, the market value of creditors claims improves. The creditors now have a more valuable asset which can be sold on the market or held as an investment. The details of the exchange are important. The creditor may want a preferred dividend and some restrictions on the firms' practices and activities. The debtor may want the right to repurchase the shares in the future. These, and other details, are part of any negotiation. The details are important because they affect the market value of the claim, but they do not present a problem that is different in kind from those that bankers face in other negotiations with illiquid debtors.

The creditors would be required to reduce the value of the claim to its market value. Their accounts would show the losses that have been incurred, but not recognised, hitherto. Those who wished to sell the claim could do so.

Some believe that the use of equity is impractical. This is far from true. Many countries permit private investment in state-owned enterprises. Brazil is one of these countries. Some of the principal creditor banks, including Chase Manhattan and Citibank, have sizeable equity positions in Brazil and other countries. The Mexico Fund, organised by Merrill Lynch a few years ago, shows that there is a market for equity investment. Yugoslavia and other Eastern European countries have, at times, encouraged equity investment under fixed rules for repatriation. There are many different forms and arrangements, but the principle is well established. The problem is that currently creditors and debtors have no incentive to negotiate a solution of this kind. They hope for a bail-out.

The proposal applies traditional banking procedures. If a homeowner is unable to pay his mortgage debt, the bank, at its option, acquires the house and typically sells it to wipe out its debt. The same principle is used in commercial lending. It seems unfamiliar in foreign lending because we have become so accustomed to the idea of government guarantees that we forget that these guarantees are only as good as a government's promise to encourage efficiency and competition in world markets and to maintain financial stability. The history of the post-war years teaches us that these promises have been devalued as often as currencies. A mistake has been made. It is not important to decide who made the mistake, whether it was an error by the debtors, or excessive zeal by the creditors or an overestimate of world growth and the future price of oil. All of these are in the past. We must work toward a solution that permits an increase in world trade, world growth and efficiency. We must recognise that the current book value of the debts on the banks' balance sheets are well above their current or prospective market value. We must both improve the claims to increase the market value and write down the book value until it equals the market value.[3] The proposed exchange of debt for equity is one of several ways in which this can be done. I believe it is the most advantageous. Debtors and creditors share the losses; the claims become marketable, and the creditors acquire an interest in the efficiency of the enterprises in the debtor countries.

LENDERS OF LAST RESORT

The capital of some creditor banks may be impaired, if a write-off of 20 to 30 per cent is used to bring the debt to market value.[4] The failure of a large bank is not an unprecedented event. The banking history of Britain and the US has many instances.

A bank failure need not cause a banking panic or a run on other banks. Banking panics are preventable, as Walter Bagehot explained a century ago. To *prevent* a panic, Bagehot insisted, the central bank must offer a credible policy *in advance* that assures depositors that the central bank will act and states the terms on which it will act.

Central banks have not followed Bagehot's advice. They have not stated the terms or conditions on which they will lend and the extent of their responsibility for domestic branches of foreign banks or foreign branches of domestic banks. In the past, some central banks have confused the issue by lending to illiquid banks to prevent failure instead of functioning as a lender of last resort.

The principal central banks should announce that they intend to serve as lenders of last resort and the terms and conditions on which they will lend. Bagehot's principle – lend freely at a high (penalty) rate – remains a desirable principle. This principle restricts lending to periods in which banks pay a premium to obtain base money in exchange for specified assets of highest quality and encourages banks to hold such assets.

No single central bank should undertake to serve as lender of last resort to the financial system. An international central bank is not required. Every central bank has the power to prevent a banking panic in its country. The problem is to prevent the panic by pre-commitment and credible action in accordance with the commitment. Central banks have abused their trust on many occasions in the past quarter century. It is important that they do not do so in the critical circumstances that may arise.

Notes

1. Data are from the *Financial Times*, 24 August 1983 citing the National Institute of Economic and Social Research and from the OECD, External Debt of Developing Countries.
2. The Amex Bank in London estimates that between 1978 and 1982, developing countries paid $126 billion in interest for the $140 billion lent to them.
3. How large is the write off? Mexico's 16 per cent bonds traded on the London market at about 80 or more in October 1983. This gives some idea of the market value. My guess is that Brazilian bonds would currently sell at a larger discount. If 20 per cent were converted to equity and all the remainder valued at the market price, the problem for Brazil (and Mexico) would be more manageable.
4. This estimate is a weighted average that recognises that Mexican and Brazilian debt is large relative to Polish or Argentinian debt. See note 3 for valuation of Mexico and a guess about Brazil. The Polish and Argentinian debts would appear to have substantially lower values.

3 A Central Banker's View about the International Debt Crisis

Brian Quinn

My views as a Central Banker are partial, not in the sense of taking sides, since I do not see it as my task to judge who should carry the responsibility for the situation in which we find ourselves, but in the sense that I do not propose to offer a thoroughgoing analysis of all the factors at work. That seems to me to be the job of the economic historian, one of the few occupations where the application of hindsight is not only permitted, but is actually required. I will instead engage in the task of looking ahead and offering a view on the prospects for a way out of our current difficulties – a much easier task since no one can actually prove me wrong.

Before discussing the prospects for solving the debt problem I nevertheless think it is important to look at some elements of the financial system as it developed over the ten or fifteen years before the problem emerged. In the Bank of England's evidence to the Wilson Committee on the secondary banking crisis in the UK, we suggested the crisis arose because a number of contemporary factors came into play simultaneously on a financial system which had undergone structural change and which had developed certain weaknesses. Even in the midst of the current problems I think I see certain similarities; and would like to examine some of them this morning.

Most diagnoses of the current situation start from the first oil price shock of 1973. I do not believe this is the correct starting point, and think some of the roots of the problem go a little deeper. During the decade leading up to 1973 generally solid economic growth in the industrialised countries of around 5 per cent p.a. had provided expanding export markets for the less developed countries, enabling them to enjoy a slightly faster rate of economic growth. Capital resources were also transferred at an increasing rate to the developing world and the financing pattern was fairly stable: the principal source of finance, amounting to 39 per cent of the total on

31

average during the 1960s was direct investment. Official finance and the commercial banks provided the rest in roughly equal shares. Both nominal and real interest rates were generally low by recent standards and the fact that much of the financing was on concessional terms meant that debt service was a relatively light burden for the borrowers.

This pattern of financing was already changing before 1973. Major banks had expanded their international operations in order to provide a full service to their multinational customers, whose number and size had grown significantly in the expansive international climate of the times. The promising growth prospects of the developing countries made them an attractive market into which commercial banks could lend. For their part, the developing countries welcomed the opportunity to borrow from commercial banks as they felt it gave them greater control over the management of their resources and conferred a certain status.

The 1973 oil price brought pressure on the developing countries on two fronts: a sharp rise in the cost of their oil imports and, at the same time, slower growth in their export markets because of reduced growth in the developed economies. The non-oil developing countries did not immediately respond to these changes. Their economies continued to grow at rates not much below what they had been previously and import volume soon recovered from an initial reduction. The current account deficits of the non-oil developing countries rose from an average of 1.7 per cent of GNP in the 1960s to an average of over 3 per cent of GNP in 1974–9.

For a number of reasons commercial banks came to be the main providers of the funds needed to finance these deficits. First, as I have said, they were already interested and involved in lending to the developing countries, and it seemed rational for them to extend this role, particularly since the recession in the industrialised countries meant that opportunities for profitable lending at home were fewer. Second, the banks were well equipped to engage in the maturity transformation which was needed. The OPEC members, which were now in substantial surplus, wished to keep their assets in highly liquid form. The need of the developing countries on the other hand was for medium and longer term development finance. Using markets and instruments tailor-made for the purpose, notably syndicated loans at floating rates, the commercial banks carried out what has come to be known as the recycling of the OPEC surpluses to the deficit countries. Although nominal interest rates rose sharply, inflation kept real interest rates at modest – even negative – levels for much of the time.

The result was that in the years immediately after 1973 commercial bank lending was providing 60 per cent of more of the external financial needs of the developing countries, while direct investment and official finance provided 18 and 19 per cent, respectively in the period 1973–8. One effect of the increased part played by commercial bank lending, which was to have important consequences later, was that the interest costs of the developing countries moved closer to market rates as the proportion of their debt at concessionary rates declined. This was particularly true of the larger, middle income, newly industrialising countries in which the greater part of the commercial bank borrowing was concentrated.

Another manifestation of the greatly increased scale of international intermediation by commercial banks was the ever larger numbers of banks wishing to be represented in the major centres. In London, for example, in the mid-1960s around 100 foreign banks were represented through branches, subsidiaries, representative offices or participations in joint ventures. Between 1972 and the end of 1974 the numbers grew from 245 to 335. Today there are over 450. Included amongst the banks seeking overseas representation was an increasing number of banks from developing countries setting up branches abroad. These banks had a limited natural deposit base and tended to rely heavily on short-term funding from the international interbank markets. Their participation in the recycling process greatly encouraged this and they, perhaps even more than other banks engaged in matching these short-term deposits with medium and long-term assets, mostly loaned directly back to their countries of origin.

To summarise, building on developments which had taken place over a period of years in the 1960s and early 1970s, banks had by the middle 1970s come to occupy the central position in financing the needs of deficit countries. In the circumstances of the time this was vital: the scale of internal adjustment that would have otherwise have been demanded of these countries would, I have no doubt, been impossible to achieve without massive upheaval – although there is certainly room for argument that there was greater scope for adjustment than actually occurred. However, certain structural changes had taken place: channels designed for financing trade had been converted to conduits for deficit and development financing; borrowers had become more fully exposed to movements in nominal and real interest rates; the proportion of short-term borrowing by debtor countries was already rising fast; and debt service ratios, so much a preoccupation of those in the official agencies in the 1960s, had risen sharply, largely unremarked.

The second oil price shock in 1979–80 brought similar consequences to the first: another fall in growth in the developing countries' export markets and an increase in the cost of their imported oil. There was, however, one crucial difference. This time the policy adopted in the industrialised countries was to give the highest priority to resisting the inflationary impetus of the oil price increase, and not to seek to offset its effects on real incomes by adopting expansionary macroeconomic policies. Instead those policies were consciously and persistently anti-inflationary in their thrust, restraining demand and output, raising interest rates sharply, first in nominal terms as the policies were applied and, subsequently, in real terms as prices responded. In an associated development, the effective exchange rate of the dollar – in which perhaps 80 per cent or more of the developing countries' debt was denominated – shifted sharply upwards, greatly increasing the costs in terms of the domestic transfers of resources needed to service these debts.

Both the banks and the borrowing countries were slow to see these changes coming and reacted much as they had done during the first oil shock. The developing countries continued to finance their balance of payments deficits through commercial bank borrowing, and the share of finance in this form rose to over 70 per cent.

Given the sizeable stock of debt which the banks already held, and the sharp increase in interest rates, banks began to feel uneasy about the weight of debt on their books and an emerging anxiety about the implications for the capacity of the borrowing countries to service these debts. Some banks had taken a more cautious attitude to their involvement in sovereign lending and made only marginal adjustments to their international activities. Others, more deeply engaged but, if you like, less committed reacted differently: they lent first at shorter term and then showed an increasing reluctance to lend at all. For their part, the borrowers too were reluctant to accept the need for adjustment and continued to borrow at shorter and shorter term. Before Mexico declared a moratorium in the latter part of August 1982 the scene was therefore set in which its difficulties could pass rapidly and dramatically to borrowers in a similar – or in some cases dissimilar – position. The channels and instruments which had proved effective in the recycling exercise were also those which ensured that the problems encountered by Mexico were communicated swiftly to others.

The response of the world's monetary authorities, of the banks and of the borrowers to the threat posed to the international monetary system by the events of the autumn of 1982 are well recorded and need no elaboration here. I will add only one or two observations of my own. First, a crisis was averted only because all of the parties involved were prepared to do things which went against instinct. The most responsible banks continued to lend when their conventional training would have indicated they should cease and withdraw. Central banks effectively committed part of their liquidity and foreign exchange reserves before they could be sure they would retrieve them quickly. Borrowing governments, both through the IMF and directly, took politically unpopular courses of action and embarked on domestic adjustment programmes which were probably unprecedentedly severe. Finally the IMF stepped away from its customary cautious and arms-length relationship with the banks and encouraged more explicit and formal links between Fund programmes and bank finance. Courage was required on all sides for habitual reservations to be set aside.

Secondly, this has been done without, in my judgement, causing fundamental damage to the operation of the international markets. Of course, certain markets have suffered a knock; and the relationships between borrowers, commercial bankers and official institutions has altered, for how long we do not yet know. But it has been a central concern of the world's monetary authorities to work through existing institutions and markets; and to avoid, where possible, fundamental changes in major institutions and markets which may be either premature or wrong in principle.

In coming to the prospects for a longer-term solution it is, I think, natural to start by asking about the nature of the problem. It is not, however, easy to see at this stage what that is. It may, of course, differ as between cases. A distinction that is sometimes used is between a 'liquidity problem' and a 'solvency problem'. I have trouble with this approach. A good deal of what we have seen in 1982 has certainly included problems of liquidity. But in considering policy solutions the concept of solvency is not really applicable to country risks. I suppose it may be possible to imagine a case where a country had incurred debts which exceeded its total assets, such as infrastructure and mineral resources; but such a calculation, even if it could be made, would ignore the people and managerial capacity of the country – which, as we all know, is what really counts. From the point of view of finding a solution, however, it is surely nonsense to talk about liquidating a country's tangible assets or distributing them to creditors. Such suggestions seem to me to be irrational since they fly in the face of political and practical realities – to say nothing of their likely effect on those whose cooperation is essential if we are to continue to work our way out of our collective difficulties.

An alternative approach and one which avoids the need to fit our thinking into established accounting definitions, is to try to assess the time-scale over which a country's debt servicing problems will last. This could help answer the question which I find great difficulty in answering – namely, has the country over-borrowed in some fundamental sense? Using this approach, the gauge of a country's return to financial health would be its ability to return to normal market financing, without recourse to special packages or co-ordinated loans, within a reasonable period. I acknowledge that this does not depend on some fixed and measurable event, but on the subjective judgements of banks and investors. However, we would be wrong to think decisions about lending will ever be reduced to complete reliance on objective criteria. Judgement will always play a central part.

Given these uncertainties it is very hard to judge how long the current difficulties are going to be with us; but there are indications that at least in some cases the problem is not transitional, in the sense I have indicated. For such countries the question arises whether the transfers of resources which would be necessary for them to meet their obligations without some kind of ameliorating arrangements are such that they would have difficulty in obtaining access to normal market finance for some considerable time.

If you assume, as I do, that the current debt difficulties are not purely transitory, but may persist for some little time, what then should be done about it? Looking around at the range of options on offer, I think there are three possible classes of action which have been suggested: to do nothing; to look for a single 'big' solution to all the problems; or to continue with *ad hoc* management. The first option, to do nothing, has two variants: the first of these is to allow a collapse to take place which will teach banks and borrowers the discipline necessary to avoid a recurrence for many years ahead, and puts the burdens where they belong. There are no points for guessing that I find this solution unacceptable. I believe the lessons are capable of being learned short of such puritanical treatment; that there are lively and serious risks that the collapse would spread and create immeasurable difficulties; and that the burdens would almost certainly not be distributed equitably – whatever that might mean.

The second variant of the first option to do nothing rests on an assumption that, so to speak, a rising economic tide will be able to float the vessel off the rocks. It cannot be denied that this is a possibility: economic recovery may arrive sooner and be stronger than we now expect, bringing lower interest rates and expanding export markets for the developing countries, a reduction in the effective rate of the US dollar, and allowing them to service their debts and return to the market with restored confidence. First there is a real risk that we may wait for an economic upsurge, and it may not arrive. Economic forecasting has scarcely become a more confident occupation in this last decade. Second, and much more important, what may be true for the generality of debtor countries may not apply to some crucial cases. I have reservations about an approach which reduces the solution to a required rate of growth for the OECD or any other group of countries. I do not know whether growth of 2 per cent, 3 per cent or any other percentage will suffice to solve the problems of some of the largest debtor countries; and it is no solution if a way forward cannot be found which assures that these borrowers' problems will be taken care of.

Unless we look to more radical solutions, such countries will therefore be obliged to continue to make their contribution by continuing adjustment. But a sustained period of adjustment is only possible in my view if there is a continued flow of bank finance. Such finance could only be forthcoming if it were managed in something like the way it has been recently, and this negates the principle of the 'do nothing' option which we are considering. I have to conclude, therefore, that the odds against such a solution are too high for it to be wise to rely on.

The second possible course of action is the radical approach, usually taking the form of a scheme which tackles, within a coherent framework, all the problems of both debtors and commercial banks. This proceeds on the assumption that, in broad terms, the balance sheets of borrowers and lenders have become so seriously out of balance that a piecemeal solution provides no lasting benefit, and early action to restructure these balance sheets offers the only hope of avoiding a further marked and possible terminal deterioration of the situation. There are a number of schemes available, some involving the establishment of new institutions, some building upon existing institutions.

To be successful, it seems to me that there are a number of things which a well-constructed scheme could do: it could ensure a contribution from the borrowing country, probably through a continuing formal link with an IMF programme; it could ease the burden of existing debt at the same time as stimulating a flow of new finance; it could also, by transferring some risks away from the banks, reduce the fears of a bank collapse and so make them less vulnerable to a loss of confidence. But I have yet to see a scheme which deals with the costs of these transfers in a way that finds unanimous acceptance from those who would have to bear any significant part of it. You may think such an observation is a counsel of perfection; a case of the best being the enemy of the good. However, we cannot wish the problem away; nor should we. Any scheme which fails to recognise realities fails to meet a crucial test. Even if the technical problems of such a scheme are overcome, I have to say I judge that the present time does not seem opportune for launching initiatives of this kind. No doubt Minos Zombanakis and, perhaps, our Brazilian colleagues will wish to argue otherwise; but they will have to spell out how to deal with this central issue.

This leaves only the final course of action: continued management on something like the present lines for some time to come. I recognise that this suggestion lacks appeal on a number of counts. In the first case, it may be argued that it does not seem to deal with my definition of the underlying problem, but it merely pushes it back in time. For although in the short term the financial position of the borrowing countries may improve as the result of current measures, further ahead maturities are starting to bunch from loans which have been rescheduled, and the new loans which have been granted.

This approach also seems rather precarious, vulnerable to accidents, and to changes in what the lawyers call material adverse circumstances – and very hard on the nerves. It would be a course of action which would require constant fine judgements on the balance to be struck between the interests of debtors and creditors. From the creditors there would be repeated calls for new money, and from the debtors there would be the need for continued adjustment. There would be the ever-present danger of stalemate. The scarce time of senior officials and government ministers could be taken up by a never ending round of negotiations. For the tidy minded it all seems rather 'seat of the pants' and lacking in coherence.

I do not find these criticisms as damning as others do. For example, I am not persuaded that the market mechanisms, supplemented by IMF programmes and official support, could not themselves develop and adjust, given time, ingenuity and the will to succeed. Already the bankers are showing awareness of the problem created by the bunching of maturities: new money in substantial amounts is being made available for eight and nine years, with grace periods of four and five years; and spreads and fees are being reconsidered, not only because of political pressures.

The new relationships which have emerged between commercial banks, borrowers and the IMF are also capable of development. There is no doubt at all in my mind that the leadership provided by Mr de Larosière was absolutely right in the circumstances, although it may have come as something of a shock to both commercial bankers and borrowers at the time. If these initiatives should lead to a more systematic management of the problem I would expect to see the Fund naturally retire somewhat from the position of prominence which it occupies at present – although I would not necessarily expect a return to the status quo ante. Exactly how it comes out is a matter for the banks as well as the Fund and I am sure both parties will be giving active consideration to the question of their relations in the period ahead. But there is, I am confident, no desire to interfere with the market mechanism for a moment longer than necessary.

I think the fears of a continuous period of agony, absorbing the energies of Ministers and officials for years ahead, may also be exaggerated. If the initial rescue efforts go reasonably well and if one or two crucial successes are recorded I can easily imagine that the form and content of these negotiations could alter covering, for example, needs for two or more years ahead. Indeed, it is the very flexibility of the current approach that appeals to me most – its capacity for adaptation to particular cases. I have little shame in confessing that I can see ahead very imperfectly, and that my vision has become weaker rather than stronger in the last decade. I therefore shrink a little from global schemes that solve the problem for years ahead; the problem itself may change.

You will see that of the three courses of action I have described my leaning is towards the process of continued management. I do not rule out the possibility that at some time in the future the time may be right for a substantial reshaping of debts. In the meantime I feel we must continue to pick our way carefully forward. If all the parties continue to show goodwill and commitment I think there is a good chance that we will make it.

4 The Lessons of the Crisis: a Developing Country View*

Carlos Geraldo Langoni

In 1982 the financial earthquake produced by the Polish, Argentinian and Mexican debt crises began to deeply change the course of life of many countries, particularly those classified as developing nations.

The financial crisis was at the same time brutal in its impact, and unexpected in its timing. Neither Central Banks, nor commercial banks, not to mention the governments of developing countries, were prepared to take the action necessary, if not to avoid it completely, at least to minimise its disruptive consequences. Especially after the trigger-point represented by the Mexican default, it became clear that an institutional framework capable of dealing with the crisis in an orderly fashion was not in existence.

Quite the opposite, the first reactions to this new scale of uncertainties together with acute liquidity problems of some countries with large external debts, were clearly procyclical and did much to magnify the difficulties. The best example of this was the frustrating IMF meeting in Toronto in 1982 when it was understood by the developed countries that there was no need of any special action, neither with respect to reinforcing the capital basis of the multilateral institutions nor to establish a liquidity window, which could assist third countries not yet directly involved in the exchange crisis to go through the difficult coming months.

At that stage of the game, the industrialised countries seriously underestimated the extension of the crisis which was just beginning. They stressed their concern about the need for more adjustment by the developing countries and sat back waiting for a 'natural' market correction which would be facilitated by lower interest rates and the expected economic recovery.

* Published in *Euromoney*, September 1983 (IMF Essay).

THE CRISIS AND ITS DIMENSIONS

Since the IMF meeting in Toronot about 22 countries have gone through a painful and troublesome process of rescheduling as a direct consequence of the virtual paralysis of the financial markets, as commercial banks over-reacted to the initial waves of uncertainty. The compound effects of each expected rescheduling added to the initial level of uncertainty and generated new externalities whose spill-over went well beyond those countries which have reached the stage of default under a normal functioning of the financial markets.

There is no question that the dubious and undefined role played by the major Central Banks and the governments of the industrialised countries have a great responsibility for the disorderly way by which the crisis has evolved. The basic contradiction was to try to adopt a 'non-intervention' posture, when in fact the pure working of the market forces was leading to a complete halt in loans to developing countries. The concept of risk usually applied by commercial banks has quickly evolved from country to regions in an irrational attempt to correct in a few months the overlending of many years. The Central Banks knew, of course, that the attempt of each individual bank to reduce quickly its own exposure would finally be frustrated by the destabilising effects of this action on the market as a whole to the extent that it might be followed by other banks. This process will only come to an end either by unilateral action of the debtors, which will mean market disruption, or by some compulsory action by the Central Banks, and their governments, which in the end could be understood as a way to internalise the externalities.

The Brazilian case dramatically illustrates the devastating consequences of these forces. In the first six months of 1982, Brazil was able to borrow normally in the market at an average of US $1.5 billion a month. Just after the Mexican default, the access to the market was cut by half and automatic borrowing virtually disappeared completely in the last quarter of the year. Market borrowing was substituted for negotiated borrowing and market forces replaced by bureaucratic meetings where the increasing number of jet hours involved symbolise the higher transaction costs.

Obviously, there is no logical reason to explain why the risk perception of Brazil changed so radically from one month to another. At the same time, as our own experience also illustrates, the trend for an endogenous shrink of the market could not be interrupted through the implementation of further adjustment policies by the developing countries or even by the announcement effect of an agreement with the IMF. Brazil took these two steps: in October it announced a series of measures designed to cut by half its current account deficit and by December had already reached an agreement with the IMF. However, the negative market forces proved to be more powerful. In the meantime, the country lost about US $4 billion of interbank deposits and about US $2 billion of trade related lines of credit which added to its liquidity squeeze.

It is clear from the above facts that once there is no more marketplace, we cannot go on trying to stick to the 'non-intervention' dogma. Whether we like it or not, there must be some exogenous compulsory action to stop the drain of resources whose speed and intensity cannot be affected by any conceivable internal adjustment by the debtor countries.

MARKET FAILURE?

At present, there is not a co-ordinated and relatively uniform action by the major Central Banks and their governments, geared to minimise the social costs of these 'financial externalities'. On the contrary, there are conflicting views and attitudes and even an opposite regulatory trend with the effect that still more restrictions and rigidities may be introduced in a situation whose emergent character calls for innovation and flexibility. It should be stressed, however, that in the Brazilian case some Central Banks were in fact very active in mobilising commercial banks so as to ensure the minimum needed level of liquidity. Others, on the contrary, took either an indifferent position or even stuck to the dogmatic posture that 'risks are the fate of banks'.

At the heart of the question lies the need of a broad recognition that we are facing a classical example of market failure. It is often heard that developing countries have borrowed too much. It is, however, also true that overborrowing is necessarily associated with overlending. One of the main lessons of the crisis is that the once praised automatic working of 'world money' has not led to an optimum solution from the viewpoint of resource allocation. The self-correcting mechanisms of competition, which affect expected rates of return, were not enough to lead to a gradual slowdown in the supply of resources which, by itself, would signal the need for symmetric internal adjustments in the borrowing countries. On the contrary, till recently the rates of profitability implied in international lending were considerably higher than the domestic ones and they looked attractive enough to offset expected or unknown risks.

It would be unjustified, given the extremely high social costs involved, to accept as inevitable a discontinuous and instantaneous process of market correction which is not only self-destructive from the viewpoint of the financial system as a whole, but, more important, may lead to a path of adjustment among developing countries which clearly conflicts with the social and political constraints.

Therefore, a more articulated action by Central Banks and their governments is still a key element to a gradual re-establishment of the market-place even at a substantially lower level of activity which will certainly derive from the adjustment effort now under way in many countries.

The new role of the IMF as an active element of pressure upon the commercial banks and at the same time as an indispensable collateral vector for negotiated borrowings is, by itself, concrete evidence that some form of compulsory action is needed in order to keep the ball rolling.

Firmer and more decisive action by Central Banks would certainly have avoided the sizeable reduction in the number of players in the market which by itself renders more difficult even the negotiated solution. The emphasis on this aspect derives from the fact also well illustrated recently, that under the present circumstances, destabilisation may stem not only from the balance of payments disequilibrium but from a discontinuity in the funding process involving branches of developing countries' banks abroad. This is a completely new phenomenon, extremely complex to the extent that these branches have established a direct link between one country's external situation and the market behaviour of individual banks. On the other hand, a drain of deposits in this market may force a diversion of badly needed liquidity from balance of payments needs to support individual banks, thus modifying the conventional concept of a resources gap. Mexico and Brazil have recently faced this new and crucial dimension of the actual financial crisis.

THE ADJUSTMENT BURDEN OF THE LDCs

Unfortunately, after almost a year living under a crisis, very few lessons were in fact learned. We are still facing great uncertainties which were not minimised by a great number of reschedulings of external debts, some already completed and others still under way. The whole system remains extremely vulnerable and no major institutional step was taken to ensure a smooth process in the near future. There is only one clear consequence: the burden of adjustment has fallen disproportionately upon the developing countries that are facing the recessionary consequences of the adjustment policies which are now in place. By contrast, despite the higher risks of substantial capital losses, the international banks as a whole were not severely affected in terms of rentability and, quite the contrary, there was some evidence that under the actual conditions, rescheduling has become a relatively profitable operation.

The adjustment policies now being implemented in many developing countries are of course inevitable, and even necessary to correct long-term distortions which were concealed behind the favourable liquidity conditions which have prevailed in the past. It is important to recognise that the current difficulties of the developing nations cannot be attributed exclusively to external factors. The majority of these countries reacted sluggishly and, frequently, in a mistaken manner to the events that signalled the intensity of the crisis then dawning. The roots of this inertia are to be found in the institutional difficulty of establishing suitable political mechanisms, capable of adjusting often legitimate social aspirations to the real availability of resources. In some cases, authoritarian practices were eliminated without sufficient time to replace them with mechanisms of consensus that presuppose trial and error and varied approaches to solutions. Perhaps the clearest example of these difficulties lies in the area of wages and labour relations, for in the majority of developing nations there still predominates the illusion that the State can be held responsible for determining real levels of wages, even in situations where the labour market is highly competitive. However, experience has shown that state intervention in wages almost always results in added inflationary pressures, unemployment and a reduction in investment levels.

In other cases, one must reflect on the swelling of the public sector, almost always at the cost of domestic and foreign indebtedness – a swelling destined to come up against physical limitations. The public deficit, financed by inflationary taxation, is a common element in the explanations offered for the domestic imbalances of many developing countries.

Moreover, efficiency in the use of resources is frequently distorted by concentration on investments of doubtful social benefit. Direct consumer subsidies and indirect credit subsidies are a wasteful allocation of resources and, far from helping the poor, tend to increase income concentration. In many countries, the external shock was worsened by the rigidity of exchange policies and the absence of export diversification plans. Both factors made revenues vulnerable to fluctuations in international market prices.

For these countries, the external restrictions imposed by the sudden curbing of access to the international financial markets have made it essential to correct such distortions. It will be necessary to reduce the dependence of developing countries on external resources.

THE EXTERNAL DIMENSIONS

However, even those developing countries with completely adequate domestic policies need the convergence of a number of favourable external factors. Otherwise, it is impossible to conceive of non-chaotic solutions to the present crisis.

Developing countries have to work within the restrictions imposed by the elementary necessity of preserving social and political stability. Therefore the process of adjustment needs time.

The Brazilian case illustrates this. The process of political transition towards democracy has been superimposed on the simultaneous process of economic adjustment.

Far from being an obstacle to the economic programme, political liberalisation, in our experience, has been an important trump card. It ensures long-term stability, and makes it possible for people to use legitimate channels of expression.

The true challenge of the present situation is to the industrialised nations. They have to recognise that adjustment policies in developing countries, even if successful, may not be enough.

An orchestrated action will be needed. It must include a change in the policy of industrialised countries, an innovative role by the multilateral institutions (particularly the IMF), new mechanisms to deal with short-term liquidity and long-term restructuring and, finally, a new deal between debtors and creditors. This last will require a reshaping of the commercial banks present policies. This may seem as complex and difficult as rehearsing an opera. How can this large cast be drilled, not only to sing in tune, but to sing in harmony with each other? Yet the alternative is chaos. Unilateral action by developing countries will be the natural and expected consequence, if new exogenous events generate another explosion of uncertainties.

The developing countries efforts towards institutional modernisation and economic adjustment demand a complementary contribution on the part of the industrialised nations. It would be inconceivable, for example, to have to support another financial shock, characterised by a new round of rising interest rates. The United States, in applying its own domestic policies, should bear in mind its international responsibility.

The accumulation of public deficits has long since ceased to be a characteristic mark of the underdeveloped, and has become quite common even among the developed nations, which have much less justification for the almost chronic existence of these deficits. Wild fluctuations in the value of the major international currencies ought to be avoided, for only with great difficulty can these fluctuations be offset through alterations in the exchange rates of the poorer countries. Finally, it is worth remembering that there is no economic or social justification for increased protectionism on the part of the industrialised countries, as a means of resolving balance of payments disequilibria.

THE INTEREST RATE DILEMMA

Interest rates fluctuations represent the major element of vulnerability involved in the payment arrangement between debtor countries and commercial banks. Each of the present rescheduling or refinancing schemes may become unrealistic overnight, depending solely on the trend of interest rates. Given the sizeable values of the external debts, the impact of even minor variations of the rates over future interest payments is enormous. Since at the present stage of the management of monetary and fiscal policy in the United States it is virtually impossible to ensure even a maximum range for interest rate variation, we will have to consider explicitly how to reconcile this reality with the minimum financial stability required by developing countries.

Here we have two basic alternatives. The first one is to include the capitalisation of interest explicit within the framework of the negotiations. The banks react to this idea, within the concept that rescheduling should be limited to the principal, not to the expected flow of income stream. On the other hand, this solution would minimise only the immediate impact and will be felt in the short run, requiring either further adjustment or additional finance, which should be provided by the banks themselves.

The only real alternative is to devise a mechanism for interest rate equilisation in which the interest rate agreed upon would be a normal or equilibrium long-term rate (possibly not too different from the long-run expected inflation). Any deviation from this long-term rate would be covered by a special fund. The viability of this scheme relies, of course, on the idea of a symmetric behaviour: at the end, higher than expected rates would be financed by the proceeds coming from lower than expected ones.

Over a longer period of time which, by the way, is the only viable framework for rescheduling, the system should net out. What is really needed is then a sort of revolving fund, with enough resources both from official and private sources to face the initial demand. It is interesting to notice that this scheme may be implemented without necessarily adopting fixed rates: it is only necessary to work with a long-term floating rate, defined as a fixed equilibrium real rate plus the rate of inflation. The ideal solution from the LDCs viewpoint would be a system combining both the capitalisation and a consensual maximum range of variation of Interest payments.

THE ROLE OF MULTILATERAL ORGANISATIONS

Comments should also be made on what should be expected of the multilateral organisations in this period of profound change in international relations. Even taking for granted that the adjustment efforts of the developing countries will succeed, on the one hand, and that the level of the international financial market uncertainty will be gradually reduced, on the other, there remains the conviction that it would be unrealistic to imagine that, in the near future, the rate of growth of loans by commercial banks, will return to a level compatible with the necessities (by then, hopefully, already reduced) of the developing countries. It is indispensable, therefore, that a more intense effort be made to substitute private sources for multilateral sources of funds, while not, of course, precluding complementary and harmonious cooperative actions, as in the areas of cofinancing and the assuming of risks.

In the first place, therefore, one is dealing with the strengthening of the capital and the resources mobilisation capacity of the already existent institutions. In this sense it is frustrating to see the sluggishness with which this problem has been faced and the slowness of the decision-making process in a matter of such priority and urgency. As we have already mentioned, the indecision that marked the 1982 IMF meeting in Toronto doubtlessly nourished the uncertainties that were then accumulating in the market and contributed indirectly to the crisis of confidence that then broke out and from which we have yet to recover.

For the multilateral banks, changes must go beyond the mere expansion of the capital basis. These new potential resources once available must be disbursed quicker so as to provide an extra margin of liquidity. This will require a sharp change in internal procedures, up to now excessively bureaucratic, and, at the same time, the design of new mechanisms such as advance or special accounts which reconcile the physical timing of projects to be financed with the cash flow needs of developing countries. Furthermore, we should go beyond the traditional project finance and increase sectorial finance directly related to broad structural changes that are required for the more permanent adjustment of the economy. It should be recognised that the World Bank is playing a leading role in this process of modernisation.

With respect to the IMF, there is a clear contradiction between its innovative role as a new element of pressure upon commercial banks in the rescheduling arrangements, and the set of conditionalities associated with the availability of the Fund's resources. Even the recently created 'extended fund facility' (EFF), which supposedly deals with 'structural' adjustment is relatively short-sighted and seriously underestimates the times required to implement institutional reforms which should follow short-term policies more related to demand management. As a consequence, the Fund asks too much in too short a period of time. It is interesting to notice that up to now about half of the countries in the EFF programme had to ask for a waiver, this reflecting the difficulties in achieving some of the initial objectives of these programmes. Since the need for an adjustment programme arises so suddenly, there is often a dangerous conflict between the Fund's requests and what is politically and socially viable within the country. A good example is the fact that, in contrast with the developed countries situation, in the case of the LDCs, the reduction of the public deficit is not a simple question of cutting back expenditures and/or increasing revenues. We must deal not only with rigid social expenditures, but quite often with a very complex system of state enterprises autonomous life, whose control requires new institutional devices which cannot be designed and efficiently implemented overnight. For countries like Brazil, who lived for years with a broad system of indexation, one cannot hope even with the toughest monetary and fiscal policies, to achieve a quick deceleration of inflation. Of course, in the management of demand policies, it is imperative to take explicitly into account the visible social constraints represented by excessively high rates of unemployment.

Here again, the problem is not only availability of resources but also of attitudes. Even though the label of the adjustment programme of the Fund is 'structural', in practice it applies mechanically the same system of performance evaluation used by the traditional standby arrangements. It is therefore surprising to find serious methodological flaws when, for example, one tries to measure the public sector borrowing in an economy with compulsory monetary correction or to define the needed public sector deficit reduction consistent with the current account objective. In many cases, theological, and not rational reasons, are raised to support the quantitative targets.

A longer period of adjustment appears to be a precondition in order to reach the appropriate balance between external credibility and internal viability in a Fund programme. Furthermore, there is no reason why the minimum adjustment period should be exactly the same for every country, when there are clearly sharp structural and institutional differences. As a matter of fact, an agreement about the timing of the programme should be part of the negotiation process, not a pre-fixed condition. An important consequence of a longer adjustment programme with the Fund is to open up the door for equally longer rescheduling procedures with the commercial banks. Curiously enough, we are facing a situation where there are neither enough longer-term resources nor sufficient short-term funds. The latter is critical to offset unexpected cash flow shortages frequently stemming from factors outside the realm of domestic policies and often even exogenous to the evolution of the balance of payments itself as, for example, a sudden reversal of interbank market expectations where, in most cases, classic discount mechanisms either do not exist or are insufficient.

In the recent crisis, some countries – taking bilateral action, such as in the case of the United States – and the Bank for International Settlements, sought to make up for this deficiency, but were faced with resources limitations or legal restrictions. It would, therefore, seem to be essential that mechanisms and institutional forums be developed at world level, thus making it possible to establish new automatic sources of liquidity so that countries would have sufficient time to react to a crisis or even to approach such international lending agencies as the IMF, in a less chaotic manner and at a reduced cost to the financial system as a whole. The discussions on the expansion of the General Arrangements to Borrow (GAB) would seem to stand as formal recognition of the lack of such mechanisms, aimed at minimising the destabilising effects of localised liquidity crises.

WHAT TO EXPECT FROM PRIVATE BANKS

In terms of the distribution of burdens among the different actors, the activities of the international banks are of essential importance to a rapid and equitable solution of the present crisis. First and foremost, as pointed out before, it must be recognised that excessive indebtedness can only exist when there is simultaneously excessive lending. For precisely this reason, the almost general halting of the flow of loans to the developing countries following the Mexican crisis laid bare grave distortions on the organisation of the international financial system that had remained unnoticed during the period of euphoria. For a moment, there existed the illusion that, in just a few months, it would be possible to correct levels of exposure that were once seen as indicative of profitability but had suddenly become viewed as reflecting higher risks. The almost hysterical movement subsequent to the IMF meeting in Toronto led to the emotional generalisation of the concept of risk, no longer applied as a country-by-country assessment, but rather as a concept of continental proportions (Latin America, Central America, Eastern Europe, etc.). This evolved into a still larger concept. Any developing country with a high level of foreign indebtedness was to be avoided. This clearly meant that very few nations retained access to the inter-

national financial market. Structural and institutional differences, as
well as the manner in which domestic policies were applied, were
no longer taken into account and, as a matter of practice, the operations of the international financial market virtually came to a stand-
still. In the fourth quarter of 1982, new loans on the eurodollar
market totalled only US $12.2 billion, as against US $27.5 billion,
in the same period of the previous year. The normally impersonal
nature of market activities had to be replaced by arduous negotiations aimed at ensuring the minimum flow of resources needed to
avoid the paralysis of domestic economies and the inevitable social
and political chaos certain to follow.

This situation must be modified. In tandem with the needed action
of the Central Banks the private financial system should take its own
steps to develop specific mechanisms aimed at minimising the effects
of 'financial externalities'. Decisive to this effort are the channels of
access to information on the economies of different countries, so as
to avoid the cyclothymic performance of the so-called regional banks.
These institutions represent not only an indispensable mass of
liquidity for the secondary market, but also relatively important
weight for the interbank market.

The very manner in which the crisis exploded should result in a
reassessment of the traditional banking standard that short-term
loans have lower risk. This is particularly true in the case of the
developing countries, since the major share of foreign resources is
almost always channelled into investments with relatively long
periods of maturation. Negotiation aimed at transforming these
short-term credits into long-term or medium-term operations are
almost always based on this principle. The fact of the matter is that
the stretching of the debt profile of the developing nations would
seem to be a key element towards the solution of the problems of
foreign debts for many developing countries.

This idea is still clearer when one compares the flow of export
earnings of the developed countries with the rigid stream of the
service of the debt even after taking into account sharp reductions
in the current deficit, after successful implementation of adjustment
policies. The expected ratio between service of debt and exports will
still be disturbingly high in the near future even for developing
countries which are undergoing the painful process of adjustment.

Of course, at the core of the question is the paradoxical situation
of insisting in applying market-terms to a non-market situation. The
transformation of short-term credits into medium-term committed

lines represents an important breakthrough and a surrender to reality. But still more needs to be done in order to build a relatively more stable environment. Long-term finance needs to be refinanced in still longer terms. The traditional grace period (three years) needs to be consistent with the implications of the heritage of high debt figures for most developing countries. And certainly we need to review the terms in which the rescheduling is being managed. There is no logical justification why in many cases a negotiated solution should end up with significant higher spreads than prevailed before, which will only add to more difficulties in the future. As a matter of fact, it would be more reasonable to say that with the IMF support and the close monitoring made by the banks themselves upon the countries which have renegotiated, the risks should be lower and this should be reflected upon the margins charged by the banks. Lastly, we have already commented on the need to minimise the disruptive impact of interest rate fluctuations.

All this will reduce the profitability of the commercial banks, slowing down the growth of their capital basis. But this is an inevitable consequence of the adjustment process which will also have to be implemented within the framework of the international financial system. From the viewpoint of equity, the fact is simply unacceptable that developing countries should bear the full burden of the adjustment process through declining real per-capita income, while at the same time there are partial indications suggesting that the average rate of rentability of the private banks may even increase with the rescheduling.

Unrealistic terms and conditions will react against the banks, either through a costly process of stepwise negotiations or by unilateral action by debtor countries. It may well be desirable to have a more active participation of the IMF in these negotiations, as the appropriate financing of the balance of payments is, in the end, the main objective of the adjustment programmes.

New attitudes and new practices are also urgently needed among the private banks which will have to accept pragmatically the clear trade-off between lower current profits and the possibility of large capital losses. It is also up to them to decide whether the optimisation of this trade-off will be a voluntary or a compulsory process.

THE LESSONS IN SYNTHESIS

A review of a little more than a year of the financial crisis unfortunately shows that the lessons are yet to be learned. Very little progress was made to build up safeguards that will prevent another wave of uncertainties that will have disruptive effects upon the financial system.

There is no doubt that the developing countries are suffering disproportionately the harsh consequences of the crisis. All of them, either voluntarily or compulsorily, without the IMF, are facing a very difficult process of adjustment, which is already imposing additional losses of real income and extremely high social costs. No one can predict the limits of this process from the viewpoint of political stability and what countries will be able to go through the coming years and succeed in reaching a new path of self-sustained growth.

The social costs involved, even taking into account concrete real economic constraints, are higher than need be, mainly because of the lack of a more coordinated action by the industrialised countries. The Central Banks have been acting in a relatively timid way, many of them still adopting the orthodox posture of non-market intervention, when in fact there is no more market to deal with. These confusing signs stimulate a selfish action by individual banks generating a vicious circle which caught the less developed countries. The multilateral institutions also react sluggishly to the violence of the crisis, many of them with still serious resource constraints and without being able to adapt old-fashioned internal practices and concepts to a completely new and challenging situation. That means that the process of substitution of official sources of finance for private sources is clearly lagging behind the true needs. The IMF is clearly attempting to play a new role particularly as an instrument of pressure upon the banks. But it could not yet find a reasonable equilibrium between the well understood structural nature of the economic imbalances which requires time for correction and the rigidity imposed by its internal theology. Finally, the commercial banks are still keeping a market-orientated view to a situation in which market forces are no longer playing. As a consequence, despite a tremendous amount of effort put into complex negotiations, the situation is still extremely vulnerable to exogenous factors such as interest rate variations. Furthermore, a simple comparison of expected earnings to the projected stream of the service of the debt shows how far we still are from a realistic long-lasting solution to the LDCs external debt problem.

The most important lesson of the present crisis is to show to what extent financial flows have involved the world. An adequate solution, therefore, will require an articulated international action at different levels of decision-making in a broad process in which the costs of adjustments are clearly and equitably distributed among the different participants. The developing countries will have to intensify their internal realignment efforts, and this will demand institutional modernisation and, in many cases, political, economic and social reforms. In managing their own domestic policies, the industrialised nations must take into account more and more the external repercussions of their internal action, hence creating objective conditions for self-sustained growth with free access to international trade and the financial markets. At the same time, the commercial banks cannot abdicate their responsibilities; any attempt to review in a moment, their long-term outstanding commitments, must prove self-devouring. Finally, the multilateral organisations must rapidly mobilise resources in an innovative and flexible way, so that they can make up for short-term liquidity constraints, while simultaneously replacing the permanent losses that have already occurred among the sources of long-term funds.

Let us hope that these lessons will be learned without necessarily reaching the climax of a new crisis, and that we will be able to reconstruct an international framework which will set the stage for economic progress and social well-being.

5 The International Debt Crisis – a Growth-oriented Management Approach

Paulo Pereira Lira

Much has been written about the international debt crisis. Imaginative plans concocted in the North have been suggested to handle it. Conceivably, there may be interest at some quarters in listening to a view from the South, especially when it comes from Brazil, the largest single non-oil LDC sovereign borrower.

The substance of this view was the object of one among several proposals to governments, legislatures and international organisations developed by the World Conference on Economic and Social Order. Assembling together very high calibre Northern economic policy thinkers, the conference met in Geneva, for the first time in August 1983, under the chairmanship of Robert B. Anderson, former Secretary of the Treasury of the United States under the Eisenhower administration.

Still carrying a rather Unctadian flavour to it, the proposal reads as follows:

The dominant view of the majority of the conference believes that the IMF strategy to design stabilization programs should strive to find *the right balance* between imposing excessively onerous adjustment programs on the debtor countries and being too lenient and thereby postponing the required policy changes in debt repayment. In striking the balance, the adjustment program should not set balance of payments targets which, in effect, could result in a *premature* transfer of resources by a developing country to the creditor country, to the prejudice of its *economic growth objectives*. (*verbatim*, with *the underlying under 'the right balance', 'premature', and 'economic growth objective'* supplied by the author of the chapter).

The chapter's purpose is twofold: (1) to carry out the full impli-

57

cation of the transcribed recommendation to the IMF, supposing that it had been made operative in a 'Bretton Woods II' financial world; (2) immediately revert to the harsh realities of the 'muddling through world' in which the international financial community operates today. The latter is the financial world borrowing countries have to grapple with, in a very objective way.

Before spelling out what the situation in the 'Bretton Woods II world' might be, one must clarify what Brazil was trying to do when she conceived, made operative and implemented an external debt policy in a rather pioneering fashion. Up until the autumn of 1982, the Brazilian external debt policy was regarded as 'well managed' in most international financial circles, specially as opposed, for example, to the Mexican way of handling the issue.

EXTERNAL DEBT MANAGEMENT IN BRAZIL

This clarification is necessary because the external debt question is a minefield where fallacies, misconceptions and all sorts of prejudices abound.

Acting as a *responsible capital importing country*, Brazil began to try, by the late 1960s, *to accelerate its rate of growth over and above* what could be accomplished with its domestic savings, and the transfer of resources obtained via direct investment. This was to be done through the engagement of her *economy* with the re-emerging international private capital market. The new actors in the scene were the commercial banks providing cross-border loans.

It all meant a *growth cum debt* approach to development finance utilising the International Borrowing System (IBS) (as that market was seen from the Brazilian point of view) to obtain an inward transfer of resources also.

Such transfer was to take place each year by having the value of new loan disbursements higher than that of past loans amortisation and interest payments. Those interested in checking the concept of resource transfer via the loan mechanism are referred to the 1983 World Bank's Annual Report Statistical Annex. Table 6 presents the relevant figures for resource transfer through public debt, presented according to different regional groupings of LDCs. It is rather revealing, by the way, to look at the figures for Latin America.

The acceleration of the rate of growth meant that the transfer of resources had to go into investment (not consumption). And also, if the investment was to be put to good use, that the rate of return on investment inside the country had to be higher than the international rate of interest. Moreover, if the borrowings were to take place via the market mechanism, through the voluntary action of Brazilian enterprises, private or public, this meant that you tied the level of the rate of interest in Brazil to the vagaries of the prime rate in the United States or the six-month libor rate in the Euromarkets.

However, the objective was not only to accelerate growth over and above that possible with domestic savings and risk capital associated resource transfer; having obtained it, there was need also to make the accelerated growth *sustainable over time*.

Achieving sustainability meant following a three-pronged protective strategy of the accelerated growth through: (a) export promotion; (b) actively distributing amortization payments over the years to avoid the 'bunching up' at the earlier ones, which would result from the natural desires of individual Brazilian borrowers and foreign creditors, and (c) pursuing a policy of international reserve accumulation well beyond the typical IMF rule of thumb recommendation of three months imports.

All these three protective actions had the ultimate purpose of limiting future borrowings, over the proximate years, so as to keep them adequately related to a reasonably expected growth in the size of the loan markets.

What was called an 'ostensibly comfortable' reserve position had also the very important function of giving confidence to the exchange rate level being practised. Its 'high' volume suppressed fears of an eventual real devaluation of the rate of exchange. It is well known that these adverse expectations raise the level of the domestic rate of interest way above the floor established by the international rate of interest (prime or libor).

Those familiar with the debt cycle of a capital importing country know that, in the *normal course of events* (and we will revert to this point later on) Brazil, within the scope of its 'well managed external debt policy', borrowed yearly to cover the following balance of payments needs, for finance:

(a) the inward transfer of resources, related to borrowing;
(b) the net interest rate payments;
(c) the amortisation payments;
(d) the yearly increase in reserves, over and above domestic gold production and SDR allocation.

The sum of the two items, (a) and (b), equals the yearly current amount deficit, leaving aside the item related to profit and dividend remittances. Their financing, in the case of Brazil, is normally more than taken care of by the net entry of new direct investment.

The whole accent of a well run external debt policy was to manage things in such a way that, when the *need for adjustment* would eventually appear (and this was bound to happen sometime in an uncertain world), there would be time to proceed in an orderly fashion.

The adjustment would be achieved by using the accumulated reserves, up to a point, and mobilising a responsive export structure and eliminating the inward resource transfer that was accelerating growth, if need be. But all efforts would be pursued to avoid an *inordinate* transfer of resources abroad, which would be *premature*, given the long-term objectives of a capital importing country.

(The rationale to avoid, if possible, the outward resource transfer by the capital importing country should be clear, by now. The inward transfer of resources, if added to domestically financed investment through the adequate macroeconomic policies, expedites the rate of growth and thereby the levels of consumption of the population. In the obverse case, the transfer of resource abroad can only be made, via the consequent macro-policies that promote it, through a reduction in the investment and consumption levels inside the country. Because both events are regarded from the long-term growth objective of the country, as 'undesirable', the resource transfer that occasions them is called 'premature'.)

But, then, many things happened after the second oil shock in 1979; abroad, as a consequence of the basic change in the policy stance of the FED as to monetary management in the context of a strong anti-inflationary campaign (with a loose fiscal policy, interest rates shot up); inside Brazil, in so far as unfavourable effects on debt management began to be observed.

A 'NEW LOOK' AT DEBT CRISIS MANAGEMENT

Having hopefully cleared away the question of good external debt management, one must return to the mainstream of the argument and apply the suggested recommendation by Secretary Anderson's World Conference to the 'Bretton Woods II' kind of financial world.

The latter expression is used in the sense proposed by Sir Jeremy

Morse, former Chairman of the Deputies of the Committee of Twenty. When 'Bretton Woods I' existed, until the Nixon-shock of USA abandonment of gold convertibility (1971), there was a 'body of laws and rules or conventions sufficiently strong to have an effect on both market and politics and make them other than they would have been'.

'Bretton Woods II' will necessarily have rules governing capital flows, which were non-existent in 'Bretton Woods I'. As an experienced and wise observer of Fund and Bank matters remarked, those capital flows of both short and long-term nature are currently the tail that wags the dog of international finance.

Two differences, at least, would exist between 'Bretton Woods II' and the unstructured 'non-system' of today, as far as capital flows are concerned. First: the IMF stabilisation programmes would establish balance of payments targets, so as to avoid 'premature' transfer of resources from the adjusting capital importing country. Second: differences of opinion as to the degree of 'prematureness' of the IMF desired outward resource transfer, could well emerge between the country's authorities, who are politically accountable, and the international civil servants of the IMF who, by their own function as 'guardians' of the 'structured' system, carry no such political accountability. The conscious capital importing country would be empowered in such circumstances to use the safeguard provision of a 'temporary disengagement from the IBS' (International Borrowing System), as previously described.

To make these ideas explicit, it is worth applying them to the current Brazilian critical situation.

The first order of business is to get down to some facts. There are currently 40 countries running IMF supported stabilisation programmes, including 11 of the 20 largest LDC borrowers. The obvious common cause to this rather ugly generalised payment imbalances is not a sudden rush of incompetence of economic policy managers in borrowing countries. Plenty of recognition has been given to policy actions by the authorities of the industrial countries which led to the undermining of the IBS as a vehicle for resource transfer to the South (historically high interest rates accompanied by prolonged recession).

Not enough attention, however, has been focused on the deleterious effect on the IBS resource transfer capability caused by the 'herd instinct' behaviour of the international banking community. The figures in Chapter VI of the 1983 BIS report are quite revealing.

The flow of international bank loans to non-OPEC developing countries, after increasing from US $12 billion to 16 billion from the first half of 1981 to the same period of 1982, suffered a precipitous drop in the second half: US $28 billion (1981) to US $4 billion (1982). The fall in Latin America is even more dramatic (for the two second yearly halves): US $21 billion (1981) to practically *zero* in 1982.

Maybe this frantic escape to the nearest door by the banks, after the Mexicans called 'moratorium', has some relationship to the circumstance that international bankers went to Toronto in the autumn of 1982 looking for some guidance from the authorities in charge. The answer they got certainly was not encouraging. The decision on a possible Fund quota increase of some significance was calmly postponed by the authorities until April, 1983. Upon returning to their desks at their respective capitals, they quickly redid their homework. For the first time, in many years, a top level ample ministerial meeting in financial matters was anticipated by two months to reach the IMF quota increase decision February 1983.

As its implementation is still pending decision by Parliaments, the order of the day to calm bankers in the Bank and Fund meetings of the autumn of 1983 may well be to spread the word that borrowing countries will deliver on their IMF stabilisation programmes, by 'putting their homes in order'.

Brazil is the object of particular attention, having recently signed a third Letter of Intentions after rather tortuous negotiations with the IMF, because it could not perform under the second. Mexico will be praised as an example to non-performers: the irony of it all is that at the Toronto meetings Mexico was the 'mischievious bad boy' and Brazil the 'wise guy that could manage the debt so well'.

Could it be that one reason for the current status of things, leaving aside eventual mismanagement problems, is the existence of a difference in the two countries' objectives as to the question of the outward transfer of resources?

Maybe Mexico is in large agreement with the IMF balance of payment targets in the three-year stabilisation programme providing for an outward transfer of resources. A good part of her debt reflects the financing of oil related projects at a fuel's nominal price which will not materialise in the markets for at least a decade, who knows. The external borrowings also financed transfer of funds abroad, by locals who simply could freely move them, because there were no exchange controls while the peso rate was clearly misplaced. This being the case, it makes sense to accept IMF targets resulting in a 'desired' outward flow of resources that 'kills undesirable external debt'.

It is awkward to discuss other countries' business, specially without a profound and intimate knowledge of its conditions and patterns of behaviour. What can certainly be said is that the IMF balance of payments targeting for Brazil cannot correspond to her national objective of economic growth.

After two years of practically zero growth and declining per-capita income, the three-year IMF stabilisation programme covering 1983 to 1985 contemplates a transfer of real resources of around US $12 billion for the period as a whole, with annual values increasing during the time span. This results from the fact that the postulated current account deficits – which are to be the base for the calculation of additional net loan by other sources beyond the IMF, according to the 'catalyst approach' – decline rather sharply, whereas interest payments, already larger than the deficit at the initial year, keep on necessarily growing.

Meanwhile, the Brazilian economy remains engaged with an IBS which has become entirely artificial, operating on the basis of a bank by bank quota distribution of the contemplated future 'fresh' loans. The system is very demanding on smaller bank officials who have to present to their boards a course of action they would not necessarily like to follow on their own.

The ultimate and very profound question to be calmly and objectively answered by Brazil is whether it serves her national objectives of economic growth to remain tied to an IBS which has the following characteristics:

(a) a historically high level of the international rate of interest in real terms (8 to 9 per cent p.a.);
(b) no clear trend direction in which it will move, because of the special dependence of that rate on the unresolved American Federal deficit problem;
(c) on top of that, short-term volatility of the interest rate which may impose unexpected additional resource transfer burden;
(d) lack of sure signs of strong growth in the industrial world as a whole, being dangerously interest sensitive in the US. A strong developed countries' recovery is a precondition for the adequate deployment of the protective strategy of export promotion. This situation is aggravated by the rampant protectionist tendencies

which have been set loose by the 'non-system' we operate with today.

When all this is taken into account, the same kind of cold evaluation that led the country to decide engage into the IBS in the late 1960s seems to lead to the convenience of the following decision: and advance application by Brazil of the ideas which would eventually be incorporated on 'a partial and temporary disengagement from the IBS'.

The 'disengagement' would be 'temporary' for a period of five years. This is the time horizon which might be deemed necessary for the international financial situation to give some definite signs of direction and stability.

The 'disengagement' would be 'partial' for two reasons. First, borrowing relationships would continue with the multilateral development institutions with which Brazil operates: the World Bank and IDB. These entities still provide the country with a positive resource transfer, their disbursements being consistently larger each year than amortisation and interest payments. Second, also exempt from the 'disengagement' operation would be the short-term financing facilities clearly related to trade. The excess of short-term financing, beyond what could be considered trade relatable, would receive the same treatment as all other long-term debt (original maturity higher than one year).

As to the other sources for borrowing, with the indicated exceptions for the MDI's and trade related credit, constituting the IBS, the Treasury of Brazil would assume responsibility for the loan obligations abroad of each and every borrower in the country. The *interest obligations would be paid on an accrual basis, on the same terms as on the original loans*.

In the course of the fourth year, the Government of Brazil would indicate the conditions for the actual starting up of payments to the creditors abroad on a cash basis, as of the end of the fifth year.

Given the evolution of the Brazilian economy, on one hand, and the performance of the World economy, on the other, it should then be possible to determine over how many years to spread the cash payments related to amortisation and interest.

To enable itself to make those payments, the Government would then tax the Brazilian people to raise the funds necessary to acquire the foreign exchange required *to actually pay the debt*.

At the same fourth year, the Government would decide whether to allow, as of the fifth year, Brazilian enterprises and other borrowers to resume access to the IBS.

Prior to the public announcement of the 'partial and temporary disengagement from the IBS', the Brazilian Government would reservedly communicate with the governments, under whose jurisdiction lie the different banks operating in international banking, to let them know in advance of the proposed action by Brazil.

In the communication the Brazilian Government would make clear that, even though recognising that it was a matter for individual decision by governments, Brazil would appreciate if no eventual punishment would be applicable to the banks. It is a well known fact that some constituencies desire to have banks pay for what they consider imprudent banking. Each sovereign government, however, would obviously be free to act as it would see fit.

Upon receipt of the Brazilian Government communication, the Government would instruct their respective bank examining agency that the Brazilian loans in the bank books could be considered 'as if performing', because interest would continue to be received on an accrual basis, for the next five years, on the original contractual terms.

If punishment would be considered desirable by a particular government, the ratio for 'as if performability' would be lower than 100 per cent of the outstanding value of the loans.

The proposed approach shows quite clearly that the capital importing country does not hold as their hostages the banks having a high exposure towards it, in relation to the bank's capital. As can be seen, the banks are dependent upon their respective authorities actions in interpreting their constituencies' wishes.

As a last pertinent remark on the suggested approach, it merely extends over time the procedure which has been recently applied in the case of the Mexican moratorium.

The possible operational level of the Brazilian economy, after the 'disengagement operation' would depend on two factors, among other things. If the providers of *direct investment* were keen on demonstrating their interest on the Brazilian market, they could organise themselves rapidly to demonstrate a show of support for the 'disengagement' decision. This could eventually be carried out with the concurrent leadership of the Brazilian private enterprise sectors.

The amount of *trade credit* available after the decision would determine the level of trade. As the trade credit had been not specifically assumed by the Treasury, it is possible that some of the regional banks abroad, having shown interest in retreating into their traditional line of international banking, could assume a more active role.

If the reaction were negative all around, the operational level of the economy would be severely curtailed, because export and import would settle at a low level. Two observations are valid. First, the economy would have avoided an 'undesired' and 'unreasonable' outward transfer of resources. Second, the so-called 'war economy', of which there is so much talk, could be put finally into place. It should be remarked that the Brazilian economy has traditionally had positive experiences under conditions of duress. And one should not forget the important structural changes which have taken place in the industrial base about to be seriously damaged. For example, the capital goods industry that is already in place.

Without going into many details, one of the chief results of the 'disengagement' procedure would be to let the domestic rate of interest be determined by the supply of domestic savings plus direct investment, and the demand for domestic investment. It would no longer be propped up by the abnormal levels of the international real rate of interest. It would also, and this is an important result, be freed from the expectational effects of real devaluation, which will be present for a long while if one follows current procedures to deal with the crisis.

The borrowers in Brazil would still have their debts denominated in foreign currency. But exchange rate policy would be simplified, because it could be conducted with only one market in mind, the market for tradeable goods and services. The financial market would be provisionally suspended for five years because no more 'fresh' loans would have to be obtained in the IBS.

As the borrowers would continue to pay their commitments of interest and amortisation normally into the Central Bank, cruzeiro funds would be available for many programmes. These flows into the Central Bank would have to be combined with the overall Federal deficit.

It would be possible to control 'functionally' the pace downward of inflation and re-establish monetary correction or 'indexation', with its due logic. The functional slowing down of inflation preserves as much growth as possible, under the circumstances.

A politically very important result is that the currently much discussed wage law in the Brazilian Congress (Law no. 2045) could be rescinded as there would be no undertaking next to the Fund as to the future rate of inflation. A new law could be enacted that would provide for the rational maintenance of the overall purchasing power of the wage bill, which is clearly not a cost-push factor these days.

Finally, the operation would not represent a rupture with the IMF. To the contrary, Brazil could eventually abandon some exchange restriction practices which the organisation objects to.

*   *   *

It is certainly an 'off the beaten path' solution to the problem. But, after all, business has not been as usual in Brazil for some time. The 'disengagement' operation may bring growth with control of inflation again, a path Brazil once rationally followed with great pride and optimism. One must revive the animal spirits of the enterpreneurs if one wants job creating investments again. And this forgotten environment must be brought back soon, for the sake of all the already unemployed and all the young workers that keep relentlessly arriving in waves of at least 1.5 million per year to the labour force.

It can be shown that Brazil's decision along the suggested lines is beneficial not only to the country itself, but also to the international financial community. After all, it is a decision of a responsible capital importing country.

6 The International Debt Threat: a Way to Avoid a Crash

Minos Zombanakis

International indebtedness is probably the most prssing problem on the world economic horizon. Many developing countries are facing severe difficulties in servicing their foreign debt, which in total has climbed to over US $750 billion, over half of it owed to commercial banks. Already more than 25 countries, with between them bank loans of around US $250 billion, have been forced into reschedulings.

This huge debt load stems from the large structural imbalances in countries' external payments which began to appear in the 1970s after the first oil crisis and which continue today. These imbalances were wrongly diagnosed as 'cyclical disequilibria'; as a result, the current-account deficits of the non-oil developing countries were allowed to accumulate to frightening proportions.

The correct way to deal with the problem would have been under the collective responsibility of the world community, expressed either through the International Monetary Fund (probably with an adjusted mandate) or through some other international initiative. Instead, it was left to the commercial banks to finance the developing countries' deficits under their own credit responsibility. The banks saw in this an opportunity for profit. They rushed to intermediate between the savings, in the form of bank deposits, of the newly-surplus countries (mainly Opec members) and the demand for loans of the deficit countries. And they allowed themselves a comfortable spread.

The banks' monetary authorities saw this intermediation as a function of cash flow movements in a free market-place and believed that, with time, a new equilibrium would emerge in world payments. It was an attitude of complacency, not an objective view of the necessary action at the time.

The New York banks, acting as the main money-centre institutions of the world banking system, set out to secure the largest share of the so-called recycling. They ended up, as a group, as the largest single supplier of credit, both directly to country borrowers and indirectly to the interbank system. Surplus funds from the treasuries of the large American banks were made available to smaller banks or foreign banks unable to attract directly deposits denominated in foreign currency. These other banks in turn used the funds to lend to the same community of borrowers. Exposure of the big American banks was thus ensured through the interbank markets even when loans were extended by other banks; there is no control over the end-use of funds once they are channelled through the interbank markets.

It was much the same for a limited number of other international banks, such as the leading British banks, the four large German banks and the Japanese banks – big banks which had the credibility to act as primary depositories of surplus funds.

The American authorities did not discourage these developments. The dogmatic American treasury could not see anything wrong with the intermediation of the market-place in the supply and demand of money. It set out to kill as irrelevant any proposals to face international debt problems collectively. The Kissinger safety net, the Healey plan and other such proposals were quashed.

Paradoxically, the Federal Reserve considered the dependence on the American banks in the recycling process a tool of strength for American policy in general and felt very comfortable with the large American banks taking the leading role. The European and Japanese international banks played their part, though always as second fiddles – except when Japan's current account was running a large surplus and the Japanese ministry of finance used the lending activities of its banks to export funds.

As for the non-American banks, in carrying out their lending operations through the Euromarkets to country borrowers (or other borrowers for that matter) they always assumed the American monetary authorities would act as lenders of last resort if there was a shortage of liquidity in the Euromarkets. Absurd as it may be, most of the banks still believe this today. For three main reasons:

(1) Three quarters of the outstanding international debt is denominated in dollars.
(2) American banks have provided the bulk of the funds for the credits. It is therefore implied that if the foreign banks cannot meet their liabilities to the American banks the Federal Reserve will have to provide the shortfall.

(3) The Federal Reserve adopted a policy of 'neglect' during the huge expansion of international lending by the American banks. The Europeans firmly believed this neglect was a way of expressing tacit knowledge and approval.

AN ORGY OF CREDIT

Such was the background against which the world's banking community embarked upon an orgy of credit. The Euromarket was seen as the main supplier of money, using net bank deposits as the monetary base. Credit expansion assumed huge proportions, as the *modus operandi* of the Euromarket came to resemble a Federal Reserve system without reserve requirements or central bank control. Demand, rather than supply, dictated its size.

In order to mobilise short-term deposits and credit availability in general, a system was devised whereby lenders entered into a commitment to supply money for a given term without having to match it with deposits of comparable maturities. The commitment allowed banks to revise their interest rate periodically (usually at three- or six-month intervals). As their interest rate was based on the cost of money to themselves plus a spread, the banks could borrow for every interest period and thus refinance the amount they had originally extended to the borrower.

At the beginning some efforts were made to apply credit judgement and to justify the purpose of the loan. With time, however, competition among the banks to secure a larger share of the business encouraged them to overlook creditworthiness and even to invent theories to justify an unwise extension of credit. Otherwise cautious bankers publicly rationalised past actions in order to justify the increasing dependence of their institutions on the earnings from their international loans.

Loan maturities had little to do with the actual structure of a country's requirements and loans were put together in terms of size and maturity either to meet market preference or to fit the spread over Libor (London interbank offered rate) that borrowers were intending to pay. Though the spread represented an insignificant proportion of the total cost of the borrowing some enterprising bankers – with the help of the Press – succeeded in turning it into a creditworthiness rating. Maturities, therefore, had to be shortened in many cases to fit the spread expectations.

Another notion was that a short-term loan was safer than a long-term one, because it would allow that lender to recover his asset before other creditors. Thus, when the market-place was reluctant to respond to given requirements, the maturities became shorter to fit lenders' preferences.

For all these reasons, the average life of loans became shorter. With time and attrition, big country borrowers saw their total debt concentrated in such short-term maturities that it was beyond their ability to service or repay it. Now countries began to be concerned with refinancing existing debt due for payment, as well as securing credit for new requirements.

REFINANCING AT ANY PRICE

When the lending spree started, both lenders and borrowers assumed that, with time and an expansion in international trade, countries would be able to increase their export earnings and repay their obligations. But something went wrong.

Doubt began to emerge when (1) the size of the obligations was inflated by the huge rise in interest rates, adding to the costs of servicing existing debt; and (2) economic growth began to diminish as the world entered its longest post-war recession. The high cost of new borrowings inevitably led to a further shortening of maturities and a further increase in the size of the loans needed to refinance maturing obligations. Suddenly the main preoccupation of the borrowers and of their bankers was to secure continuous refinancing at any maturity.

So 1982 began with international debt in a very fragile state. Western banks had outstanding loans of about US$60 billion to Eastern Europe (including Russia) and over US$180 billion to Latin America.

Equally important, the average life of the debt of the biggest borrowers among the developing countries – Mexico, Brazil, Argentina, Poland and Yugoslavia – had fallen and large chunks of debt were due in the following year or two. A number of international banks had large exposures in individual countries, especially American banks in Latin American countries. This forced them to extend still further credit to cover these countries' current needs in order to avert sovereign insolvency. In addition, they had to make up for the leakage caused by the unwillingness of American regional banks, and some other international banks, to renew maturing credits.

It became evident that the large banks were locked into these foreign loans. The withdrawal of any individual bank from any given country could bring the country's downfall and, in the process, insolvency of the bank also.

The large banks were preoccupied not only with the solvency of their assets; they were also anxious to see that other creditors, especially the smaller banks, did not abandon the borrowers. Their anxiety led their respective authorities to ask all banks to overlook creditworthiness and to stick with the loans – an absurd (and perhaps illegal?) position for a central bank to take, but nevertheless justified under the circumstances.

POLITICS DIDN'T HELP

The political events of 1982 did not help. The persistence of political turmoil in Poland not only weakened its own negotiating position on its outstanding debt, but it also reduced the ability of other Eastern European countries to raise funds internationally – with the exception of Hungary, which pleaded that it had nothing to do with the problems of its brothers. The rescheduling of the Polish debt met with difficulties, but in the end was done.

The Falklands war did not help the fortunes of Latin American credit in general. It contributed directly to the disruption of payments by Argentina. It also exposed the myth that Latin America is an American backyard and so, whatever happens, the United States will underwrite these countries. Under certain conditions America would take the part of 'outsiders', as it did with Britain over the Falklands crisis. And America could not tell the banks or the IMF to bail out countries – contrary to self-perpetuating, mythical assumption.

Suddenly Latin American countries met with closed doors when they approached the market for refinancing on a business-as-usual basis. The first to try – and to fail – was Mexico, which at the end of the summer of 1983 declared it could not service its debts. The IMF was consulted, the American government agreed to payments against oil, and the Bank for International Settlements put a short-term facility at Mexico's disposal. But it was soon realised that all these *ad hoc* arrangements were a drop in Mexico's $80 billion ocean of outstanding loans. In fact, the $5 billion package put together for Mexico amounts to only half of the interest payments due for 1983.

Faced with this situation, neither the banks (especially the American banks which – unlike in Poland's case – had the lion's share) nor their supervisory authorities knew what to do. Many people in August 1983 thought the financial system would collapse. Catastrophe was averted only because: (1) people who might have panicked were on summer vacation; and (2) the Federal Reserve intervened to provide both liquidity and encouragement to the banks to 'hold on'. The fear was that one of the lenders might declare its loans in default which, through cross-default clauses, would put all loans to Mexico in default and make them due for payment.

Subsequently, consultations with the IMF, strong intervention with the banks by its managing director, Mr Jacques de Larosière, consultations among the lenders and encouragement from their respective governments helped to arrest the situation in Mexico, at least temporarily. The same procedure was later followed to deal with the problems of Brazil and other countries, as they followed in Mexico's footsteps.

The case of Brazil was especially dramatic. Just before Christmas 1983 the country declared 'unilaterally' its inability to service and repay its loans. The banks had no choice but to concede to its requests by a certain date (31 March), otherwise the country would declare itself insolvent. Brazil's action gave a different perspective to the whole problem of outstanding world indebtedness. Bank loans became frozen assets.

THE BORROWER DICTATES

It exposed the fact that when lenders are involved with a borrower to the point where their own solvency is at sake, it is the borrower that dictates and the lender that follows. Unfortunately, this is where we are today. Table 6.1, reproduced from the *American Banker*, shows that in Brazil, Mexico and Venezuela (recently added to the casualty list) taken together, the 10 large American banks have outstanding loans which by far exceed their total equity.

It serves no purpose to blame anyone now, perhaps the banks less than most, for in a way they became the victims of circumstances. Instead, we must concentrate our efforts on relieving the system of pressures to avoid the consequences of its possible collapse. There

Table 6.1   Exposure of ten American banks. Outstanding loans in $ billion

	Brazil	Mexico	Venezuela	Total of three countries	Total as per cent of bank's equity
Citicorp	4.4	3.3	1.1	8.7	180
Bank America	2.3	2.5	2.0	6.8	148
Chase Manhattan	2.4	1.7	1.0	5.1	183
Man. Hanover	2.0	1.7	1.1	4.8	174
Morgan Guaranty	1.7	1.1	0.5	3.3	122
Chemical	1.3	1.5	—	2.8	143
Bankers Trust	0.9	0.9	0.5	2.2	143
Cont. Illinois	0.5	0.7	0.5	1.6	96
First Interstate	0.5	0.7	—	1.2	64
Security Pacific	0.5	0.5	—	1.0	68

Source: American Banker.

is no way the problem will solve itself without official intervention, despite the optimism of some bankers. What else can they say if they are to maintain the confidence of the public?

THE ZOMBANAKIS PLAN

Rescue schemes for countries which have been worked out so far with the IMF's help, calling for programmes of adjustment under agreed reschedulings, can only buy time: they cannot solve the basic problem. We must look for longer-term solutions while struggling to hold the system together through these *ad hoc* arrangements.

Solutions should not disrupt the international system of trade and payments. They should not require the bailing out of banks by their respective taxpayers. They must address themselves to the real problem, which is not just shortage of liquidity but, above all, the threat of insolvency both to countries and to the banks. They must fit the existing framework to the maximum extent possible, so that a new international consensus is not required – something that would be hard to obtain today, at least before the catastrophe had occurred. In a nutshell, we must look for solutions that allow Mohammed to go to the mountain rather than expect the mountain to go to

Mohammed. So far, in all the plans proposed by academics and others, the latter is the case.

The IMF is the indispensable element in any new initiative, and faith in that institution should be restated in the strongest possible terms. The proposed increase in its quota should be ratified as soon as possible. In consultation with the IMF, countries in a critical situation should try to work out realistic programmes for long-term adjustment. Such programmes should be over a longer period of time than envisaged by present schemes: we are dealing with problems of a longer span than in the past. The IMF management should be encouraged by the interim committee to take this approach.

Once a reasonable programme has been agreed between a country and the IMF, the creditors should be brought in to satisfy themselves about the plan's viability and even to offer suggestions for improvement. After obtaining the consent of the lenders, the IMF should propose a rescheduling of existing debts, taking into consideration not only immediate cash requirements but also, particularly, the projection of earnings and expenditure over a longer period of time. Let us use a period of 13 years for the sake of this exercise.

An IMF initiative

When new repayment schedules had been argreed between borrowers and creditors, the IMF would enter into an arrangement with the parties concerned under which it undertook unconditionally to guarantee the repayment of amounts due in the last three years – years 11–13 – of the programme.

The guarantee of the IMF (arranged as described below) would signify that the programme carried the IMF's approval. It would give the borrowing country time to adjust its economy to realistic goals over a period of 13 years, in the expectation that as world conditions return to normal it will be able to repay its obligations. Any such programme, by its nature, would be less restrictive for the borrowers than a short-term rescue. So it would release some restrained demand to help world recovery.

The guarantee would be looked upon by the creditors as the instrument which secures the repayment of their claims at the time when the guarantee is applicable – that is during the last years of the loan. With this security, the banks could resume their consideration of new requests from the borrowers – provided, of course, that these demands were within the framework of the new programme agreed with the IMF.

Needless to say, countries would have the right to prepay, partially or totally, their outstanding debt during the period of the adjustment process, just as they now have the right to prepay against their banking credit. This could happen, for example, in Mexico's case if the oil prices were to climb to $60 a barrel (not unlikely four or five years from now if there is a healthy world economic growth meantime). An arrangement for compulsory prepayment could apply, if required by the creditors, if a country's reserves accumulated to a certain level.

Arrangements under the agreed programme could be interrupted or their application made conditional if the IMF and the creditors were uncomfortable with the borrower's progress. If the borrower falls down on its commitments to the IMF programme, then the guarantees are revoked and would not be forthcoming. This would be a safeguard against debtors offloading their debts in years 11–13 on the IMF guarantee, having by then enjoyed ten years of easier life. Only if the borrower has stuck to IMF conditions, yet could not pay in the last years of the loan, would the IMF be called upon to make payments to creditors under its guarantee. The guarantee could serve as take-out for the banks only if the IMF allowed it to be used as such.

In order to lessen the pressures on the Eurodollar market, lending banks from strong creditor countries (which should include, as a minimum, Japan, West Germany and Switzerland) should be asked to convert claims on borrowers to their own currencies. Thus if Deutsche Bank has borrowed $10m from Citibank through the Euromarkets to lend to Mexico, by mutual agreement the Bundesbank could provide the dollars to repay Citibank and turn the Deutsche Bank dollar loan to Mexico into one denominated in D-marks. This would increase the confidence of the lending banks which would feel that, if necessary, their central bank will be a lender of last resort. It would also, incidentally, reduce pressure on the dollar.

For all rescheduled loans a new set of terms should be worked out. Under these terms:

(1) The banks should accept for the rescheduled loans an interest rate comparable to the return on government-issued or government-guaranteed paper available to them for investment. For American banks, for example, that would be American government paper of comparable maturity.

(2) The difference between the original rate and the new rate should be charged to the borrower as a guarantee fee. This amount, collected in an escrow account over the years, should go a long way towards meeting the requirements under the guarantee in case it becomes necessary.

The guarantee

The IMF is not empowered to provide guarantees, and to try to give it the right to do so out of its quota resources would be both controversial and undesirable. For guarantees to be provided, an arrangement should be made under which a group of countries – probably those in the enlarged Group of Ten – would set up a facility to be administered by the IMF in conjunction with the programmes of adjustment. It could be called a Guarantee Loan Fund (GLF).

This facility would be provided with standby letters of credit by the Group of Ten creditors under which funds would be drawn to meet payments as required under the guarantees to meet unfilled obligations by the debtor countries to the banks. Net payments (minus the funds from the escrow account accumulated with the proceeds of the interest differentials on rescheduled loans) would be repaid to the contributing countries, through the GLF, under conditions to be worked out subsequently. Alternatively, a fund could be structured on the lines of the substitution account proposed a few years ago, which could be resurrected for the purpose given the political will. These proposals are a realistic approach to a very complicated problem because:

(1) They do not require the banks to be bailed out, nor do they let the banks off the hook.
(2) They allow lenders and creditors time to make a realistic adjustment to a deep-rooted problem that cannot be handled through short-term programmes and reschedulings.
(3) Developing countries are spared programmes of extreme devaluation that expose them to the dangers of political upheaval, damaging both to their own constituency and also to their region.
(4) By rescheduling short-term assets and adding the IMF's guarantee, the banks can unfreeze their assets and resume their function of financing trade and investment with renewed confidence.
(5) The banks would no longer have to change exorbitant rates to

good customers in order to create the excess pool of profit required to be able to write off the inherent in developing countries' loans.

(6) There would be no interruption of the present *modus operandi* of the financial system. The interbank market would not be at risk.

(7) The Group of Ten countries, which will have to carry the burden of rescuing the world if there is a debt repudiation, can look forward to 13 years of breathing space for the IDCs to adjust their economies.

(8) With the right policies of growth by the industrialised countries and co-operation between the IMF, the banks and the borrowers, the guarantees would never have to be called upon.

These proposals amount to a pre-emptive rescheduling of existing debts with the object of correcting wrongly-structured maturities. They also provide a facility of collective responsibility that will act as guarantor of last resort. These measures are proposed not as a substitute for existing arrangements under the IMF and other institutions, but as an addition to them.

Part II
The 1984 Conference

7 Properties of Monetary Systems

Allan H. Meltzer[1]

A constant theme in Keynes's analytic work is the design of monetary and non-monetary arrangements. *Economic Consequences of the Peace* is a strong critique of the arrangements proposed at the Versailles peace conference. *A Tract on Monetary Reform*, as the title suggests, proposes an alternative to the return to the classical gold standard. *A Treatise on Money* takes a deeper look at fundamental properties of money and ends with proposals for world monetary reform to reduce price variability. The *General Theory* tries to show why an economy remains at less than full employment, as Britain's economy had in the 1920s, and proposes institutional reform, principally non-monetary reform, to remedy the problem of underemployment. Keynes's last major effort, the proposal for Bretton Woods, though not written as an analytic work, was a major effort to redesign the world monetary system.

In a world of costless transactions, certainty and costless acquisition of information, the comparison of monetary standards is uninteresting. Many methods of making payments and expressing values have the same costs and benefits. For economic analyses of differences in monetary standards, the reasons for using money, the way society chooses to denominate assets and express values or the role of government in the monetary system there must be costs and benefits that change with the monetary standard and the monetary system. Principal differences in costs to individuals or societies arise from three sources. Costs of producing and storing the unit used as money vary with the choice of fiat paper or commodity standards and with the choice of the commodities used as a commodity standard. Costs of organising, administering and policing the system vary with the resources used to co-ordinate decisions, nationally and internationally, and the resources used to prevent fraud and counterfeiting or to monitor debasement of the currency units. Costs vary also with the type and degree of uncertainty that individuals and society bear. No monetary system can provide complete price, exchange rate and interest rate stability. There are differences in cost and in the distribution of the cost burden that depend on the properties of the monetary and economic systems and on the nature of shocks or disturbances. Keynes (1936, p. 170) reaches a similar conclusion about the effect of uncertainty on liquidity preference.

The choice of monetary arrangements and a monetary standard has elements found in many collective decisions. Each person's net benefit depends upon the actions that others take. The fact that the choice has elements of collective choice does not mean that the choice of monetary arrangements and the monetary standard must be made by governments. There is considerable historical evidence that the evolution of monetary systems began as a private solution to a local problem and only later governments assumed certain functions.[2] The role of government in the monetary system changed many times in the centuries that followed. The design of monetary arrangements has been drawn and redrawn in the market-place and in the parliaments as a response to prevailing conditions, beliefs, hopes and fears about future conditions, technology, and the tastes expressed in the market-place and in the voting booth or by the dictator or sovereign.

The twentieth century provides a rich and diverse history of choices and a lively discussion about the merits of various alternatives. The rest of this section briefly surveys the history and its background. Keynes is a central figure – probably the central figure – structuring the choices and comparing the alternatives during the first half of the century. The ideas associated with his work, or based on it, dominated monetary and non-monetary arrangements in the quarter century following his death in 1946. The international monetary agreement, known as the Bretton Woods system, was the product of many minds, but Keynes's blueprint provided the structure around which discussion occurred and from which the international monetary arrangements of the post-war years evolved. The monetary and non-monetary policies of many countries are – properly or improperly – called Keynesian, testifying to the belief that these policies are based on theories propounded by Keynes.

Keynes was born in 1883, at a time when the classical international gold standard was firmly established. Britain's commitment to the standard, about 150 years earlier, fixed the value of the pound sterling at 113 grains of fine gold and sustained the commitment by offering to buy and sell gold at that price. Since the Bank of England kept its notes convertible into gold at the fixed price, other banks could maintain convertibility of their notes either by buying and selling gold at the price fixed by the issuing government or by maintaining convertibility of their note issue, and later their deposits, into Bank of England notes. Exchange rates were determined by the relative gold content of a currency for countries on the gold standard. As an example the US dollar was reset in 1900 at 23.22 grains of find gold, so £1 was the equivalent of $4.8665. The fixed exchange rate between the two currencies was maintained by both countries' commitment to maintain the gold content of its currency.

The British commitment to buy and sell gold was suspended from 1793 to 1821 and from 1914 to 1925. In 1821, Britain restored the commitment at the former price and returned to the gold standard. The return to gold was accompanied by a 50 per cent deflation from 1814 to 1824 to restore convertibility at the former exchange rate of gold for notes (Viner, 1937, p. 174). The 1821 resumption, and a number of temporary suspensions and resumptions of convertibility of notes into gold at the Bank of England later in the century, reinforced anticipation about the long-run fixity of the price of gold in pounds sterling but left no doubt that there was uncertainty about convertibility on any specific future date.[3] The commitment to gold was not as fixed as the constant of gravity. It seems proper, however, to regard the public's belief in the commitment to the gold price at the end of the century as being as firm as any political or economic arrangement is likely to be.

During the last quarter of the nineteenth century, social decisions suggest that belief in the social and private benefits of the gold standard was high. Many countries formally committed their monetary authorities to buy and sell gold, and by extension to buy and sell other currencies on the standard, at fixed price.[4]

The commitment to gold at its historic price was widely accepted as a norm in Britain and the United States. After the First World War, the Governor of the Bank of England, Montagu Norman, and Benjamin Strong, Governor of the Federal Reserve Bank of New York agreed to work for the restoration of the prewar exchange rate between the British pound and the US dollar. Both countries had inflated during the war, so the Governors agreed that both would have to deflate to restore the former exchange rate, $4.86 to the pound. Mutual deflation imposed excess burdens on both countries, including the relatively severe recession of 1920–21. The return to gold at the prewar price is usually offered as a principal reason for persistent unemployment in Britain's export industries during the

1920s. Money wages had increased in the export industries, relative to foreign wages, so the prewar parity required a reduction in money wages or a reallocation of resources. In either case, the return to the prewar price of gold imposed a burden. Some of the burden would have been avoided by devaluing the pound in terms of gold, but that option was dismissed.

Keynes actively opposed the return to the prewar gold standard in 1925. He believed that the social costs of returning to gold were larger than the benefits and, from a broader perspective, he opposed the gold standard as a vestige of *laissez faire*. Keynes favoured greater intervention in the economy and, at the time, worked to change the position of the Liberal Party toward greater activism in economic affairs (Harrod, 1951, pp. 331–4). He was not a socialist, but 'he was not a great friend of the profit motive' (p. 333), or of the prewar liberal order. He saw the gold standard as part of that order and, although he changed his opinions on many issues during the next twenty years, he always opposed the classical gold standard and worked actively to develop alternatives.

Although the return to the gold standard was brief, its effect was long lasting in Britain and elsewhere. The return to gold did not restore the competitive position of the export industries and was not followed by a reduction in unemployment. Belief in the standard as a means to prosperity seems to have been eroded by the experience and its aftermath. The tide of opinion shifted away from the commitment to gold and toward greater experimentation and management of monetary affairs.

Britain once again left the gold standard in September 1931 after the start of the depression of the 1930s. During the years until the start of the Second World War, most of the world's currencies devalued against gold and against each other. Countries imposed exchange controls and trade restrictions seeking relative advantage or to increase the government's control of interest rates and resource use. Monetary and trade arrangements, and the growing threat of war at the end of the decade, heightened uncertainty about future values. Many countries continued to use gold to settle international payments. They paid the resource costs of a commodity reserve currency without obtaining the benefits that come from the avoidance of exchange controls and a credible commitment to domestic and international convertibility at a fixed exchange rate.

At the end of the Second World War, the governments of both Britain and the United States hoped to avoid a return to the instability of the interwar period. Planning of post-war monetary arrangements began as an effort by the two governments to establish a more stable international economic order. The Bretton Woods agreement and the General Agreement on Tariffs and Trade set up institutions that imposed restrictions on member countries' freedom to restrict trade or to change relative values or currency parities. Countries did not entirely avoid the cost of holding gold, but the stock of dollars and convertible currencies increased relative to the gold stock, and most countries held reserves in dollars. Eventually, the increase in dollars relative to the US gold stock, and the failure of the US to slow the rate of increase, raised doubts about the future values under the standard. Uncertainty about future values rose. Efforts to restrict *de facto* convertibility into gold added to the uncertainty and the cost of the system.

In 1971, the Bretton Woods system formally ended when President Nixon ended *de jure* convertibility of dollars into gold. Exchange rates became market determined, and countries were free to choose fixed or fluctuating rates.

Milton Friedman had argued earlier (1953, pp. 157–250) that the gold standard and other commodity standards with fixed exchange rates are more costly than a system of fluctuating exchange rates with a rule fixing the rate of money growth. Friedman calculated the resource cost of a commodity standard for the United States but neglected costs arising from uncertainty about future values. He claimed that, in addition to lower resource costs, a system of freely fluctuating exchange rates can benefit countries by encouraging trade and allowing government to pursue policies that keep exchange rates and domestic prices relatively stable (Friedman, 1953, p. 158).

A decade or more of fluctuating exchange rates has not borne out Friedman's hope or prediction. Governments have not chosen to reduce barriers to trade but have, instead, imposed quotas and trade restrictions. Although inflation was reduced in the early 1980s, governments have not used monetary policy to stabilise either domestic prices or exchange rates, and they have not refrained from intervention in currency markets in their attempts to alter the outcome of private decisions.[5]

The brief sketch of monetary arrangements conveys some of the diversity of arrangements during the past century. The sketch also suggests the way in which costs change under different systems and brings out several issues that must be resolved in the design of domestic and international arrangements. First is the division between public and private functions. Monetary systems and arrangements are social institutions, but they may arise or change either through private action or by law. Second is the level and type of risk that society bears under different monetary arrangements. The choice between fixed and fluctuating exchange rates, or between rules and discretionary monetary management, impose different types of risk on society and call forth different arrangements for pooling, diversifying and reducing risk. Third is the level of consumption, output or welfare achieved. Some arrangements may increase or reduce efficiency by introducing or removing uncertainty, by facilitating or hampering trade expansion, by increasing resource costs and in other ways.

A monetary system cannot provide high employment at rising real wages if other institutions inhibit efficiency or shift resources toward present consumption. But it is also true that society's opportunity set is not independent of monetary institutions or arrangements. If the monetary system increases risk and uncertainty, investment is likely to be smaller or a smaller fraction of wealth will be invested within the country. If the financial system is highly regulated, resources will be used to circumvent controls instead of searching for opportunities that increase aggregate wealth. If the financial system does not develop, opportunities for trade and exchange are restricted. For these reasons, among others, the opportunity set depends on the type of monetary system. See Brunner and Meltzer (1971).

OPPORTUNITIES, RISKS AND THE ROLE OF GOVERNMENT

The changing role of governmental and private institutions, and their coexistence, suggests that no single arrangement has been found to dominate all others. Money is produced by privately owned banks and by government central banks. While many central banks began as private banks, today most central banks are owned by governments or operate as government agencies. Even where equity in the central bank is owned privately, as in the United States, government has the power to appoint the managing directors and to restrict their policies and operations.[6] Where governments have nationalised ownership of the central bank and placed the central bank under the control of the Treasury, as in Britain, the central bank retains some independence within the government. The bank has, at times, resisted the government's proposals for changes in monetary arrangements and operating procedures.

Different monetary arrangements introduce different explicit or implicit norms for government and devolve different responsibilities on the public and private sectors, on governments, private institutions and individuals. Each choice distributes risks and opportunities in different ways. This section discusses the role of government and the distribution of risks and opportunities arising from four choices: the medium of exchange, the standard of value, private or public production of money, the international standard – fixed or floating exchange rates.

The medium of exchange

Social choice of a medium of exchange has elements found in all collective decisions. Each person's net benefit from using a small number of assets to make payments depends on the information, knowledge or beliefs that others have about the units or commodities offered. A main item of information about a medium of exchange is the knowledge that third parties accept the unit in exchange for a wide range of goods and services and in diverse locations.

The collective aspect is widely recognised. The term 'general acceptability' is typically used to define 'medium of exchange'. 'General acceptability' conveys that the cost of using a particular asset decreases as the frequency of use within a social group increases.[7]

Collective choice of the assets used as mediums of exchange does not require that the choice be made by government. Monetary theory offers many examples of market practice moving ahead of law or treaty to establish trading and exchange arrangements. Traveller's cheques issued by privately owned banks and non-banks are modern examples of privately developed means of payment that are used internationally. But these means of payment, though widely used, are used mainly for current transactions. They are not much used to settle deferred obligations or contractual agreements. And they are denominated in units previously established by law or agreement within a group.

The use of a medium of exchange reduces costs of transacting and reduces uncertainty about the quality of the objects received in payment for goods and services. The knowledge that objects received in payment will be accepted in payment by others reduces time spent, or resources used, in many exchanges. Reduction of the risk that the objects received will not be acceptable to others increases the utility of risk averse transactors. Both the reduction in resources and the reduction in risk permit the market system to expand. Expansion of the market opens opportunities by permitting increased specialisation and division of labour (Brunner and Meltzer, 1971; Alchian, 1977).

Collective choice of a medium of exchange does not require government action or law. The history of money shows that the choice of a medium of exchange within social groups often preceded the development of governments with the power to specify the means of payment used by all parties to the exchange. Then, as now, trade extends beyond the hegemony of particular governments. To find reasons for government's role in monetary affairs, we must look beyond the role of money as a medium of exchange.

Standard of value

Payment of obligations raises an issue about what constitutes payment or discharge of debt. Conventions about payments may start by summarising practice, but eventually laws restrict practice. When laws specifying methods of payment are embodied in statutes, as they have been for centuries, the choice of the standard of value becomes a governmental function.[8]

Keynes regarded the money of account – the use of money to express prices – as the primary concept of money (Keynes, 1971, p. 3). He saw the choice as a governmental function, part of its function of enforcing contracts (1971, p. 4). Money is held, according to Keynes, because it is a standard. He repeated this view in the *General Theory* (1936, pp. 236–7) where he emphasised the difference between the premium paid for 'liquidity' and the carrying cost of money as a principal determinant of the assets used as money.

Choice of a unit of account and a standard of value has some elements in common with the choice of standards of weight and measure. Specification of weights and measures, like value, requires the choice of an arbitrary unit in which measurement is expressed. Governments can lower the cost of achieving consensus about these units by legislating or imposing the choice. Both monetary units and weights and measures remain fixed for long periods of time, although monetary units are susceptible to destruction by high inflation. Cheating may occur in setting weights and measures, as in the weight of coins or in counterfeiting, but these departures from the norm are correctable in principle where standards have been defined.

There are important differences between 'money' and units of weight or measure. Monetary units differ from other standardised units in comparisons across space or time. A contract to deliver an acre of land or a metre of cloth can be converted into hectares of land or inches of cloth by arithmetic. Whenever the conversion is properly made, the result is the same. Whether a contract for future delivery is written in one unit or another is unimportant for this purpose.

Contracts expressed in different units of value can be equivalent on one date and different on another. Relative prices of units change with changes in taste and technology or because one is produced under conditions of increasing and another under conditions of decreasing cost. This is a principal problem faced by those who have tried to define an 'ideal' commodity standard.

The history of monetary units provides many instances of changing relative values. Attempts to maintain bimetallism at a fixed exchange rate between gold and silver, or to maintain any two units with different costs of production, often gave rise to the problems made familiar as Gresham's law: Bad money drives good money out of circulation at a fixed exchange rate. People pay using money of lower current or anticipated market value and hold the unit that is expected to appreciate.

Monetary history also provides examples of failed efforts to measure value by specifying commodity baskets or by developing index numbers or formulas as a means of comparing values intertemporally. Keynes considered the problem in the *Treatise*, where he emphasised effects of price change on the distribution of real income and concluded that 'the right way to compare the purchasing powers of money in two positions is to compare the total money incomes of two "similar" persons in the two positions' (1971, p. 89). He acknowledged a difficulty in finding persons for comparison, and he was careful to note at several places that tastes must be constant, but he did not see the general nature of the problem.[9]

The impossibility of defining an ideal or exact index number is the reason that there is an irreducible uncertainty about value in intertemporal comparisons and in comparisons across regions or locations at a given time. Whenever tastes or technology change, relative prices, relative product demands and the utility of any standardised basket change. No index number or weighted commodity standard can be devised to keep a measure of value stable in the sense in which a standard of weight or measure is stable.

Standards of value differ in the degree to which they reduce uncertainty. If people are risk averse, they prefer lower risk and uncertainty. Other things equal, they will choose the unit of value – and the monetary system – with lowest risk.

There are three restrictions on the public's ability to make the choice, however. First, there must be broad agreement on the standard or it will not be widely used in contracts. The costs of acquiring and disseminating information about alternative standards is large relative to the benefit that any individual, or small group can obtain. For this reason, people may continue to use less stable, established standards for long periods rather than incur the costs of shifting to a more stable standard. Second, there is no agreement on the ideal standard or on the best way to minimise instability of value. Stability of value is a main point of contention between those who favour gold or commodity money, or private production of money, or some type of monetary rule. Third, enforcement costs are high and may become infinite.[10] Governments often have little incentive to either maintain the value of nominal contracts or to pursue policies that reduce variability and uncertainty.

The benefits of a common unit of value are not fixed. They depend on the rules or arrangements for producing money and the degree to which the rules increase or reduce uncertainty about value.

Production of money

The choice of a unit of account, a standard of value, and a medium of exchange or the enforcement of deferred payment obligations does not require that governments produce money. Governments specify systems of weights and measure and enforce these standards without engaging in the production of scales or yardsticks. Governments have a greater incentive to produce money than to produce yardsticks if the public accepts paper money in place of full-bodied money. The government collects revenue, seigniorage, and society saves resources when paper replaces gold, silver or other metals as money.[11] It costs no more to produce a ten dollar bill than to produce a one dollar bill, but the same cannot be said about the cost of producing ten ounces rather than one ounce of metal.

In a fractional reserve system, paper substitutes for metal as money. Confidence in the ability of the issuer to convert paper into metallic money is established and maintained by a record of payment. Default and counterfeiting lower the confidence that people place in paper money and raise the cost of using paper money. Small changes in the gold stock are amplified. The social saving arising from the substitution of paper for metallic money is, therefore, not a net gain to society. Where governments have broad discretion to increase or reduce money, significant resources are used to conduct, monitor and predict the actions of central banks and governments. Costs of acquiring information and costs of monitoring are part of the social cost of uncertainty about future prices, output and the real value of nominal assets.

Private production of money can reduce these monitoring costs if there are sufficient private incentives to produce money that has greater stability of value. Other costs increase, however. Money produced by government can be made free of default in nominal value. The government, or the central bank, has the power to print money and to suspend convertibility into specie when the public chooses to increase its holdings of government money. Bagehot (1873), Schwartz (1983) and many others have described the financial crises of the past. These authors show that prompt action by a lender of last resort reduced the severity of crises and brought each crisis to an end. Failure of the lender to lend, or otherwise expand the monetary base, as in 1931–3, made the recession in the United States deeper and longer, bankrupted large numbers of banks and firms and sharply reduced wealth and welfare.

A private bank can suspend convertibility and offer to lend to the market at a penalty rate during financial crises also, but its ability to act as lender of last resort is limited. A private lending institution can only be kept free of default risk during a financial panic if it holds relatively few risky assets. If the lender makes loans to households of firms, holders of its liabilities bear the risk of failure in a financial crisis. To reduce risks of this kind, the lender must sacrifice return by holding relatively riskless assets like Treasury bills. This reduces the profitability of the lender or requires a user fee to be paid by the public.[12] Government can reduce costs of this kind by authorising a lender to issue obligations that are free of the risk of default on nominal value. The reduction in risk is not costless. Unless the power to issue money is restricted, granting the government power to issue money raises the risk of inflation or deflation and increases uncertainty about future values.

Again, there are different combinations of resource cost and uncertainty and different types of uncertainty under different monetary arrangements. Any monetary system based on commodity reserves uses resources to produce money or to control its production. Strict commodity reserve systems make the value of money depend on the relative price of the commodity. Uncertainty about future relative prices and costs of production affects asset allocation. Any effect on the allocation of assets between money and real capital or between long-term and short-term capital affects output and consumption. If, instead, government produces fiat money and controls the quantity, resource costs of producing money are lower, but monitoring costs are likely to be higher, and the risk that government will tax the real value of nominal assets by inflating is higher. A central bank permits the government, or its agent, to function as lender of last resort and to reduce risk of default by private banks. These risks, too, affect asset allocation.

Fixed or fluctuating exchange rates

Systems of fixed and fluctuating exchange rates are most easily discussed by treating polar positions and neglecting mixed systems. In a regime of freely fluctuating exchange rates, the monetary authority controls a particular quantity. The price level of domestic goods and services and the exchange value of domestic for foreign money adjust to that quantity. The relevant quantity of money is the monetary base – the net liabilities issued by the monetary authority for use as reserves of other issuers or as a means of payment. In a fixed exchange rate regime, the authority fixes a particular relative price and accepts the quantity of money and the general price level resulting from the choice. The pre-set price is usually the price of a particular commodity, such as gold, or of some basket of commodities. The monetary authority agrees to issue and withdraw money in exchange for the commodity at the pre-set price.

The operating characteristics of each system depend on other institutional arrangements, including the fiscal system, the types of shocks to demand or supply that people experience and the relative frequency and durability of the different shocks. Characteristics of a fixed exchange rate system vary, also, with the conditions under which the commodity reserve is produced, on changes in the demand for the commodity in alternative uses and on the extent to which the system is based on a unilateral commitment by a single country or a multilateral agreement.

A rule setting a growth rate for the quantity of money reduces the resource cost of operating the monetary system. Commodities do not have to be stored as a monetary reserve, and monetary growth does not require additional storage (Friedman, 1953). A credible monetary rule can also reduce the variability and uncertainty that people experience. By fixing the growth rate of money, the monetary authority eliminates the variability of money growth and any covariance between money growth and velocity growth. The variability of aggregate output is, then, equal to the variance of velocity growth. This latter variance differs under a monetary rule from the measured variance under existing standards.

A rule for money growth cannot maintain domestic price stability on average unless the difference between the average growth rate of real output and average velocity growth is constant. Prices of foreign goods and services consumed domestically will reflect influences abroad mediated by the adjustment of exchange rates of domestic for foreign moneys. Further, the variability of velocity growth is not independent of the choice of monetary regime. If the variability of velocity growth is sufficiently lower under fixed than fluctuating exchange rates, or if the covariance of money growth and velocity growth is negative, fixed exchange rates can reduce the variability of nominal income growth and the risks that people face.

Keynes apparently believed that fixed exchange rates would increase stability if temporary payment imbalances gave rise to lending and borrowing instead of expansion by creditors and contraction by debtors. His plan for Bretton Woods fixed exchange rates internationally but permitted central banks to pursue domestic objectives. If domestic policy produced sustained inflation (or deflation), the country could devalue (or revalue). Neither the exchange rate of a country's currency nor its domestic price level was fixed permanently under the Bretton Woods system, but the presumption was that principal countries would achieve approximate price stability on average and would borrow and lend to stabilise output and prices. Nothing enforced stability or prevented inflation, however, and the lack of enforcement was a major reason that the system did not endure.

Earlier, in the *Tract*, Keynes favoured discretionary control of money to achieve domestic price stability, but he recognised that the system would provide greater benefits if other countries, particularly the US, stabilised prices also. In the *Treatise*, he proposed a type of commodity reserve standard based on prices of internationally traded raw materials. He did not, then or later, claim that the proposed system was ideal, but he believed it was an improvement over the classical gold standard (Meltzer, 1984).

Keynes's objective in each of his proposals was to reduce uncertainty by reducing the variability of prices or incomes. He presumed that governments or central banks would share his objective and work to achieve it. Early in his career, he rejected the classical gold standard, and what he described as *laissez faire*. Throughout his life, he remained a proponent of activist policies. Activism was limited, however, by the rules of the monetary standard. Each of his proposals permitted discretion, within rules that limited discretion. He never proposed a system of freely fluctuating exchange rates with determination of money growth left to the judgement of the central bank or government or determined by a rule that reduced or removed the role of government.

An activist system has as one of its main objectives reducing fluctuations in prices and, if prices and anticipations are less than fully flexible, reducing fluctuations in employment and real income as well. If fluctuations can be predicted with sufficient accuracy to make smoothing profitable, private speculators enter to capture the gain. The fluctuations that remain can be reduced by collective action only if governments or central banks have superior information or if there is some gain from pooling across individuals and over time that private speculators cannot (or do not) capture.

Without risk and uncertainty about future outcomes, the design of monetary (and other) institutions would be a simpler task. All outcomes would reflect any gain from using money and having an established medium of exchange and standard of value. Differences in outcome would reflect the excess burden imposed by institutions that are less than optimal arrangements from the standpoint of efficiency. Risk and uncertainty change the size of the burden by changing costs and benefits faced by a risk averse public. Institutional arrangements may absorb or augment the risks that the public bears and, thus, raise or lower the burden.

An important difference between monetary arrangements determining the medium of exchange, standard of value, production of money and choice of international regime is the degree to which these arrangements reduce risk toward the minimum level inherent in nature and trade. Unfortunately, there is no obvious way to compare alternative monetary systems on *a priori* grounds. I turn, therefore, to consider some evidence.[13]

SOME EMPIRICAL DIFFERENCES BETWEEN STANDARDS

US monetary experience in the twentieth century includes six different policy regimes. None of the regimes lasted less than ten years. Gordon (1982) developed a set of quarterly data for several variables of interest – prices and real and nominal income – beginning in 1890. Friedman and Schwartz (1970) constructed quarterly data for the stock of money (M_2) – currency and total deposits – beginning in 1907 and for currency and demand deposits (M_1) beginning in 1915. The series on nominal GNP and money are raw material for the construction of quarterly series on monetary velocity starting in 1907 and 1915. In this section, I use these data to draw some tentative conclusions about monetary regimes.

The tentative nature of any inferences must be emphasised. The quarterly GNP series is interpolated from data that has been constructed long after the event (see Gordon, 1982). Although interpolation most likely reduces the variability of the data for the earlier years, this is far from certain, and data for nominal GNP remain relatively variable in some periods. No less important is the inability to separate real shocks, including weather and wars, from monetary shocks. Data for war years are included. Agriculture had a much larger role at the turn of the century and in the 1920s, so variability of real and nominal GNP may have been larger for that reason alone.

The data are divided into six periods corresponding to six monetary regimes in the US. The starting and ending dates and brief descriptions of each regime are shown in Table 7.1. All data are quarterly rates of change computed from first differences of logarithms.

These data can be used to compare the variability of GNP, money and velocity growth under the six monetary regimes. The comparison is a first step, since no attempt is made to distinguish types of change. Some of the variability reflects anticipated changes, while some changes are unanticipated. The costs of anticipated and unanticipated changes differ. Further, part of the variability arises from transitory changes in growth rates that promptly reverse, while some reflects permanent changes in the growth rate. The costs of bering variability arising from transitory and permanent changes differ, and the proper responses differ. An unanticipated, transitory change cannot be offset and requires no adjustment. The proper response to a permanent change is to adjust once the change is expected to persist.

Table 7.1   Description of six monetary regimes

Period	Starting date	Ending date	Number of observations	Description
	Year and quarter			
1	1890 – 1	1914 – 4	100	Gold standard, no central bank
1B	1907 – 3	1914 – 4	30	Gold standard, no central bank quarterly monetary data available
2	1915 – 1	1931 – 3	67	Gold exchange standard, central bank
3	1931 – 4	1941 – 4	41	Managed exchange rates, discretionary policy
4	1942 – 1	1951 – 1	37	Interest rate pegging
5	1951 – 2	1971 – 3	82	Bretton Woods
6	1971 – 4	1980 – 4*	37	Floating rates and discretionary policy

* M_2 data end with change of series in 1979 – 4.

The computed values for the variances of nominal GNP growth, money growth and velocity growth can be used to compute the covariance of money growth and velocity growth for periods 1B through 6 using the standard formula.

$$\text{Cov } MV = \frac{1}{2} (vGNP - vM - vV)$$

with v denoting the variance of the growth rate. Table 7.2 shows these data for the variances of M_1 and M_2 growth.

The principal differences between periods reflect the changing contributions of the variance of M and the covariance of money and velocity growth. There is no apparent systematic relation between monetary regimes in the distribution of the variance of GNP growth between the three components. The covariance is always positive, however, suggesting that in each monetary regime, the variabilities of money growth and velocity growth are positively related.

Under a stabilising monetary regime, money growth offsets

Table 7.2 Distribution of variance of GNP growth

Period	Variance GNP growth	vM$_2$ (%)	vV$_2$ (%)	2Cov M$_2$V$_2$ (%)	vM$_1$ (%)	vV$_1$ (%)	2Cov M$_1$V$_1$ (%)
1B	0.76	25.9	5.3	68.8			
2	2.07	21.9	5.3	72.8	26.0	7.0	67.0
3	3.73	40.1	6.5	53.4	24.1	7.2	68.7
4	1.02	53.8	5.7	40.5	68.5	6.2	25.3
5	0.12	53.8	3.4	42.7	46.2	4.3	47.9
6	0.10	28.0	2.0	70.0	52.0	2.0	46.0

changes in velocity growth. Relatively high variability of money growth can have a stabilising influence on nominal GNP growth if the covariance of money and velocity growth is negative. That negative values of the covariance are not found in any sample period suggests that a rule that kept money growth constant would lower the variability of nominal GNP growth in two ways: the variability of money growth would be zero, and the covariance would be zero also. The data in Table 7.2 suggest that the arithmetic effect of constant money growth is a reduction of 93 to 98 per cent of the variance of GNP growth.

The arithmetic effect is not the final effect. Most likely the variability of velocity growth is not invariant to a regime change of this kind. The variance of velocity growth would have to rise by a factor ranging from more than 14 to more than 50 to increase the variability of nominal income growth following the institution of a rule fixing the rate of money growth according to the estimates in Table 7.2.

Additional evidence on this issue is found by Benjamin Friedman (1984, Table 7). Friedman computed the variances and covariances of money growth, velocity growth and nominal GNP growth for post-war expansions and contractions in the US from 1948 to 1982. He found that the comparable percentages to those in Table 7.2 for vM$_1$, vV$_1$ and twice the covariance are, respectively, 36, 38 and 26 per cent.[14]

An earlier study by Brunner and Meltzer (1983) computed the variances and covariances of deviations of money growth and velocity growth from the values estimated using time series models on quarterly data for 1953 to 1980. The deviations are a measure of unanticipated growth of money and velocity. They found (1983, Table 1) that the variability of unanticipated velocity growth never dominated the variability of unanticipated GNP growth, but constant money growth reduces the variance of GNP growth much less than is shown by the data in Table 7.2. This suggests the importance of separating anticipated and unanticipated changes before drawing firm conclusions.

None of these data provides evidence on the direction of causation. The data show that the substantial post-war reduction in the variance of GNP growth is distributed over all components. Each is substantially smaller in the post-war, periods 5 and 6, than in earlier periods. Prewar variability is smallest in period 1B, the classical gold standard without a central bank, and largest in period 3, the era of managed exchange rates and discretionary central bank policy. Period 3 includes part of the depression of the 1930s and the recovery from the depression, but the depression does not explain why the variances of M_1 and M_2 growth or the covariances of money with velocity are as much as two or three times the variances or covariances in other prewar periods.

The remarkable decline in the variability of real and nominal GNP growth, money growth and velocity growth under the Bretton Woods agreement appears to confirm Keynes's belief that variability can be reduced by changing monetary arrangements. Keynes believed that, with lower variability, risk averse individuals hold smaller money balances. The demand for money falls, and the demand for capital increases, lowering real rates of interest. The decline in interest rates encourages investment raising the equilibrium stock of capital and the level of real income. Meltzer (1981, 1984) Variability of real income growth remained relatively low in period 6 and the post-Bretton Woods era, so we cannot conclude that the Bretton Woods agreement was the principal cause of the post-war reduction in variability.

Keynes believed that the principal way to lower variability was to reduce the variability of the demand for money. The data for the six periods in Table 7.2 suggest that the variability of velocity growth explains a relatively small part of the variability of GNP growth in all periods. The variability of money growth and the covariance of money and velocity growth appear to account for the largest part of the variability of GNP growth.

A more direct test of Keynes's conjecture is provided by evidence that the demand for money per unit of income is lowest when variability is lowest. Rank correlations of money per unit of income for the six periods for which M_2 is available, and the five periods for which M_1 is available, do not support the hypothesis. A stronger test of the effect of monetary variability on interest rates and the demand for money produces some evidence rejecting the hypothesis. Mascaro and Meltzer (1983) test for the effect of increased variability of unanticipated money growth, unanticipated velocity growth and the covariance on interest rates. They conclude that increased variability of unanticipated money growth raises the rate of interest and the demand for money, but they fail to find a significant effect for the variability of unanticipated velocity growth on interest rates. This evidence suggests that the monetary regime may properly be described as the cause of an excess burden that would be reduced by changing monetary arrangements to reduce uncertainty, lower interest rates and increase real income but not for the reason Keynes suggested. The reduction in excess burden is more closely related to the reduction in the variability of the money stock.

CONCLUSION

A monetary system has four elements of choice. There is a medium of exchange, a standard of value, an arrangement for producing money and a decision about the international monetary arrangement, fixed or fluctuating exchange rates. Each choice has some collective elements, but not all the collective elements involve government.

The choice between private and governmental responsibility changes the nature of risks or uncertainty borne in the society. Some risks are unavoidable; they can be reduced but not eliminated. The choice of a standard of value is an example. There is no way to eliminate risk of fluctuations in value or uncertainty about future values. Other risks can be eliminated, or nearly so, by monetary arrangements. The creation of a lender of last resort to prevent the spread of defaults on nominal values is an example.

Monetary experience in the twentieth century includes very different arrangements for specifying value and producing money. An examination of this experience shows that the variability of real and nominal income growth differed markedly under different arrangements. The social choice of monetary arrangements appears to be associated with differences in variability. If variability of income is a measure of risk or uncertainty, the choice of monetary arrangements has been associated with large differences in uncertainty.

Decomposition of the variance of nominal income growth into the variance of money growth, velocity growth and their covariance shows that the variance of velocity growth – or growth in the demand for money per unit of output – makes a relatively small contribution to the variance of nominal income growth. Further, the covariance of money growth and velocity growth is positive in each of the six monetary regimes considered.

The use of an identity, the quantity equation, precludes the assignment of any causal significance to particular factors. But the use of the identity assures that all factors affecting the variability of nominal GNP growth have been considered. The relative small contribution of the variance of velocity growth, and the much larger contribution of the variance of money growth, suggests the fruitful direction for research on the sources of variability.

The findings suggest that risk or uncertainty in the growth of real and nominal income is more likely to be reduced by arrangements that reduce the variability of money growth than by policies that attempt to offset fluctuations in the demand for money or velocity. A monetary rule that held money growth constant eliminates the covariance with velocity growth and the variance of money growth. The data suggest that a rule of this kind would reduce risk below the level observed under any of the standards. This conclusion differs, of course, from any of the conclusions reached by Keynes.

Notes

1. I am grateful to Karl Brunner and to Alex Cukierman for helping me to work my way through parts of the problem, but they are not responsible for what emerged.
2. The use of cigarettes as a medium of exchange in the prisoner-of-war camps during the Second World War and the use of stone money among the Yapese are well-known examples of private solutions. Toynbee (1954, p. 309) claims that government assumed responsibility for production of coins in the seventh century BC by establishing a monopoly and fixing the sizes and weights of coins.
3. See Viner (1937) for details of the controversy about resumption and devaluation. Ricardo favoured resumption but predicted that prices would fall only 8 to 13 per cent. The additional decline, he claimed, was largely the result of mismanagement. See Viner (1937, pp. 176–9).
4. Bloomfield (1959) and Bordo and Schwartz (1984) discuss the extent to which countries followed the rules of the gold standard without intervention. The verdict appears to be that they did not, but they maintained multilateral fixed parties and gold exchange rates until 1914.

5. Friedman (1984) continues to favour fluctuating rates. He now proposes to fix the level of the monetary base – currency and bank reserves instead of fixing the growth rate of money.

6. Responsibility for US international monetary policy, for example decisions to devalue or revalue, to intervene in foreign exchange markets and to operate the Exchange Stabilisation Fund have not been given to the central bank.

7. Recent work by Fama (1980) on the theory of banking ignores this collective aspect and misses one of the main services that a monetary system provides – the services of a medium of exchange.

8. Specification of legal tender for payment of taxes gives government an interest in the choice.

9. Keynes's discussion of Fisher's ideal index number, or of earlier work by Marshall and Edgeworth, suggests that there cannot be any precise comparison (see Keynes, 1971, pp. 100–3).

10. Courts upheld the right of the US Government to abrogate the gold clause in private contracts. The British Government required people to sell their foreign assets to the government during the war thereby preventing them from limiting the loss of value.

11. The saving of resources refers only to the cost of production. The net social benefit need not be positive. The choice of optimal monetary arrangements depends on the latter. The government can collect the seigniorage by taxing private producers of money.

12. Private producers of travellers cheques charge a fee, even though they do not function as lenders of last resort.

13. Evidence for shorter periods and particular policies is given in Mascaro and Meltzer (1983) and Evans (1984). See Brunner (1983) for a related discussion of the issue.

14. The covariance is positive for the expansions and negative in the contractions, but the negative value is less than ¼ the variance of money growth.

References

ALCHIAN, A. A. (1977) 'Why Money?' in A. A. Alchian (ed.), *Economic Forces at Work* (Indianapolis: Liberty Press) pp. 111–123.

BAGEHOT, W. (1873) *Lombard Street*. Reprinted Homewood: Irvin, 1962.

BLOOMFIELD, A. I. (1959) *Monetary Policy Under the International Gold Standard* (New York: Federal Reserve Bank).

BORDO, M. and SCHWARTZ, A. J. (eds) (1984) *A Retrospective on the Classical Gold Standard, 1821–1931* (Chicago: University of Chicago Press).

BRUNNER, K. (1983) 'Has Monetarism Failed?' *Cato Journal*, vol. 3 (Spring) pp. 23–62.

BRUNNER, K. and MELTZER, A. H. (1971) 'The Uses of Money: Money in the Theory of an Exchange Economy', *American Economic Review*, vol. 61 (December) pp. 784–805.

BRUNNER, K. and MELTZER, A. H. (1983) 'Strategies and Tactics for Monetary Control', *Carnegie-Rochester Conference Series on Public Policy*, vol. 18 (Spring) pp. 59–104.

EVANS, P. (1984) 'The Effect on Output of Money Growth and Interest Rate Volatility in the United States', *Journal of Political Economy*, vol. 92 (April) pp. 204–22.

FAMA, E. (1980) 'Banking in the Theory of Finance', *Journal of Monetary Economics*, vol. 6 (January) pp. 39–57.

FRIEDMAN, B. M. (1984) 'Money, Credit and Interest Rates in the Business Cycle', NBER Working Paper (March).

FRIEDMAN, M. (1953) *Essays in Positive Economics* (Chicago: University of Chicago Press).

FRIEDMAN, M. (1984) 'Monetary Policy for the 80's', in J. Moore (ed.) *To Promote Prosperity: U.S. Domestic Policy in the Mid-1980s* (Stanford: Hoover Institution), pp. 23–60.

FRIEDMAN, M. and SCHWARTZ, A. J. (1970) *Monetary Statistics of the United States* (New York: Columbia University Press for the National Bureau of Economic Research).

GORDON, R. J. (1982) 'Price Inertia and Policy Ineffectiveness in the United States, 1890–1980', *Journal of Political Economy*, vol. 90 (December) 1087–1117.

HARROD, R. (1951) *The Life of John Maynard Keynes* (New York: Harcourt, Brace).

KEYNES, J. M. (1936) *The General Theory of Employment, Interest and Money* (London: Macmillan).

KEYNES, J. M. (1971) *A Treatise on Money*, Vol. 5 of the *Collected Writings of John Maynard Keynes* (London: Macmillan for the Royal Economic Society).

MASCARO, A. and MELTZER, A. H. (1983) 'Long and Short-term Interest Rates in a Risky World', *Journal of Monetary Economics*, vol. 12 (November) pp. 485–518.

MELTZER, A. H. (1981) 'Keynes's General Theory: A Different Perspective', *Journal of Economic Literature*, vol. 19 (March) pp. 34–64.

MELTZER, A. H. (1984) 'Keynes on Monetary Reform and International Economic Order', The Henry Thornton Lecture (London: City University).

SCHWARTZ, A. J. (1983) 'Real and Pseudo Financial Crises', NBER xeroxed.

TOYNBEE, A. J. (1954) *A Study of History*, Vol. 7 (London: Oxford University Press).

VINER, J. (1937) *Studies in the Theory of International Trade* (New York: Kelley (1965).

Comment on 'Properties of Monetary Systems'

Geoffrey E. Wood

In recent years Allan Meltzer has published several analytical studies of Keynes's *General Theory* (see, e.g., Meltzer, 1981, 1983a). He wrote of the *General Theory*:

> I find in Keynes' General Theory an economic argument based on the belief that fluctuations in output impose social costs that cannot be removed by private action. (Meltzer, 1983a)

In the present chapter, a central part in Allan Meltzer's analysis is again played by a divergence between private costs and benefits and social costs and benefits.

The chapter has four sections. First there is a brief discussion of Keynes's views on the choice of monetary standard. Second there is consideration of why governments are involved in the creation and issuing of money. Third, there is a brief review of the choice between fixed and floating exchange rates. Finally, there are some statistics on the performance of the US economy under various monetary standards.

The sections of the chapter are discussed in that order.

An initial issue is what exactly is meant by the term 'monetary standard'. The term is frequently used but seldom defined, probably because most people have both an idea of what it means and an assumption that other people have the same idea. For the sake of clarity a definition should be set out. The one used here is that a monetary standard is a particular type of economic policy regime – it is the particular legal and institutional setting that determines monetary behaviour. The choice of whatever is to serve as money is, of course, an important part of the 'monetary standard'. It is now possible to turn to Allan Meltzer's chapter.

KEYNES ON GOLD

Allan Meltzer observes that 'Keynes actively opposed the return to
the gold standard in 1925'. This was, he argues, because Keynes
favoured 'greater invervention in the economy'; Harrod is quoted as
saying that Keynes was 'not a great friend of the profit motive'.[1]

In summary, Allan says, Keynes 'always opposed the classical gold
standard'. That is an over-simplification – inevitable when
summarising the views of one such as Keynes, who wrote so much
and so frequently, but an over-simplification which does miss an
element in Keynes's views important for the conclusion of Meltzer's
chapter, and influential in the Bretton Woods system.

Keynes was opposed to the return to gold in 1925. But his oppo-
sition was to the choice of parity rather than to the standard itself.[2]
Evidence for this can be drawn from two episodes – 1925 and 1931.[3]
First from 1925, we have Keynes's famous Purchasing Power Parity
calculation – that sterling was over-valued by 10 per cent against the
US dollar. That calculation has twice been challenged – at the time
by T. E. Gregory (1926) who maintained that when a more appropriate US price index was used, sterling was not over-valued against
the dollar; and recently by Redmond (1982) who claims that on a
trade-weighted basis, sterling was actually over-valued by some 25
per cent.

From our point of view, however, the rightness or otherwise of
Keynes's calculation is irrelevant. What matters is that he made
it, and considered the result important. Had he wanted a flexibly
conducted, domestically focused, monetary policy, the argument,
advanced time and again by Keynes, that what was wrong with the
1925 decision was the parity was really beside the point.

A second type of evidence from 1925 emerges from the correspondence columns of *The Times*. Keynes and Sir Henry Strakosch
carried on a correspondence about the morality of devaluation.
Keynes argued for a once-for-all devaluation to avoid a period of
deflation when unemployment was already high. Strakosch maintained that was morally wrong, and would defraud Britain's creditors;
in *The Times* of 3 July 1925 he wrote of 'devaluation – more appropriately called repudiation'. Again, Keynes's position is that he wanted
a fixed parity, but at a new level. He wanted a devaluation not a
float.

Third, Keynes wrote to the City Editor of the *Morning Post* (1
August 1925) that his position had been misrepresented in the Press,

and that he wished price stability as much as did any of his critics, but that the old gold parity for sterling would not deliver that, but would involve deflation.

Moving to 1931, we find Keynes defending staying on gold at the existing parity. Sterling had been under pressure for sometime. There were several official committees on different aspects of economic policy. Keynes argued in one of these, the Macmillan Committee, that sterling should not be devalued, and that even protective tariffs were preferable, because they would leave the international monetary system undamaged.

In summary, then, Keynes was opposed to the decision of 1925, but because he thought the parity was wrong. He was not a complete and consistent opponent of the gold exchange standard. Unquestionably, however, he also seemed to favour freedom to change the parity occasionally.[4] (See, for example, Keynes's, 'Tract on Monetary Reform', and Meltzer (1983b).) This ambivalence towards fixed rates was built into Bretton Woods, and helped the system's demise, for it was never quite clear what the rules were. (This lack of clarity was, of course, at least as much the fault of White as of Keynes. The Bretton Woods agreement had more of the White Plan than the Keynes Plan in it (see Cooper, 1968).)

THE ROLE OF THE GOVERNMENT

The use of money makes a society better off. It lets the economy attain consumption/leisure bundles that would be unattainable without money. But the same is true of other things – telephones, bicycles, refrigerators. Why do we need governments to supply money, but not these other things? Or do we? This is the central issue of part two of Meltzer's chapter; that is followed by a discussion of how the 'distribution of risks and opportunities' is affected by the nature and extent of the role of government in this area. The second part of this section is clear and persuasive, and opens up promising lines of research, but there is a difficulty with the first part. It is argued that 'Collective choice of a medium of exchange does not require government action or law. . . . To find reasons for government's role in monetary affairs, we must look beyond the role of money as a medium of exchange'.

That sharp separation of the medium of exchange function from the other function of money is artificial. It was made by Hicks (1967), who grafted a simple banking system on to a commodity-money using society, and claimed that bank balances did not act as a store of value in his model because at the end of the 'market day', no individual was left with either a credit or debit balance at the 'bank'. The problems with that approach are first, its arbitrariness, and second, its neglect of what goes on *during* the day. It is not utility maximisation which leads people to have zero bank balances at the end of the day; it is just a restriction which Hicks imposed. Second, in the course of the day bank balances serve as a store of value, in the gap between an individual's making a sale and making a purchase. Money is always and everywhere a 'temporary abode of purchasing power' (Friedman, 1956).

One cannot separate the medium of exchange function from the store of value function. A medium of exchange must, at least to some extent, serve as a store of value.[5] Hence if private collective action introduces a medium of exchange, it can, and does, introduce a store of value. For this reason, separating the two functions cannot help to bring in government. Nor is the argument that the lender of last resort function requires government persuasive. Bagehot did, after all, lay down his guidelines for action in a financial crisis to what was still a privately-owned bank. And, just like a government, a private bank can print more notes in time of crisis – privately produced money can also be free of default in *nominal* value.

All this said, Allan Meltzer is surely on the right track when he argues that government money emerges because of externalities or enforcement costs of some sort that exist with private money. It is noteworthy that most episodes of 'free banking' have occurred in small, cohesive, societies, where everyone was well informed about everyone else's business.

In concluding this section there is a further point to note. The line pursued by Allan Meltzer was to ask what it was about money that led to governments being involved in its production. In at least some cases, money was produced by government not because it was beneficial for society that it be so, but rather was imposed on society by government as a demonstration of sovereignty. This was, for example, done by Athens; the use of local rather than Athenian money was illegal in Athenian subject states after around 480 BC (Burns, 1927).

FIXED OR FLOATING EXCHANGE RATES

Whether a country should have fixed or flexible exchange rates has been frequently discussed, either directly or as an aspect of the theory of optimum currency areas. This section of Allan Meltzer's chapter draws attention to the extensive contribution of Keynes to this discussion. As he also points out, the question of whether a particular country should have fixed or floating exchange rates cannot be resolved in the abstract. The answer depends on a large number of institutional and empirical factors. Some of these – degree of openness in particular – are not discussed by Allan Meltzer; but some are. This therefore leads to the empirical section of the chapter.

EMPIRICAL DIFFERENCES BETWEEN STANDARDS

This section is largely, and deliberately, atheoretical. The behaviour of nominal money, GNP, and velocity are examined, within the framework of the quantity identity, across the six policy regimes the US experienced since 1890. The 'stylised facts' are; a striking decline in variability of nominal GNP after 1945; that the variability of real growth dominated the variability of nominal GNP throughout; and that the variability of money growth and velocity growth are positively correlated. What is to be made of this? The atheoretical approach has both benefits and costs.

A benefit is that a clear organising framework, which 'ensures that all the factors affecting the variability of nominal GNP' (Meltzer, 1984) have been considered, is imposed on the data. A cost is that we really cannot draw any conclusions until we use these data to test or reject theories. It is notable, indeed, that Meltzer's clear (and I think correct) claim about the result of adopting a stable money growth rule is reached after imposing the view that money fluctuations cause velocity fluctuations.[6]

It would be worthwhile to carry the analysis a little further. There is now an extensive body of analytical work which relates the unpredictability of government actions to their effect on the economy. A paper by Roy Batchelor and the present author (1982) has found that unpredictable exchange rate variability increased with official foreign exchange intervention not conducted by some systematic rule. Robert Barro (1981) has found that only the unpredictable component of money growth affects real output in the US. There is now work on the predictability of money growth under different standards in the UK, and I believe the US. This predictability seems to vary with standards. Examination of the relation between predictability of money growth and the behaviour of the economy would have considerable bearing on the monetary rule argument. Certainly at first glance the UK evidence would support the argument for a rule; the unpredictability of money growth was much lower between 1950 and 1970 than in the interwar years, as was the variability of economic activity.

CONCLUSIONS

In conclusion, it is worth briefly setting out the main lessons of Allan Meltzer's chapter. First, it directs attention to the unifying, albeit not totally unified, analytical framework of Keynes's work on international monetary policy, and links that to the analysis of the *General Theory*. It has thereby given us a clearer overall view of Keynes's work. Second, it sharpens discussion of an issue which economists have only recently started to grapple with. Why do governments issue money? That is a question the analytical complexity of which is fully matched by its practical importance; the steps towards answering it taken in this chapter are therefore doubly welcome. Finally, and most important, the chapter directs our attention towards thinking of monetary policy in terms of alternative monetary standards rather than, for example, in terms of alternative money growth targets. This refocusing of attention is a natural extension of the work of Robert Lucas on economic policy regimes, and is of equal importance. Altogether, this chapter by Allan Meltzer is enjoyable, stimulating, and useful.

Notes

1. Harrod on Keynes is a dangerous witness. Harrod's *Life of Keynes* is better regarded not as history, or as biography, but as hagiography. Robert Skidelsky shows clearly how Harrod worked on the evidence so as to produce a Keynes such as Harrod thought he should have been.
2. This sets aside for the moment that one may not be entirely independent of the other. See Note 4 below.
3. Higonnet (1981) cites also a paper on the Indian gold exchange standard which Keynes gave in 1911, and which was the basis of *Indian Currency and Finance*.

4. It should be noted that a change in parity at other than time of war may *be* the end of the standard. This was certainly the view of W. A. Kiddy, Editor of the *Banker's Magazine* who, in the course of a speaking tour advocating a return to gold at the old parity, regularly argued that once the parity was changed it could be changed again, and therefore all guarantee of stability was gone if the old parity was not resumed.
5. The converse is of course not true.
6. Despite the last sentence of Allan's paper, it seems that at least some of the time Keynes would have agreed with Allan's recommendation.

References

BARRO, R. J. (1981) 'Unanticipated Money Growth and Economic Activity in the United States', in *Money, Expectations and Business Cycles*.

BATCHELOR, R. A. and WOOD, G. E. (1982) 'Floating Exchange Rates; the Lessons of Experience', in *Exchange Rate Policy*, ed. Batchelor and Wood.

BURNS, A. R. (1972) 'Money and Monetary Policy in Early Times' (reprinted by Augustus M. Kelly, 1965).

COOPER, R. H. (1968) *The Economics of Interdependence*. (Columbia University Press, New York.)

FRIEDMAN, M. (1956) 'The Quantity Theory of Money; A Restatement' in *Studies in the Quantity Theory of Money*, ed. M. Friedman (The University of Chicago Press).

GREGORY, T. E. (1926) *The First Year of the Gold Standard* (London, P. S. King).

HICKS, J. R. (1967) *Critical Essays in Monetary Theory* (Oxford, Clourand on Press, 1967).

HIGGONET, R. (1981) 'Keynes and the Gold Exchange Standard', University of Florida Discussion Paper in Economics and Banking.

MELTZER, A. H. (1981) 'Keynes's General Theory: A Different Perspective', *Journal of Economic Literature*, March 1981.

MELTZER, A. H. (1983a) 'Interpreting Keynes', *Journal of Economic Literature*, March 1983.

MELTZER, A. H. (1983b) 'Keynes on Monetary Reform and International Economic Order', Fifth Henry Thornton Lecture, The City University, Centre for Banking and International Finance.

REDMOND, J. (1982) 'The Norman Conquest of $4.86, was the pound overvalued?' (University of Birmingham Discussion Paper No. 9).

8 The Costs and Benefits of International Banking

Shelagh A. Heffernan

INTRODUCTION

In investigating the case for an international central bank (ICB), it is useful to begin by reviewing the functions normally associated with a domestic central bank. These duties have evolved over time, the Bank of England Act (1844) setting the ground rules for the growth of central banks. The passage of this Act was a victory for the Currency School.[1] This school identified the stabilisation of the price level, through control of the money supply, as the primary role of the central bank. It demanded adherence to the strict quantity theory of money, reflecting the earlier acceptance of the Palmer Rule in 1832. This Rule had called for a fixed volume of securities and a passive exchange of gold against notes.[2] The strict money supply rule was applied until 1914. Over this period, the average annual rate of growth of the money stock was less than 1 per cent, compared with a 2.5 per cent average annual rate of growth of output.[3]

At the time the Act was passed, officials were confident the new regulations would serve to eliminate monetary crises. Based on the idea that speculative manias preceded monetary crises, it was hoped that adherence to the strict money supply rule would lead agents to realise that in the event of speculative manias, there would be no accommodating institution. However, the crises of 1847, 1857, and 1866 proved them wrong, the government having to suspend the Act as the reserves held by the Banking department dwindled to nothing.

A second important function which central banks began to assume is associated with the Banking School.[4] According to this school, the central bank's primary objective should be the minimization of financial crises. Adherents to this principle opposed laws which restricted the quantity of notes issued, arguing for measures which would guarantee the quality of issue, through strict convertibility to gold. In 1844, this school had suffered a defeat at the hands of the Currency School. However, their arguments did receive attention in the revised Bank of England Act (1914). The Act permitted the Bank to adopt discretionary monetary policy in place of the strict money supply rule. Thus, while control of the money supply continued to be one of the functions of the Bank of England, it was now assigned the task of minimising financial crises, a potentially conflicting function. Further measures aimed at reducing the occurrence of financial instability gradually evolved. The deposit of reserves by private banks at the Bank of England became an informal convention. Further, while the Bank was never explicitly made lender of last resort (LLR), it did have a re-discounting function, a precursor to the LLR.

The central bank functions in the United States evolved in much the same way as they had in the UK, with a greater formal stress on financial stability. The Federal Reserve Act of 1913 singled out the provision of an 'elastic' currency as the primary function of the newly created Federal Reserve system. Members of the system were also granted powers of rediscounting and lending. In 1934, the passage of the Glass Steagall Banking Act stressed the promotion of financial stability. The Act gave authority to the Federal Reserve system to adjust its reserve requirements (prior to 1934, this requirement could only be altered by legislation) and provided for the establishment of a public deposit insurance scheme, a measure designed to increase confidence in the banking system.

A third, more recent function of the central bank has been the placement of government debt on the most favourable terms possible. The growth of fiscal deficits has increased the importance both of this function and correspondingly, seigniorage income, the implicit tax yield from the state's non-interest bearing liabilities. Clearly, this is potentially in conflict with the first two primary functions.

In this chapter it is argued that with the advent of international banking (defined as cross-border private banking activities), the case for an international central bank (ICB) has been strengthened. However, the ICB would not be assigned the potentially conflicting functions normally associated with a domestic central bank. If the goals of the post-war international economic order established at the Bretton Woods conference are accepted, then there is a need for a neutral central body whose primary duty would be the maintenance of international financial stability. Since it would assume one of the key functions of a domestic central bank but at an international level, this body is referred to as an international central bank. The study also identifies a secondary function for the ICB: the reduction of real resource costs associated with international banking. This is shown to contribute (indirectly) to the promotion of international financial stability.

The chapter is divided into the following sections. Section 1 reviews the meaning of financial crisis and illustrates how the current situation could provoke an international crisis. In Section 2 it is argued that as the exogenous shocks of the 1970s created serious balance of payments difficulties for many developing countries, the IMF's apparent failure to effectively intervene went against the spirit of the Bretton Woods agreement. A newly defined 'IMF' in a flexible exchange rate, mobile capital world would assume a principal feature of a central bank, the preservation of international financial stability. The real resource costs and benefits of international banking are reviewed in Section III and in relation to these, a role for third party intervention is identified. Moral hazard and free rider problems which could be associated with an ICB are discussed in Section 4. Section 5 concludes.

1 FINANCIAL CRISES

Historically, a primary function of the domestic central bank has been the insulation of the economy from financial crises. This was evident in the evolution of duties assigned to the Bank of England and the Federal Reserve. However, their histories also demonstrate that it took several crises before these institutions were granted adequate facilities to deal with the problem. The question is whether it is possible, in the 1980s, to prevent economic history from repeating itself at the international level.

The most all embracing interpretation of a financial crisis is that of the 'real' school.[5] In this interpretation, the financial crisis is an endogenous part of the business cycle. An exogenous event explains an upswing in the cycle, creating profitable opportunities for investment in key sectors of the economy. With the rising prices and output in these sectors, profit rates increase, stimulating further investment. Interest rates rise, a consequence of rising demands for finance. The financial system becomes increasingly 'fragile' (Minsky, 1977, 1979). Four factors contribute to this: an increase in debt finance (especially if inflation rates are rising faster than the nominal rate of interest), a rising predominance of short-term over long-term debt, a reduction in the financial institutions' margins of safety, and a switch from 'hedge' to 'speculative' to 'Ponzi' finance. If a unit's cash payments on debt are significantly less than its cash receipts, the unit is engaging in hedge finance. Under conditions of speculative finance, a unit's cash flow payments either exceed or are expected to exceed its cash receipts over a relatively short period. If the speculative unit finds it has to increase its debt to meet its existing debt servicing commitments, the unit has moved into a state of Ponzi finance. The increasing fragility of the financial system exerts a further upward pressure on interest rates. The vicious circle which ensues precipitates a refinancing crisis and 'distress selling' (Fisher, 1932), when firms, unable to roll over their debt, are forced to liquidate their assets. At this point, catastrophe theory is useful in explaining how the liquidity problem spreads until the situation reaches crisis proportions. If any one firm is forced to liquidate its assets, their value will decline. The asset values of a bank or banks will also fall if these institutions are associated with a sufficiently large number of insolvent firms. The insolvency of the single firm or bank would have no impact on the position of other enterprises in a world of perfect information. But with less than perfect information the investor/depositor may use the problems associated with the single firm or bank to revise down his estimates of the relative safety of other firms or banks (see Batchelor, 1983). This reaction is the well known contagion effect. It arises in situations of less than perfect information where lenders (or depositors) perceive that the risks of default (bank insolvency) are positively correlated across firms (banks). If one firm or bank experiences liquidity problems, a crisis of confidence causes the problem to spread to other firms or banks. Prices decline as asset values fall further.

It is possible to draw parallels between this description of financial crisis and the current international debt problems. The 'firms' are the debtor countries. Banks with a relatively high sovereign loan (external debt incurred either directly by the public sector or by a private debtor, guaranteed for repayment by a public entity) exposure are those subject to potential bank runs. Exogenous shocks (see Section 2 for an elaboration) to the world economy were responsible for creating conditions on the demand and supply sides of international lending which increased the fragility of the international financial system. On the supply side, oil rich economies sought markets for the investment of their new wealth. On the demand side, non-oil developing countries searched for a solution to their increasing balance of payments difficulties. Western banks, through the facilities of the Euromarkets, brought these two groups together.

Sovereign loans became the dominant form of finance for the non-oil developing nations. The banks were inexperienced with the new types of risk attached to sovereign lending, probably because unlike a firm, it was difficult (if not impossible) to define an 'insolvent' country. This inexperience in turn led to inadequate provision of margins of safety. Throughout the 1970s the developing countries moved from hedge to Ponzi external finance largely because of adverse economic conditions caused by exogenous shocks. But this continuous increase in the demand for funds was not matched by an equivalent rise in the rate of supply. Resulting pressure on interest rates was exacerbated by monetary policies in Western economies which squeezed international credit markets still further.

These events contributed to the increasing fragility of the international financial system. With the Mexican announcement in 1982, all the ingredients for a financial crisis were present. Saunders (1983) provides evidence of the spread of contagion effects in the international loan markets in the recent past (1978–82). He finds interest spreads to be rising (on average) and demonstrates a positive correlation in their movements across borrowing groups. The apparent absence of runs on Western banks with a relatively high debtor country sovereign loan exposure is probably explained by the relative speed with which rescheduling packages have been put together and the existence of deposit insurance (for all but the largest depositors) in the United States.

The costs associated with a collapse of the international financial system fall into two categories. First, international capital mobility would be severely curtailed if not eliminated. In Section 2, the life cycle hypothesis of economic development is used to explain the demand for external capital by developing countries. Countries borrow to capitalise on expected future income streams now, thereby raising current living standards. Provided the social welfare functions of developing countries are defined in this way, a shut down of international capital markets could seriously diminish their welfare. In addition, all the benefits from international banking (see Section 3) would be lost.

The second category of costs are associated with a decline in economic activity following the financial crisis. Friedman and Schwartz (1963) illustrated the adverse effect on US aggregate output in the 1930s, arising from the rapid decline in the money supply and (less important) the reduced wealth of bank shareholders. In the context of the present threat these effects would be minor given adequate lender of last resort (LLR) facilities. However, the existing domestic LLR facilities have gaps which must be filled (see Section 4) if, in the event of a crisis, contractions in the world money supply are to be avoided. A collapse of the Euromarkets is unlikely to have any serious effects on the world money supply given that the Euromarket money multiplier, if measurable, appears to be very small.[6]

Recently, Bernanke (1983) has shown that during a financial crisis, output can be affected in a non-monetary way through an increase in the real cost of credit intermediation. The disruption of financial services between 1930 and 1933 hampered the ability of the US financial system to provide costly information services. With the rising cost of credit intermediation, credit for certain types of borrowers (small farms, firms, and households) was severely curtailed or only available at a relatively high price. This has implications for the current international problems. Debt servicing difficulties have raised the cost of credit intermediation (as evidenced by the rising spreads in the Euromarket) and reduced the supply of sovereign loans to developing countries. The share of net external borrowing from private sources (for non-oil developing countries) is expected to be half its 1978–80 share by 1983, largely because of a reduction in short-term credit facilities. This decline will be countered by an elevenfold increase in the use of IMF credit. The IMF intermediation will go some way in helping to avoid the negative implications for output identified by Bernanke. Also, if a central body assumed responsibility for the pooling of information (see Section 3) the costs of credit intermediation could be substantially reduced.

This review of the costs suggests that they could be substantial. Of course, the amount of 'fragility' required before the international financial system would collapse is a matter for debate. Certainly the US banking crisis from 1929 did provoke a prolonged suspension of a workable financial system. Other historical precedents include the collapse of the River Plate and Australian financial systems in, respectively, 1889 and 1893. On the other hand, no such collapse came about after two English banking crises in 1866 and 1890 (see Batchelor, 1983). If a systematic comparison of these and other outcomes were conducted, it would probably be found that in cases where crises did not precipitate financial collapse, there was some form of third party intervention. Unfortunately, time and space prevent this chapter from properly addressing this question. However, there can be no doubt that the likelihood of an irreversible international crisis will increase with the fragility of the financial system. Much of the current fragility has been caused by adverse international events, the probability of which no single nation has a vested interest to reduce. This strengthens the case for an international body whose principal objective would be the promotion of financial stability. The next three sections discuss the mechanisms by which this might be achieved.

2   BRETTON WOODS, THE IMF AND AN ICB

The 1944 conference at Bretton Woods and the resulting IMF Articles of Agreement gave official sanction to a paradigm for the post-war international economic order. While the newly created International Monetary Fund was never granted the full status of an international central bank, some of the features were there. However, post-war events, particularly those in the 1970s, have been responsible for an unofficial erosion of IMF authority. This section illustrates how the failure of the IMF to play a major role in response to world economic shocks in the 1970s went against the grain of the Bretton Woods agreement. In the interests of financial stability, the powers of IMF intervention need to be explicitly redefined. This encapsulates an argument for an international central bank.

Southard (1979) summarises the primary objective of the International Monetary Fund:

> to assist members to finance payments deficits and to monitor their exchange rate and policies. (p. 15)

The task of dealing with serious balance of payments difficulties parallels one of the primary functions associated with a domestic central bank but at an international level. To achieve their objectives, the Fund assumed two important functions. First, under the adjustable peg exchange rate system, the IMF had the power to approve or order changes in par values if the problem underlying a member's Balance of Payments difficulties was classified as one of 'fundamental disequilibrium': situations where a country's external balance was incompatible with full employment and free trade in goods and services. Second, if the difficulties were not of a fundamental nature members were granted access to the financial resources of the IMF, to help see them through the temporary difficulties. Today, Fund resources include the Credit tranches, the Compensatory Financing facility, the Extended facility, facilities for Buffer stock and Supplementary financing, the Reserve tranche and Special Drawing Rights (SDRs). All but the latter two facilities have conditions attached to their use. The borrowed resources must be repaid within a specified period of time and the IMF has to approve a programme of economic adjustment before the facilities can be used.

With the collapse of the adjustable peg system between 1971 and 1973, a key method by which the IMF could intervene to fulfil its objectives was eliminated. The resulting confusion over the role of the IMF occurred at a time when IMF type intervention was in greatest demand. A review of the external debt problems of non-oil developing countries lends support to this contention.

Over the period 1973 to 1982 real external debt for non-oil developing countries[7] doubled. While the average annual growth rate in real GDP was 4.5 per cent per annum, the average rate of growth in real debt was roughly double this figure. Economic theory lends support to a developing nation's growth rate in external finance temporarily exceeding its growth rate in output. According to the 'life cycle' hypothesis of economic development,[8] expectations of higher future income streams give rise to a demand for external credit by developing economies in order to finance higher levels of current consumption and investment. An inadequate domestic capital base causes them to import capital from abroad. This is supplied by a 'first world' group of developed economies whose supply of capital is in excess of their domestic requirements. Arbitrage leads to a trade in capital between the two worlds.

Accepting this hypothesis, the optimisation problem for the developing country will be to choose the level of external capital which maximises expected national product in future periods. The steadily rising investment share of national income[9] through the 1970s suggests that external capital was being used to finance future growth. However, capital was also being imported for other reasons. In a recent study Cline (1983, p. 25) estimates that the rise in external debt can be attributed largely to four external factors: the oil price rise (in excess of US inflation rates), relatively high real interest rates (in excess of the average for the period 1961–80), deterioration in terms of trade and the world recession which cut export volumes. Demands for external financing were even more pronounced for countries who supported domestic policies which encouraged large fiscal deficits and over-valued exchange rates.

From Cline's estimates one can infer that much of the rapid growth of developing nation external debt through the 1970s is explained by their need to deal with serious balance of payments difficulties brought on by external shocks. Accepting that the principal objective of the IMF is to intervene in such circumstances, major involvement by the Fund should have taken place. However, the figures tell a different story. Table 8.1 gives the sources of external borrowing for non-oil developing countries.

Table 8.1   Non-oil developing countries: sources of external borrowing

Sources of external borrowing (percentage share)	1974–7 (Average)	1978–80 (Average)	1981	1982	1983
Official finance	40	30	35	56	69
(i) Long-term capital	33	29	28	36	47
(ii) Fund credit	7	2	7	20	22
Private borrowing	60	70	65	44	31
(i) Long-term capital	50	47	49	47	79
(ii) Short-term capital	10	23	16	−3	−48

Source: IMF, *World Economic Outlook*, p. 66.

Table 8.1 illustrates that the traditional role of the IMF had been usurped by the private international capital markets. First, one observes the large rise in the percentage share of external borrowing from private sources. Prior to 1973, commercial bank loans to developing countries accounted for approximately 30 per cent of external financing. Between 1974 and 1982 they become the primary source for external borrowing while the percentage share from official sources fell. Second, the table reveals that Fund credit contributed to only a small proportion of external financing. Finally, by the late 1970s, much of the growth in external debt was in the form of short-term credit (loans with a maturity of less than one year). This increased fivefold between 1978 and 1980, compared with a rise in long-term credit of just over half its 1978 figure. While rescheduling agreements will reduce these short-term obligations, the figures reveal a mismatch between lender and borrower: the private capital markets were supplying short-term external capital to countries who should have been demanding it to finance long-term growth objectives.

Recall that the primary objective of the IMF was to help countries deal with balance of payments difficulties, be they caused by fundamental or non-fundamental disequilibria. According to Cline's evidence, the rapid growth in external financing was largely in response to balance of payments problems caused by exogenous forces. In the 1950s and 1960s, this would have been a classic case for IMF intervention. But with the collapse of the adjustable peg system, one of the tools for IMF intervention was eliminated with no provision for a replacement. The statistical evidence reveals the consequences of this. The ambiguity surrounding IMF functions caused the private capital markets to fill the vacuum left by the collapse of Bretton Woods. This is completely at odds with the original objectives of Bretton Woods: the paradigm of the international economic order has changed. Had the Bretton Woods participants foreseen the resumption of international capital mobility in the post-war period, the IMF may well have been assigned duties closer in line with those of the International Clearing Union, proposed by Keynes.[10] The ICU was to be a clearance centre for all international payments and a new international currency unit, 'bancor', was to be created. But in absence of international capital mobility, Keynes's proposals appeared unwarranted. Indeed, as Williamson (1978, Ch. 2) points out, the adoption of the adjustable peg and the creation of the World Bank reflected a Bretton Woods attitude that the post-war international economy would be one without mobile capital.

This section has illustrated that when the adjustable peg was abandoned, the IMF lost much of its ability to make an effective contribution to the promotion of world financial stability. The subsequent failure to provide an adequate replacement has contributed to the financial system's growing fragility. If the Bretton Woods paradigm of the international economic order is accepted, then at the very least, the IMF functions must be explicitly redefined. These would have the objective of promoting financial stability in a flexible exchange rate, mobile capital international economy. As such the 'new' IMF would assume a characteristic normally associated with an international central bank. It may well be that the Bretton Woods paradigm is unacceptable. For example, there is a large body of economists who advocate the monetary approach to the balance of payments and reject the concept of fundamental disequilibrium.[11] To ensure international growth rates in the money supply and output were in line with each other, thereby stabilising exchange rates and the financial system, this group would favour an international central bank with powers to regulate domestic monetary policies of member countries.

Whatever the economic philosophy, the analysis points to a need for a 'Bretton Woods' in the 1980s to define the international economic priorities and to decide how best they might be achieved. The ambiguous climate only contributes to financial fragility and, unlike the IMF Articles of Agreement drawn up in the 1940s, the current situation has been reached without the official consent of the major actors.

3 THE COSTS AND BENEFITS OF AN INTERNATIONAL BANKING SYSTEM

The rapid growth in the international banking system from the mid-1960s is largely explained by regulatory practices in most Western domestic banking systems. The imposition of reserve requirements and interest ceilings on deposits was standard. While exchange controls restricted the movement of capital across national boundaries, financial autarky prevailed. As these controls were removed, an increasing number of agents turned to offshore banking. In this section, attention is focused on the resulting costs and benefits of transnational banking. The question to be addressed is whether an international central bank could minimise the associated costs.

To identify these costs and benefits, begin with a simple model of domestic banking under financial autarky. Assume (Case A) that interest rates are set by market forces but the central bank imposes a reserve ratio requirement. In this case, market forces will ensure that in each country:

$$(1 - z)f(r) = g(q) \tag{1}$$

$$q = c + x + r(1 - z)^{-1} \tag{2}$$

where:

z: the reserve ratio requirement.

x: the profit margin on loans. This will depend on the quality of competition or the degree of collusion in oligopoly. Under perfect competition, $x = 0$.

q: the loan rate established by market forces.

r: the deposit rate established by market forces.

c: the cost of financial intermediation. This is assumed to be constant and loan related.

f: supply of deposits, D.

g: supply of loans, L.

The reserve requirement, a form of taxation on the banking system, is a source of government revenue. In this case, government revenue is:

$$zf(r)q \tag{3}$$

where the loan rate (q) is identified with the rate paid on interest bearing government debt.

If the interest and profit rates are set by the central bank (Case B) then:

$$(1 - z)f(\bar{r}) < g(\bar{q}) \tag{4}$$

$$\bar{q} = c + \bar{x} + \bar{r}\,(1 - z)^{-1} \tag{5}$$

and

$$\text{government revenue} = zf(r)\bar{q} \tag{6}$$

where the bars denote the rates set by the government. The assumptions that $\bar{r} < r$ and that $\bar{x}$ is not high enough to prevent an excess demand for loans at $\bar{q}$ make eqn (4) an inequality.

Now grant the facilities of offshore banking to agents in the domestic banking system. The growth of supply and demand for offshore banking facilities resulted from the unique combination of regulations in different Western economies. For example, reserve requirements and regulation of interest rates in West Germany and the US created a demand for offshore facilities which were supplied by countries like the UK who imposed no controls on non-resident loans and deposits (McKinnon, 1979, pp. 204–5). In this analysis it is assumed that offshore banking facilities have the characteristics of the Euromarkets. That is, they are facilities primarily for wholesale banking, catering to only part of the domestic market. Thus, while the offshore deposit rate (r^*) will be higher and the loan rate (q^*) lower (a result of the absence of regulations), the specialised nature of the market prevents rates from being equalised across markets because of insufficient competitive pressure. This means there will be a differential between offshore and domestic banking rates, whether or not the market is regulated.

Suppose a fraction s_i of country i's total supply of deposits migrate offshore. Then the total supply of offshore deposits from the i countries will be $\Sigma_i s_i f_i(r^*)$, where s_i is a non-decreasing function of the interest differential $r^* - r$ or $r^* - \bar{r}$. The total demand for offshore loans will be $\Sigma_i v_i q_i(q^*)$ where a fraction v_i of country i's total demand for loans migrates. v_i is assumed to be non-decreasing in $q_i - q^*$ or $\bar{q}_i - q^*$. If domestic credit markets are rationed, the demand for offshore loans will be reinforced.

If international banking services are supplyable with negligible reserves and perfectly competitive conditions prevail, the equilibrium is characterised by:

$$q^* = c^* + x^* + r^* - c^* + r^*$$

where the * denotes offshore rates. For domestic banking equilibrium, eqns (2) and (5) are unchanged while (1) and (4) become:

$$(1 - z)(1 - s)f(r) = (1 - v)g(q) \qquad (1^*)$$

$$(1 - z)(1 - s) f(\bar{r}) = (1 - v)g(\bar{q}) \qquad (4^*)$$

Government revenue is now:

$$z(1 - s)f(r)q \qquad \text{for } r = r \qquad (3^*)$$

$$z(1 - s)f(\bar{r})q \qquad \text{for } r = \bar{r} \qquad (6^*)$$

The welfare effects of offshore banking may be analysed in the context of the simple model outlined above. Throughout, all agents are assumed to have an identical marginal utility of money. Surplus gains will accrue to agents depositing and borrowing in the offshore banking system. Assuming f and g may be approximated by linearisation these will be:

$$\tfrac{1}{2}[\textstyle\sum_i (r^* - r_i)s_i f_i(r^*) + \sum_i (q_i' - q^*)v_i g_i(q^*)] \tag{11}$$

where, for countries with no interest ceiling, $q' = q$ while q' is the shadow value of domestic loans for countries with an interest ceiling set by the central bank. There may be additional surplus gains (or losses) for agents who continue to deposit with or borrow from domestic banks if domestic loan and deposit rates change in response to the emigration offshore. It is more likely to be a gain because the offshore competition erodes central bank monopoly power and may make $(1 - s)f$ and $(1 - v)g$ more elastic than before. Central banks will re-optimise by setting a lower z_i and higher r. By the same reasoning, x should also be lower. Domestic borrowers may gain or lose, depending on the effect of offshore banking on q. In the absence of central bank interference (Case A) q will fall but if interest ceilings and deposit rates are set, q could well rise (see eqn (5)). This makes the effects on domestic agents ambiguous. Nor is it possible to say whether there is a net gain accruing to residents of a given country. For while competitive pressures will likely lower q and raise r, international banking also leads to discrimination in interest rates, those having access to offshore banks obtaining more favourable terms than co-nationals.

Another gain will come from any *new* international capital movements which are a consequence of the emergence of international banking. This will arise if, in autarky, interest rates differ across countries. With governments as the primary borrowers and banks channelling deposits from other countries (especially the OPEC members), there is no doubt the Euromarkets facilitated the transfer of capital between countries. Over the period 1974–80, of the \$317 billion cash surplus accruing to oil exporting nations, \$47 billion went in the form of direct finance to developing countries while \$147 billion was deposited in private banks (including the Eurobanks) who re-lent the cash.[12] However, as was noted in the last section, it is questionable whether this was the optimal source of external finance for developing countries, given their balance of payments difficulties.

The diversion of banking activity from inshore to offshore also gives rise to changes in real resource costs. These are:

$$(c^* - c_i)r_i(1 - z)f_i \gtrless 0$$

The sign of this equation is governed by the cost differential between inshore (c_i) and offshore banking (c^*). It is likely to be positive given enforcement problems (bank legislation varies widely across countries) and the relatively greater difficulty of acquiring information on loan applicants. A second form of real resource costs may come from additional distortionary taxation levied by national governments to make good revenue losses from the implicit tax on domestic bank reserves. The revenue loss is found by subtracting eqn (3^*) (or (6^*)) from (3) (or (6)).

The analysis of the welfare effects from the introduction of offshore banking points to two reasons for an international central bank. First, with the exception of new international capital movements, all the welfare gains cited could be achieved if the restrictive practices of national central banks were relaxed. Some countries have been forced to do this with the emergence of the international banking system. In the UK, reserve requirements and exchange controls have been removed and in the US, regulation Q and the interest equalisation tax have been abandoned. However, if the real resource costs associated with offshore banking are high, a central agency which put pressure on nations to deregulate their system could well have achieved the same gains at a relatively lower cost. This would be a financial version of GATT, encouraging the free trade of financial transactions both across and within national frontiers.

Second, if the current international banking system is accepted as a permanent feature of the international economy, a central bank could act to reduce the real resource losses associated with it. These arise primarily because there is no body which pools information on the creditworthiness of potential borrowers. Euromarket lending differs from the standard lending facilities associated with domestic banking systems in two respects. First, it is the norm for the bank officer in the domestic banking system to assess creditworthiness based on direct knowledge of the lender. In the Euromarket only the final bank has certain knowledge of who the lender is, the average deposit passing through several banks before being loaned to a non-bank borrower. Second, the absence of collateral in the majority of Euroloans (certainly those to national governments) adds a new dimension to the risks associated with lending. Enforcement difficulties exacerbate the problem. The current debt problems of non-oil developing countries highlight these difficulties. The nature of operations in Euromarkets caused banks to increase their exposure without explicit knowledge of the activities of other lenders. The total size of sovereign loans to any one country was unknown. Further, the recent 'involuntary' lending[13] by private banks illustrates how it is impossible to exercise enforcement privileges in the usual manner.

Some private banks have responded to these problems by forming the Institute for International Finance (IIF), its primary objective being the pooling of information on developing countries. However, from the standpoint of international welfare, this may not be the first best solution to the information problem. Radner and Stiglitz (1984) have shown the existence of a non-concavity in the net benefit from acquiring information. This suggests there are increasing returns to pooling when information is costly. Thus a formal institution making information more symmetric may be more efficient than piecemeal exchanges by a small coalition of agents. Also if the pooling of information is left to a private group of international banks, new undesirable oligopolistic tendencies could be created.

The pooling of information, apart from reducing real costs, could also promote confidence in international banking and so contribute to financial stability. Should the pooling of information prove insufficient in meeting either task, the central bank could resort to requesting reserves on international deposits. The existence of SDRs mean the mechanics for this are already in place and in the absence of any revenue raising goals for the ICB, there would be no potential conflict of interest associated with the meeting of reserve requirements by domestic central banks.

4   MORAL HAZARD AND THE INCENTIVE TO FREE RIDE

Apart from administrative costs, two problems, moral hazard and the incentive to free ride pose potentially serious drawbacks for an international central bank whose principal aim is the maintenance of financial stability. These problems are associated with most types of third party intervention and appropriate action must be taken to minimise their effects.

Problems of moral hazard will arise on both the borrowing and the lending sides. Moral hazard was initially identified as a cost incurred by insurance companies, the insurance agreement shifting the risks, thereby modifying the incentives of the insured and changing the agent's behaviour. With respect to international banking, the presence of an ICB will alter the risk profile of international loans. This could give rise to moral hazard on the part of the lender and borrower. It is the latter which differentiates moral hazard problems associated with domestic banking from those of international banking.

On the lending side, moral hazard can arise from two sources. First, the presence of an ICB will alter the risk profile of sovereign loans and second, insolvent banks may attempt to conceal this information from the ICB. These problems are linked to the lender of the last resort (LLR) function normally associated with a central bank. According to Guttentag and Herring (1983, p. 4) the central purpose of an LLR is to assume risks which are unacceptable to the market place, providing loans to illiquid but solvent banks and thus minimising the effects of a financial crisis. It is this function which gives rise to the moral hazard problems just cited. The consequent weakening of private bank lending responsibility is the main argument against a LLR function being assigned to a central bank.

An ICB should not be assigned a direct LLR function on the lending side. Its role should be the exertion of pressure on domestic central banks to ensure adequate coverage. For on the lending side, the problem is not unique to international lending activities: a bank encounters liquidity difficulties and traditionally the domestic central bank takes the decision to intervene. However, there can be an ambiguous relationship between the central bank and offshore activities of the bank. As was pointed out earlier, it was domestic bank regulations which played a significant role in inducing banks to set up offshore operations. Also, as pointed out by Guttentag and Herring (1983, p. 4), the domestic central banks represent national interests. Unless international activities interfere with these interests, they have no incentive to provide LLR assistance to international banks. This creates a gap between domestic and international central banking responsibilities, and a neutral international agency could close the gap. It would be unnecessary (and potentially costly) for an ICB to assume full LLR responsibilities. Rather, its function would be to act as a coordinator of domestic central bank LLR activities, minimising the number of gaps which exist.

The present situation is as follows. The 1983 'Basle Concordat' (reached between the central banks of the Group of Ten plus Luxembourg and Switzerland) dealt with the subject of supervisory activities. For solvency problems arising with subsidiaries or liquidity problems associated with either a branch (no legal independence from the parent) or subsidiary, joint supervisory responsibilities would be assumed by the host and parent countries. In the case of a solvency problem associated with a branch, the responsibility would lie with the parent. Note, however, that the emphasis is on supervision: the LLR function is not explicit. Further, in the cases of joint action, the practical difficulties of distinguishing between illiquidity and insolvency could be a source of friction between central banks. The ICB could act as adjudicator in these cases, strengthen the existing agreement to include LLR responsibilities, ensure that to meet these responsibilities, an adequate level of reserves are held by central banks, and expand the agreement to include all member countries of the ICB. In particular, the ICB must act to eliminate three types of vulnerable banks, as identified by Guttentag and Herring (p. 20–21). These include banks headquartered in countries with no LLR facilities (e.g. Luxembourg), inconvertible currencies, or a shortage of foreign exchange reserves and subsidiary banks with ambiguous access to the parent's central bank facilities.

The possibility of country insolvency creates a unique moral hazard problem associated with international lending. This is where the ICB's role would have to be more direct. If the ICB facilities change the risk profile associated with sovereign loans it could increase the incentive of debtor countries to either default or threaten default on their sovereign loans.[14] Or it could dull their incentives, thereby making them more likely to use these loans for high risk projects. In domestic situations, the problem of carelessness is minimised through deductible insurance and to discourage default on loans, collateral is demanded. In the case of sovereign loans, the lender is faced with both of these problems. For in addition to their normal activities as lenders, participation in rescheduling agreements has turned the banks into insurers against exogenous shocks to borrowing countries. However, the usual remedies are not open to it. If, in the event of rescheduling the banks impose penalties which are too severe (a form of deductibility), this could well increase the probability of default, the bank having little recourse to action in the latter situation.

A neutral ICB would be better able to minimise the moral hazard problems on the lending side than the individual bank engaging in international loans. The ICB would assume two responsibilities in this area. Its first task would be to convince governments of borrowing countries that default probabilities have to be minimised in order to persuade potential lenders to grant loans. The ICB could argue that if lenders perceived a near zero default incentive, the cost of the loan would be lower. Second, the ICB would act as an enforcement body. Member countries would agree that in the event of default or rescheduling, the country in question would grant economic sovereignty to the ICB until the latter was satisfied all was being done to prevent an exacerbation of debt difficulties. This would also deal with the incentive problem of potentially careless economic management. IMF conditionality attached to the recent rescheduling packages has forced participating debtor nations to forego much of their economic sovereignty. However, the informality of the IMF role has contributed to uncertainty in the international climate. Such problems could be alleviated if its role was formalised. Also, the resentment in debtor nations caused by IMF conditionality indicates that the reasons for it have not been adequately explained. As members of an ICB, they would recognise that the net import of capital, be it in the form of foreign direct investment or sovereign loans, will entail a loss of economic independence. The ICB would emphasize that it is for the country to choose whether their central social welfare objective is the maximisation of expected future income streams and if so, how best to import capital to minimise their loss of independence. But having made these choices they must play the game.

The incentive to free ride will be associated with marginal international banks: those banks with a relatively small exposure to international loans. These 'small' banks will have an incentive to give false signals to the ICB in order to derive an *external* benefit from its existence. Assume the central role of the ICB is to minimise the occurrence of international financial crises. If participation was voluntary, marginal international lenders would have no incentive to join. Such banks, in opting out of membership would falsely signal a lack of interest, false because the ICB, in stabilising the financial environment, would significantly affect the performance of all international loans. On the other hand, unlike the large banks, the decision not to participate by a small bank would not affect the ability of the ICB to achieve its objectives. The marginal bank 'free rides': it gains from the benefits of the ICB without incurring any of the costs. To prevent this, the ICB would have to be given authority to exclude non-members from participating in international banking activities. This could create a 'black market' in international lending because some borrowing countries may also want to avoid ICB monitoring. However, any such market would be small since the large banks have no incentive to free ride. This would prevent it from undermining the ability of the ICB to achieve its objectives.

5 CONCLUSIONS

This chapter has investigated the case for an international central bank. Unlike a domestic central bank where two, perhaps three primary functions have evolved over time, the central objective of an ICB would be the preservation of international financial stability. The world financial system has become increasingly fragile over recent years, the result an absence of third party intervention at a time when exogenous shocks to the world economy demanded this. It is likely the IMF would have been assigned this role had the participants at Bretton Woods foreseen a post-war world where capital was mobile across countries. If a body did assume the task of preserving international financial stability, it would take on one of the major characteristics normally associated with a central bank. A secondary but important role of the ICB would be the minimisation of real resource costs associated with the emergence of international banking. It was shown that the pooling of information would be the principal means by which this could be achieved. This would complement the ICB's primary function.

What of current international problems? There is no doubt these have reached crisis proportions. Action should be directed at the prevention of international financial collapse. In terms of the existing debt difficulties, all parties must accept the potential long-run nature of the problems, which could take over twenty years to resolve. While the new rescheduling packages have provided a breathing space until (approximately) 1986, another serious downturn in the world economy could create a need for further rescheduling of this debt. It would be neither possible nor desirable for a newly created ICB to assume the debt, estimated to be over $600 billion for non-oil developing countries alone. The ICB would have to assume the role as the neutral negotiator of rescheduling packages. To minimise moral hazard and the incentive to free ride, careful monitoring should be conducted by an ICB. With respect to new international lending, this would be subject to ICB regulations as outlined in this chapter. No attempt should be made to single out a scapegoat, such an exercise would prove unproductive. Rather, all parties should look upon the existing difficulties as lessons to be learned from a relatively new economic experience, the emergence of a sophisticated system of international finance.

What has become increasingly evident in these 'reflections' is the need for a 'Bretton Woods' conference attended by all countries who rely on the international financial system. Its objective would be to grant official sanction to a course of action, be it the preservation of the status quo or the creation of an ICB. Utmost in the minds of the decision-makers should be the trade-off between the costs associated with the growing 'fragility' of the world economic system and those associated with the regulation of international finance. Aware of the trade-off, it is for the participants to reach a decision.

Notes

1. For an elaboration of the principles of the Currency School and the main proponents of it, see, among others, Andreades (4th edn, 1966), Part I, Chapters 4, 5, 6.
2. See Andreades (1966), Part I, Chapter 2.
3. Nagatani (1982), p. 11.
4. See Andreades (1966), Part I, Chapter 4.
5. See, among others, Fisher (1932), Kindleberger (1978) and Minsky (1977), (1979).
6. See, among others, Crockett (1977) and McKinnon (1979).
7. This employs the IMF definition for non-oil developing countries. It includes two major divisions, net oil exporters and net oil importers, the latter subdivided into three groups. See Appendix B in IMF, *World Economic Outlook* (1983) pp. 168–9.
8. See, among others, Beenstock (1984).
9. In the IMF survey of 20 non-oil developing countries, the propensity to invest in the period 1968–72 averaged 18.9 per cent of GNP rising to an average of 23.6 per cent in the period 1978–81. See IMF (1983) Appendix A, pp. 140–44.
10. See J. M. Keynes, vol. xxv, pp. 33–40 and for interpretation, Harrod (1972), pp. 622–9 and the Appendix in Williamson (1983).
11. See, among others, Frenkel and Johnson (1976).
12. See Table 22 (p. 129) in IMF, *World Economic Outlook*, June 1981.
13. See Cline (1983), p. 74.
14. On default incentives, see, among others, Eaton and Gersovitz (1981) and Heffernan (1984).

References

ANDREADES, A. (1966) *History of the Bank of England, 1640–1903*, 4th edn (London: Frank Cass and Company).

BATCHELOR, R. A. (1983) 'The Avoidance of Catastrophe: Two Nineteenth Century Banking Crises', Monetary History Discussion Paper No. 10, Centre for Banking and International Finance, The City University, October, 1983.

BEENSTOCK, M. (1984) *The World Economy in Transition*, Second edn (London: George Allen & Unwin).

BERNANKE, B. S. (1983) 'Non-monetary Effects of the Financial Crisis in the Propagation of the Great Depression', *American Economic Review*, vol. 73, June, 257–76.

CLINE, W. R. (1983) *International Debt and the Stability of the World Economy* (Washington: Institute for International Economics, MIT Press).

CROCKETT, A. (1977) *International Money: Issues and Analysis* (London: Nelson).

EATON, J. and GERSOVITZ, M. (1980) 'Debt with Potential Repudiation: Theoretical and Empirical Analysis', *Review of Economic Studies*, vol. 48, pp. 289–309.

FISHER, I. (1932) *Booms and Depressions* (New York: Adelphi).

FRENKEL, J. A. and JOHNSON, H. G. (eds) (1976) *The Monetary Approach to the Balance of Payments* (London: George Allen & Unwin).

FRIEDMAN, M. and SCHWARTZ, A. J. (1963) *A Monetary History of the United States, 1867–1960* (Princeton: Princeton University Press).

GUTTENTAG, J. and HERRING, R. (1983) 'The Lender of Last Resort Function in an International Context', *Princeton Essays in International Finance*, no. 151, May 1983.

HARROD, Sir Roy (1972) *The Life of John Maynard Keynes*. London: Pelican Books (first published by Macmillan in 1951), pp. 622–9.

HEFFERNAN, S. A. (1984) Country Risk Analysis: The Demand and Supply of Sovereign Loans. City University Business School Working Paper no. 52, 1983. Revised Version, 1984.

INTERNATIONAL MONETARY FUND (1983) *World Economic Outlook*. Occasional Paper no. 21, Washington.

KEYNES, J. M. *The Collected Writings of John Maynard Keynes*, vols I–XXX. London: Macmillan, XXV, pp. 33–40 (for the Royal Economic Society).

KINDLEBERGER, C. P. (1978) *Manias, Panics and Crashes: A History of Financial Crises* (New York: Basic Books).

McKINNON, R. (1979) *Money in International Exchange* (New York: Oxford University Press).

MINSKY, H. P. (1977) 'A Theory of Systematic Fragility', in E. J. Altman and A. W. Sametz (eds), *Financial Crises: Institutions and Markets in a Fragile Environment*. (New York: Wiley), pp. 138–52.

MINSKY, H. P. (1979) 'The Financial Instability Hypothesis: A Re-statement', *Discussion Paper No. 7, Confederazione-Generale dell' Industria Italiana*. Rome, 1979.

NAGATONI, K. (1982) 'What Central Banks Really Are', Department of Economics, The University of British Columbia, Discussion Paper, No. 82–07, March 1982.

RADNER, R. and STIGLITZ, J. E. (1984) 'A Non-concavity in the Value of Information', in M. Boyer and R. E. Kihlstrom (eds), *Bayesian Models in Economic Theory* (Amsterdam: North-Holland Press).

SAUNDERS, A. (1983) 'An Examination of the Contagion Effect in the International Loan Market', Mimeo.

SOUTHARD, F. A. (1979) 'The Evolution of the International Monetary Fund', *Princeton Essays in International Finance*, no. 135, December.

WILLIAMSON, J. (1977) *The Failure of World Monetary Reform*, 1971–1974. (London: Nelson).

WILLIAMSON, J. (1983) 'Keynes and the International Economic Order', in D. Worswick and J. Trevithick (eds), *Keynes and the Modern World* (Cambridge: Cambridge University Press), pp. 87–127.

Comments on 'The Costs and Benefits of International Banking'

D. Fitzgerald

There has been much interest recently, largely inspired by the apparent crisis in the world financial system, in the possible role for an international lender of last resort, or in the terminology of the author an 'International Central Bank'. The chapter, however, presents an unconvincing case for an institution, for which it would be very hard to find a convincing case. Much of the argument for an 'ICB' rests upon the 'increasing fragility' of the world economic system. The author presents no substantive evidence that the world economic system is any more fragile now than it was before. She says 'with the Mexican announcement in 1982, all the ingredients for a financial crisis were present'. But there is no sign of a financial crisis on the horizon. Indeed, all the evidence seems to be that banks are managing to write off problem loans slowly but surely out of high profit levels, and that as long as bankers refrain from further reckless Third World country lending, the problem will have disappeared with a small number of years. The success of the West German banks in writing down their Polish loans, which were of a similar order of magnitude, is a lesson in this regard.

Of course, it is certainly true that individual banks could conceivably get into trouble over international lending, although it is interesting none of the most spectacular banking crashes of recent years has concerned Third World lending. And doubtless the 'contagion effect' of which the author makes much could cause a run in a wider sense on international banks. The Continental Illinois case suggests though that the Central Banks of individual countries will certainly be willing to protect major money centre banks from their own follies. If that is true, and I think it clearly is, then the demise of one or two smaller banks seems unlikely to contribute too much 'fragility' to the system. Moreover, I find it unconvincing to argue that the possibility of contagion is best handled by a lender of last resort in the person of an International Central Bank. The author correctly points out that in a world of perfect information, the insolvency of a single bank or financial institution will have no essential impact on the system. If you want a regulatory agency, therefore, it seems to me that its aim should be to create an availability of information that will produce this effect. This could be solved as suggested in Batchelor and Fitzgerald (1982) by an organisation publishing details of variable risk-related insurance premiums that *would* be charged *if* an insurance scheme operated. Such premiums would convey all the information required by depositors to set appropriate equilibrium rates of return consistent with a true knowledge of the composition of the bank portfolio. This seems infinitely superior to creating an institution which would be likely, whatever the original intentions, to be seen as providing infinite amounts of deposit insurance at zero cost.

There is also the question here of a severe agency problem in the relationship between international banks and their shareholders. The old-fashioned but still attractive objective function in financial management has always been to maximise shareholder wealth. What are banks doing involving themselves in the type of Third World financing they have been doing, lending more money so interest on the original loans can be paid etc. It would be a very strange commercial organisation which invested in a capital project costing say $500 million expected to yield $50 million per year and ended up yielding nothing, and then followed that up by investing another $500 million so $25 million per year could be yielded by the original project. But this is an exact parallel with the major money centrebanks with respect to Third World lending. It would be better in my view for the world financial system if the international banks stopped worrying so much about international financial 'fragility' and started acting in the pedestrian money-grubbing interests of their shareholders.

Finally, there is the question of how an International Central Bank would operate. The author quotes Guttentag and Herring (1983) describing the lender of last resort facility as assuming risks which are unacceptable to the market-place. I may be old-fashioned but I cannot conceive of any welfare gain that is obtained by such action, which in any case would be unnecessary with the information system described above. Even so international lender of last resort facilities are one thing – the totalitarian and despotic nature of the International Central Bank described by the author are another. 'The ICB must act to *eliminate* three types of vulnerable banks.' 'The ICB would act as an enforcement body.' 'The country in question would grant sovereignty to the ICB.' 'The ICB would have to be given authority to exclude non-members from participating in international banking activities.' The current state of the international financial system may be fragile, disorganised and inefficient, but would anyone really prefer to operate in one run by a grandiose bureaucracy of the type suggested by the author – certainly not me, brother.

To sum up I totally disagree with the author on most of her basic premises. There is no evidence international problems have reached crisis proportions. There is no need for a new 'Bretton Woods'. The international financial system seems in pretty good shape, dealing with its problems in the spirit of *ad hoc* response and innovation which is the mark of a resilient system. The author's solution of a super bureaucracy to run or at least regulate world finance went out with the ark.

References

BATCHELOR, R. A. and FITZGERALD, M. D. (1985) 'Financial Regulation: A Survey', in R. A. Batchelor and M. D. Fitzgerald (eds), *Finance Regulation*, Macmillan, forthcoming.

GUTTENTAG, J. and HERRING, P. (1983) 'The Lenders of Last Resort Function in an International Context', *Princeton Essays in International Finance*, No. 151, May.

Reply to Comments by D. Fitzgerald

Shelagh A. Heffernan

In reply to these comments, several points need to be raised. First, at three different points in his commentary, Dr Fitzgerald equates an international central bank with an international lender of last resort. As those who have read the original chapter will observe, the author stressed the need to avoid the synonymous treatment of these two terms. The primary role of the ICB would be the preservation of international financial stability, a goal *partly* achieved through the co-ordination of the LLR activities of national central banks. The need for co-ordination is underlined by Fitzgerald's inference that while national central banks appear willing to bail out 'major' private banks, smaller banks need not be protected in the same way. What distinguishes the two types of banks when it comes to the provision of LLR facilities? Surely the inferred distinction could create severe distortions in the financial system. I only cite Fitzgerald's comment as an example of why greater co-ordination of domestic central bank activities may be necessary.

Second, Fitzgerald claims there is no 'substantive' evidence of increasing financial fragility in the world economy. In the chapter the author described how world economic events in the 1970s created an international economy which closely fits the Minsky description of fragility: an increase in international debt and Ponzi finance, the rising predominance of short-term over long-term debt, and a reduction in the international financial institutions' margins of safety. The author also noted the difficulty in estimating the amount of financial fragility necessary to provoke a financial collapse. But this does not mean economists can pretend the problem does not exist.

Third, Fitzgerald believes the problem will disappear within a few years provided bankers refrain from further 'reckless' Third World lending. One wonders what type of sovereign lending fits the description of reckless. Is it Cline's 'involuntary' lending which made up 50 per cent of new net lending in 1983? If so, the rescheduling agreements associated with this type of lending merely postpones the threat to financial stability, they do not necessarily eliminate it.

Finally, Fitzgerald's concern over the totalitarian nature of the ICB points to the hazards of quoting authors out of context. Readers of the chapter will find that the ICB would be anything but totalitarian given its primary function of preserving stability through the co-ordination of national central bank activities, the gathering of information and the minimisation of moral hazard–free rider problems which could well arise with its creation. As for Fitzgerald's concern over bureaucracy, it is already in place in the form of the IMF. Unfortunately, the role of the IMF has been undermined in a world of flexible exchange rates and internationally mobile capital. In light of these changes in the world economy it seems sensible to provide the IMF with a new set of tools which would enable it to achieve the goals for which it was established. This would be in the spirit of the Bretton Woods agreement. On the other hand, world leaders may hold opinions similar to those of Dr Fitzgerald, in which case it is time to abandon the principle of third party intervention in the world economy. But these are issues which need to be debated at a formal conference, just as they were in the immediate post-war period.

9 International Lenders of Last Resort: Are Changes Required?

Stephany Griffith-Jones and Michael Lipton

1 INTRODUCTION

> Theory suggests, and experience proves, that in a panic the holders
> of the ultimate Bank reserve (whether one bank or many) should
> lend to all that bring good securities, quickly, freely and readily.
> By that policy they allow a panic; by every other policy they
> intensify it. (Bagehot, 1873)

As the national lender of last resort (LLR) needed clear exposition
just over one hundred years ago, so international lender of last
resort (ILLR) needs it now. Bank activities are much more complex,
internationalised and interlocked. Not merely the welfare of depositors, but the capacity of sound firms at home and abroad to borrow
– as well as the capacity of many developing countries to grow –
depend on the maintenance of a liquid base for the banking system.
We concur with Kindleberger (1978), IMF (1983) and others, that
formalised, known international lender-of-last-resort arrangements
are increasingly necessary not mainly to 'allow a panic', but to
prevent one.

However, to construct a proper ILLR requires an improved understanding of LLR functions in two respects. First, while most
observers appreciate that LLR's purpose is not 'to bail out banks' –
indeed, a major problem is to prevent banks from relying on this
perception – neither does LLR exist mainly to protect depositors;
its main purpose is to ensure a stable, and if possible steadily
growing, flow of credit to sound borrowers. Second, in this task,
reliable LLR and really adequate supervision are two sides of one
coin, the latter acceptable to banks only with the former; as supervision should smooth upswings, so LLR should buffer downswings
of bank credit. This chapter tries to suggest ways in which ILLR

arrangements can be achieved, without unacceptable increases in moral hazard,[1] by changes in supervisory arrangements and other matters. First, however, we would stress the importance of confidence in ILLR for maintaining, despite recent shocks, the flow of capital to developing countries. This applies even to low-income countries, although they seldom borrow much from commercial banks. The present operations of the system, without clear ILLR facilities, may hurt the poorest countries in two ways. First, pressures to avoid default divert official flows from low-income to middle-income countries – and, recently, towards shorter-term and less concessional official lending. Second, as we shall explain, the inadequacies of ILLR, even without crisis and especially during early recovery, exercise steady deflationary pressure on growth, trade, and hence development prospects.

The lack of an appropriate ILLR – which can take account of the enormous complexity, scale and internationalisation of commercial banking – makes two undesirable developments more likely. Firstly, there remains a possibility that widespread financial distress now characterising the world economy may turn into a major financial crisis. Secondly, and more plausibly, the combination of actual reschedulings (reducing the banks' liquid base) and fear of defaults may continue to constrain private bank lending to developing countries. *Ad hoc* anticipatory contractions – by them or banks – are mutually deflationary, and further weaken the prospects of a sustained world economic recovery.

More generally, insufficient ILLR facilities give commercial bank scant reason to accept really effective supervision. This contributes to patterns of capital flows, especially of bank lending to developing countries, in which 'euphoric' over-expansion (Kindleberger, 1978) alternates with over-contraction. Such swings tend to accompany, not to stabilise, business cycles, both at country level (Griffith-Jones, 1980) and world-wide. Adequate supervision would control, diversify and, when necessary, limit 'euphoric' expansion. Moreover, such supervision relates each bank's behaviour to the total exposure, not just of that bank, but of the borrowing and lending country. It considerably transcends traditional supervision,[2] and would be acceptable to commercial banks only if backed by reliable, even if potentially costly, ILLR facilities. With supervision moderating upswings and ILLR buffering downswings, private credit flows would be more regular. The package would produce much more desirable credit patterns – not just for developing countries but for the world economy, and ultimately for the banks as well, even though some apparently profitable business would from time to time be frustrated.

This chapter focuses on issues closely linked to the need, or otherwise, for ILLR. However, this problem cannot be treated in isolation from other major issues. In particular, any ILLR facility is complementary to – and by no means a substitute for – measures to make its use less likely or less necessary. This covers, in general, measures to promote sustained world economic recovery, and, in particular, the expansion of official and private flows, which may be more appropriate to finance lending in some developing countries than is current short- or medium-term bank lending with floating interest rates (ICIDI, 1983). We share doubts about the genuine appropriateness of medium-term variable-interest bank loans for the finance of some developing countries. However, such flows remain essential, particularly while alternative mechanisms – either private or official – remain only as proposals.

In Section II, we define the role of an LLR, pointing to the key issue of how 'onerous terms' for its use must deter imprudence by potential users. We then ask why a special ILLR is needed at all (Section 3). Next – in the context of the central bankers' decision to make ILLR deliberately uncertain and vague, so as to create a form of 'onerous terms' – we outline existing ILLR facilities, and associated supervision procedures (Section 4). We then assess (Section 5) whether they are – and are perceived to be – sufficient to contain a 'crisis' that might be caused by various sorts of non-repayment of foreign debt. In that context, we also enquire how these uncertain ILLR facilities affect the level and stability of commercial bank lending and of world flows of credit. Do these facilities encourage banks and customers to distribute credit among users in ways that favour steady and sound economic expansion, especially by developing countries? Finally, in Section 6, we review our conclusions and make our proposal – to replace damaging uncertainty about ILLR by a revival, in a form that suits today's needs, of Bagehot's original conditions for 'onerous terms'.

2 ROLE OF NATIONAL LLR, AND INTERNATIONAL ASPECTS

An LLR is a central bank, group of banks, or treasury that has the power, and accepts the responsibility, to lend without limit – or to the limit of plausible requirements – but on onerous terms, to institutions in trouble or crisis. 'Institutions' were taken by Bagehot to mean 'all comers' but nowadays are confined to banks, or, at most, institutions taking financial deposits against interest for onlending.

'Trouble' has normally been taken to mean a significant risk of not being able to repay depositors and creditors on request, either because the bank is unusually illiquid, or because depositors seem likely to ask for their money in unusually large numbers (a run); if depositors are confident of LLR facilities they will, it is assumed, be prepared to restrain withdrawals. In fact, 'trouble' could be more broadly defined as incapacity by a bank, even well short of any risk of collapse, to carry on with normal lending operations. For instance, when British commercial banks recalled money from discount houses and forced them into the Bank of England at the 'penal' Bank Rate, this was often conventionally taken as a first-stage LLR operation, though nobody suggested that either commercial banks or discount houses were in danger of not meeting obligations; recourse to the central bank was in order not to forfeit normal, profitable business. Similarly, recent 'liability management' by US banks implies that 'even borrowing from the Fed should be considered a source of funds' (Cargill, 1979).

It is crucial, in understanding the case for LLR (ILLR) as a 'social good' like health or roads to be provided by the State, to realise that this case depends not only, nor mainly, on the wish to rescue depositors. The main basis is the need to maintain the capacity of the banking system to lend: to prevent 'trouble' facing one bank, especially if it threatens to degenerate into a 'crisis' of confidence in many banks, from stifling the flow of credit to countries and enterprises. Of course, panic transfers of cash among banks by depositors, or rushes by them into cash (or foreign currency, or physical or financial assets bought with foreign currency), would make it even harder for firms to borrow, as banks became more cautious and less liquid. But the principal reason for an LLR to commercial banks is not to safeguard depositors (which can be achieved by other mechanisms – see below); it is to preserve and stabilise productive activity, by underpinning the capacity of the banking system to lend to enterprises and countries.

Before we define 'onerous terms', we should build on these points to clarify what an LLR is not. LLR is sometimes vaguely or inexactly used to describe three entirely different sorts of operation. The first is deposit insurance. This covers, for example, US deposits below

$100,000 – about two-thirds of the total, but excluding almost all major foreign deposits. Since 1934, deposit insurance through FDIC has been dramatically successful in reducing US bank failures (Cargill, 1979) and since 1967 Canada, France, Germany, Japan, Netherlands, Switzerland and the UK have set up similar schemes. Coverage is usually incomplete or small (e.g. 75 per cent of deposits up to £10 000 in Britain) and foreign-currency or company deposits are sometimes excluded (IMF, 1983). These schemes provide valuable safeguards for small depositors, but their extension would probably create larger and less predictable burdens for central banks (and ultimately taxpayers). More fundamentally, deposit insurance does not fulfil the prime function of LLR as a social good – maintenance of the commercial banks' capacity to lend in support of economic activity. Repayment of depositors by an official deposit insurance agency normally implies the winding up of the institution in question; and while its assets may be transferred to a viable competitor its new lending activity will be lost, with no clear guarantee that other institutions will replace it, especially in a climate of impaired confidence.

Support for depositors is different from LLR. So is support for borrowers. We share the widespread fear that the recently agreed enlargement of IMF resources is insufficient. We share, too, the fear that IMF conditionality can be inappropriate; although aimed at financial realism for each borrower, it involves – when simultaneously applied to many countries – contractions of demand, including mutual export demand, that will make it harder for the borrowing community as a whole to meet its new and old obligations. Countries with repayment problems, if there are many countries and large problems, certainly need new funds conditional on their adjustment in a manner that does not induce general and mutual deflation. However – while additional provision of such funds (and new modalities for conditionality) may reduce the risk of calls upon ILLR – provision of such funds to borrowers is distinct from LLR facilities for banks.

Both depositors and borrowers, if their activities have not been speculative, may be provided with emergency facilities through some sort of safety net. Such help for customers, while it may ease the strain on an LLR, is not truly a substitute for LLR to the banking or near-banking intermediaries. Nor, third, are general open-market operations a true form of LLR in near-crisis. Generalised new liquidity will not unless enormous – go to distressed banks, or their clients.

To advocate provision of LLR proper, as Bagehot did – and to deny the adequacy of substitutes – is not to express general lack of trust in the operation of financial markets. A series of bank troubles, leading to a crisis that feeds on itself for want of an LLR, is not a market, but a gap, a discontinuity, between two sets of situations, in each of which market forces can operate, but between which they can no more mediate than people can see round sharp corners. LLR is not a substitute for financial markets, but a necessary condition for their contribution to stable growth.

However, if an LLR is not to be transformed into a mechanism to 'bail out the banks', and if LLR facilities are not to encourage reckless lending in the belief that there is no lender's risk, then a precise content must be given to the concept of 'onerous terms'. Three different methods for applying the concept of 'onerous terms' today seem possible:

(a) Bagehot did this with a twin condition: lending had to be on 'good collateral', and there should be 'a very high rate of interest' (Fetter, 1965).
(b) Another approach is to define clearly conditions where LLR will not be available, e.g. if there is good reason to suspect fraud, or if there has been gross breach of banking practice and/or explicit supervisory conditions.
(c) A final approach is to maintain uncertainty about the nature, duration, entitlement or cost of LLR facilities.

We shall argue that current reliance on (c) in ILLR has gone too far for the health and stability of the banking system – but that (a) and (b) can be revived only with supervision, redefined, as the counterpart to a more assured ILLR.

3   THE INTERNATIONALISATION AND BANKING AND OF ITS RISKS

Why cannot the requirements of ILLR facilities simply be met by national authorities? Six trends in international banking since the early 1970s have increased the need for an ILLR, and for new forms of international central-bank co-ordination and supervision. These are well known and have been analysed in depth elsewhere; we sketch them very briefly here.

1. The growing dependence of developing countries on commercial lending: private bank lending to oil-importing developing countries grew at 19.7 per cent annually at constant prices between 1970 and 1980 (World Bank, 1982). Recently a very high proportion of such countries' current-account deficits has been financed by borrowing – and more recently by short-term borrowing – from international banks. Of all such deficits, in 1977–81, 53 per cent was financed on average by increases in international bank claims. (For the large borrowers, the ratios were much higher.) Thus, by end-1981, the total obligations of non-oil developing countries to banks reached on average 3.56 times the level of their official international reserves and as much as 45 per cent of this debt was due in less than one year (IMF, 1983).

2. The rapid increase in the financing needs of the developing countries: the current-account deficits of the non-oil less developed countries (non-oil LDCs) increased from $11.6 bn in 1973 to $100 bn in 1981 and $87 bn in 1982 (IMF, 1983).

3. The rising trend of debt service ratios: By mid-1982, the debt service 'ratio' (DSR) to annual exports of goods and services was 38 per cent for oil-exporting LDCs, and 24 per cent for oil-importing LDCs as a whole (IMF, 1982). In 1965–74, when risks were smaller, difficulties arose in 38 of the 102 cases where and LDC had a DSR above 20 per cent in a particular year, but only in 2 of the 478 cases with a DSR below 20 per cent (Feder, 1979; Lipton, 1981). Nor, on past evidence, need 'recovery' – especially if patchy – reduce the risk; for some debtors, it could even worsen terms of trade and/or raise interest-rates. Hence there is no validity whatever in popular, and populist, claims that the internationalised threat to financial stability is somehow unreal, or no greater than before (Lal, 1983), or that urgent demands for ILLR or other action constitute some sort of 'banker's ramp'.

4. The concentration of bank lending: the debts – and risks – are the more alarming for being very concentrated on a few big debtors and banks. At end-June 1982, of $347.5 bn owed by the hundred-plus developing countries to BIS reporting banks (excluding offshore centre), some 49.6 per cent was owed by Argentina, Brazil, Mexico and Venezuela (Morgan Guaranty, 1983) all of whom in early 1983 had reported DSRs well over 100 per cent. Exposure to the first three alone by the 10 leading US banks was $38 bn – over 40 per cent of the countries' bank debt, and over 140 per cent of the banks' total equity! (*The Economist*, April 1983).

5. The concentration of bank deposits: 'Recycling' of OPEC funds meant that, by December 1981, 16 per cent of total deposits of private banks in the BIS reporting area originated from the oil-exporting countries; and about 38 per cent of these banks' net external resources (deposits minus credits) came from oil-exporting countries, mainly Saudi Arabia, Kuwait and the UAE (BIS, 1981, 1983).

6. The changing supervisory needs of the market: the internationalisation of banking – through (a) syndicated lending, with the participation of banks from different countries to finance developing country and Comecon borrowing; (b) the rapid growth of a much larger, international interbank market; (c) a growing search by banks for legal means to avoid exposure limits and to reduce tax liability – has resulted in a great variety of foreign branches, subsidiaries, affiliates, so-called holding companies, etc., largely in offshore centres with parent banks based in other countries. As a result, a large proportion of operations and flows do not clearly fall within the purview of any national supervisory or LLR authorities.

4 EXISTING PROVISIONS FOR ILLR FACILITIES

There is now, as we have stressed, uncertainty about LLR for foreign activities. Central bank representatives repeatedly argue that even indications of the possible provisions of their support as ILLRs, or any apparent generalisation from past cases where their services were provided, may reduce bank prudence. Governor Wallich (1978), of the US Federal Reserve Board, has stated:

> There are dangers in trying to define and publicise specific rules for emergency assistance to troubled banks, notably the possibility of causing undue reliance on such facilities and possible relaxation of caution . . . The Federal Reserve has always avoided comprehensive statements of conditions for its assistance to member banks. Emergency assistance is indirectly a process of negotiation and judgement, with a range of possible actions varying with

certain circumstances and need. Therefore, a pre-determined set of conditions for emergency lending would be inappropriate.

Bank of England Executive Director (now Deputy Governor) McMahon expressed a very similar view (1978):

> close consideration and cooperation among the central banks most concerned with the security of the international banking markets is essential. By the same token, however, it is not possible for them to define in advance with any precision the circumstances in which last resort finance might be forthcoming. Indeed, if they tried to do so, banks might be tempted to sail too close to the wind with the presumption that support would automatically be forthcoming if they got into difficulties. The primary purpose of agreement among central banks on the provision of last resort finance is to safeguard the international banking systems on which that is founded. The provision of such a safeguard does not – indeed cannot – entail automatic support to any bank facing difficulties regardless of the particular circumstances.

Central bankers, therefore, deliberately do not make explicit existing ILLR arrangements. Thus the major official statement, the September 1974 Communiqué, issued by the Central Bank Governors of the Group of 10 and Switzerland, a few months after the collapse of Bankhaus Herstatt, is kept brief and unspecific (IMF, 1983):

> The Governors also had an exchange of views on the problem of the lender of last resort in the Euromarkets. They recognised that it would not be practical to lay down in advance detailed rules and procedures for the provision of temporary liquidity. But they were satisfied that means are available for that purpose and will be used if and when necessary'[3]

Note that this leaves open the possibility that 'temporary liquidity' may be supplied to borrowers, to lenders, or through open-market operations. It is not explicitly assured to the troubled bank.

In April 1980, the same Group – in a further communiqué, mainly about supervision – referred even less explicitly to ILLR issues:

> In view of the present volume of international bank lending and

of its prospective future role the Governors are agreed on the importance of maintaining the soundness and stability of the international banking system and of seeking to avoid any undesirable effects either worldwide or on the conduct of policy in particular countries.

This 1980 Communiqué announced the creation of the Standing Committee on the Euromarkets. This has been interpreted (IMF, 1983) as a responsibility for 'coordination of responsibilities of lenders of last resort'. It has also been suggested that the BIS 'bridging loans' in 1982 and 1983 represented a sort of ILLR facility; and that, behind the 1974 Communiqué, there lay 'an agreed plan with respect both to the allocation of responsibilities of lender of last resort and the circumstances under which such support would be provided to banks experiencing difficulties' (IMF, 1983). However, supervisory authorities (in conversations with us) questioned all this; they suggested BIS functioned, in respect of ILLR, not independently but as a monthly meeting-place for central bank Governors of the Group of Ten and Switzerland. Moreover, as the IMF document (1983) itself points out, 'subsequent developments with respect to individual banks, as in the case of Banco Ambrosiano, have cast doubts on whether such firm commitments exist'.

Some indirect evidence on the distribution of ILLR responsibilities can be extracted from the actions of central banks following the few recent failures of individual banks with significant international operations: Bankhaus Herstatt, the Franklin National Bank, the Israel-British Bank and Banco Ambrosiano.[4] Except for Franklin, all four cases revealed important ambiguities as to final responsibilities in case of bank failures.

The ambiguities were much greater in the case of Ambrosiano, leading (so far) to the loss of money by creditors of Banco Ambrosiano Holdings of Luxembourg, though the parent bank's creditors were granted full protection. The Luxembourg authorities, and naturally the creditors of Banco Ambrosiano Holdings, objected. The issue was made more difficult by technical questions;[5] and it has also been put to us that the problem arose from open fraud, not from international over-exposure as such. However, we are unconvinced that existing ILLR-overview facilities would prevent even a perfectly 'innocent' bank from failing, if its overseas operations were overstretched.

The Ambrosiano failure clearly points to gaps in the coverage of both supervisory and ILLR facilities. Luxembourg lacked an indigenous central bank, or any other LLR capacity for Euro-banks; while according to many observers Italy did not supervise adequately Ambrosiano's consolidated accounts. These elements could surely be repeated in other cases – Italy and Luxembourg are relatively sophisticated financial centres, after all.

More generally, the problems of non-banking (and other) subsidiaries, etc., without clear supervision from their parent country, particularly in centres with no LLR obligations, do reveal a more serious gap, both in supervisory and ILLR facilities. It is not clear whether this case has led to adaptations of these facilities.[6]

Our fears that major deficiencies and gaps exist in supervision and ILLR facilities are supported by the Group of Thirty report on bank supervision by Dale (1982):

> It is a matter for concern that lender of last resort facilities differ considerably from country to country. A few financial centres have no LLR capacity. Some national authorities can provide only temporary liquidity assistance on a secured basis, while others are able and willing to sustain even insolvent institutions in order to protect depositors. These disparities apart, there is a danger that some authorities may be prevented from extending collaterallized assistance to banks' foreign branches where national laws confer on branch depositors preferential claims to branch assets.

International bank failures since 1973 have been at fairly long intervals, and each has been relatively small. It has been reasonable, therefore, to see the main ILLR task as being to safeguard the interests of depositors and other creditors. If a major international bank – or a closely-spaced sequence of minor banks – were to be 'in trouble' or to fail, the main issue would not be to safeguard those interests, but to sustain that bank's (and others') lending capacity. It is in this context that true ILLR – not just deposit insurance, which in essence is what was applied to these four cases – acquires fundamental importance. (Even deposit insurance may require international coordination, if it is not to cut across and destabilise ILLR operations.[7]) Reliance on *ad hoc* solutions, however brilliantly managed, may be acceptable for a Herstatt case, or even an Ambrosiano case, but the prospect of open default by LDC or Comecon creditors requires formal ILLR safeguards.

The inadequacy of existing safeguards is well summarised by Dale

(1982). The main disparities and gaps in LLR operations at a national level, which create problems at an international level, are in his view:

(i) When monetary authorities provide financial assistance to commercial banks experiencing temporary liquidity difficulties, there are varying national distinctions made between formalised routine use of the official discount window, and longer-term support operations undertaken on a discretionary basis.

(ii) Although emergency assistance is typically extended directly by the central bank, there are different alternative methods of support in different countries (e.g. special joint facility of th₋ authorities and the banks; lending below market rates to institutions prepared to acquire or assist the problem bank; general support, with or without official encouragement, by one or more large domestic banks).

(iii) Crucially, several financial centres – notably Luxembourg, Hong Kong and Singapore – have no indigenous central banks. (Luxembourg has no LLR at all.) This (and other problems) would appear even more widespread and serious among financial centres not included in the Group of Thirty study (e.g. Cayman Islands, Bahamas).

(iv) Frequently emergency support can be offered only on a secured basis to solvent institutions. Some countries have broader powers of intervention where insolvency is threatened; elsewhere, the deposit insurance agency has LLR powers which – for potentially insolvent institutions – may exceed those of a central bank.

(v) Some central banks are permitted to act as LLR in domestic currency only, although these funds may in principle be converted. Elsewhere, the capacity to provide foreign currency assistance has specific limits.

(vi) To varying degrees, countries conceal the precise scope of LLR, as a matter of policy. In general, they expect foreign parent banks to provide all necessary assistance to their local subsidiaries, although the threat of shareholders' actions could limit their commitment.

(vii) Finally, where banks do fail, national liquidation proceedings sometimes favour local depositors. (US and many other deposit insurance schemes, too, leave big and/or foreign depositors virtually unprotected.) For this, several countries treat branches

of foreign banks as separate entities requiring their own liqui-
dators; such creditors may also enjoy a preferential claim to
branch assets.

5 ILLR AND INTERNATIONAL EXPANSION: ACUTE AND CHRONIC PROBLEMS

Are ILLR facilities – and the accompanying supervision – adequate
to limit damage in times of crisis or widespread distress? Perhaps
even more important, in less 'abnormal times', do existing arrangements encourage the right scale of lending; do they avoid 'euphoric'
lending, followed by panicky curtailment of lending; and do they
promote, without over-centralist 'hands-on' intervention (McMahon,
1983), an appropriate structure (by types of loan) and distribution
(amongst developing countries) of bank lending?

A first conclusion of this study – shared by many other analysts
– is that current arrangements, based on general uncertainty and
attempted *ex post* coordination of ILLR in cases of distress, are
dangerously insufficient.

There are a number of reasons – some familiar from the historical
literature, others arising from the current situation – which make a
reliable, predictable ILLR essential amid the complexities of international banking today.

As Kindleberger (1978, 1982) has pointed out, responsibility for
international banking stability (like health and welfare) is a public
good, even if public provision of it may somewhat diminish private
self-reliance. The good is too risky, and fraught with externalities to
be provided by one, or even several, private agents acting alone.
This approach does not necessarily rest on the perception of some
analysts that the US and other banking systems are inherently fragile,
but on the possibility that the international capital market is mostly
resilient but can very occasionally break down, with huge, unpredictable, lasting and maldistributed costs.

National LLRs cannot cope with the problems of an international
bank. As central banks or other national authorities represent their
own national interests, they will be unlikely to take a cosmopolitan
view of their responsibility in a crisis – unless, implausibly, potential
loss from absence of ILLR, and potential cost of ILLR rescue, are
in the same ratio for all creditor countries involved. It may be feared
that as a consequence no single lender of last resort may be willing

to save a given bank (whose activities transcend its frontiers) from a liquidity crisis, because the domestic effects of inaction do not seem to be larger than the cost of support, even though the world consequences may be.

Inevitable conflicts of interest will arise where parent banks, subsidiaries, holding companies, depositors and borrowers have varying nationalities. Each central bank will try to minimise its proportion of the costs of any ILLR operation. Delays and disputes about responsibility can themselves reduce confidence and deepen crisis. We repeat: the world can put up with such costs in the event of a Herstatt or an Ambrosiano; but in the event that overt default, in one or several developing countries, threatens the liquid base of major banks? We should perhaps thank the Ambrosianos for alerting us, in time, to the crucial need for a formal, transparent, swift ILLR. But are we in fact alerted?

The review of existing national LLR facilities, and more importantly the recent experience of international bank troubles – with interlocking, multiple losers and unclear responsibilities – raised concerns that the financial crises of the 1870s and 1930s may be repeated, and showed that these concerns are not merely theoretical and historical. Furthermore, even if a national LLR had – and if it was willing to commit – unlimited resources in domestic currency, the fact that international deposits and loans may be denominated in foreign currencies could cause it serious problems and lead to its unwillingness to provide foreign currency to support commercial banks' international operations.

Amongst industrial countries' central banks, this problem has so far been overcome by mutual balance-of-payments support operations. Such operations, however, could be much more clearly and swiftly handled in the framework of an ILLR. The role of the US Federal Reserve would necessarily be crucial, as such a large proportion of international banking operations are still in dollars. Therefore, the position of the US Government and of the US Federal Reserve Board in these matters will inevitably have a great influence on arrangements agreed.

Guttentag and Herring (1981) also stress special characteristics of international banking that make a transparent ILLR essential. Interbank credit lines may cause one bank's failure to damage the solvency of other banks. Furthermore, several of the largest international banks hold similar assets in their portfolios. Here, one bank's weakness may raise suspicions about other banks. On either ground, failure of one bank may result in deposit outflows from other banks. Thus uncertainties about ILLR may make uninsured depositors more prone to abrupt reassessments of the creditworthiness of banks. This creates, under current conditions, unacceptable risks to the stability of the international banks.

Such authors as Guttentag and Herring recognise the problem of moral hazard, but attempt to overcome it by mechanisms which they perceive as far more efficient (i.e. effective bank supervision). Moreover, if uncertainty is used to control moral hazard, private banks may not know what behaviour would disqualify them from support; they will therefore not know what activities they should avoid (Shafer, 1982). Most important, 'uncertainty' in time of crisis must involve delay, speculation and dangers of further destabilisation – especially if uncertainty is combined with unclear division of responsibility among central banks.

So much for the problems of ILLR in time of fear of crisis. Even in more normal times, the lack of clear ILLR protection, and of appropriate supervision, not just of the prudence of individual bank lending but of the adequacy and stability of the structure of total bank credits especially to LDCs, has serious disadvantages. Great swings of expansion and contraction, e.g. in lending by banks to Mexico or Brazil, indicate several things. First, each bank, initially lending in hope of a sound return, continues to do so to defend its previous lending, or to avoid admitting past erros. Then, when a country's balance of payments deteriorates, the withdrawal of some banks imperils the position of others, and they too withdraw. Finally, in the downswing, erosion of the cash base – and measures, by banks and borrowers, to anticipate it – reduce the volume of sound lending and delay recovery (McNamara, 1982; Lipton, 1981).

6 TOWARDS A SOLUTION

Neither more lending nor less lending – only more appropriate lending, with better structure, distribution, steadiness and insurance (e.g. via ILLR) – can remedy this recurrent, deepening, and more and more destabilising sequence. Recovery alone cannot. If it turns out to be sustained and ideal for debtors – pushing up oil prices for Mexico, and commodity prices and general export demand (but not interest rates) for other LDC and Comecon lenders – 'men of affairs' may, as in Britain in 1858–65, conclude all is well; credit will again be blown hard into the balloon marked 'sovereign risk'. But more lending on the same pattern as before will only mean bigger problems later. As for less lending as such, that either destroys recovery or precipitates default; national and international authorities realise this, as the recent frenzied, brilliant, and largely successful attempts to ensure that large numbers of banks continue to lend to the large debtors (e.g. Brazil, Mexico) show.

What does 'more appropriate lending' mean, and how could a more clearly defined ILLR help? More appropriate lending involves three things: better information; sustained, counter-cyclical flows; and diversification.

Commercial banks considering loans to country X, which is likely to have a given production structure implying a particular set of foreign-exchange flows to and from X, would ideally know (a) what, in total, other banks and official institutions propose to lend to X, and have already lent to X – and what are the maturity structures; (b) what are the prospects for X's future trade flows, both as regards their volumes and their prices. That sounds a frightening require-ment, almost a world economic model, and if taken too far would choke off all credit; but what is needed is something much more modest. Unless a loan is secured very firmly, a commercial bank needs to know – from its own sources, and from the central bank and perhaps indirectly from BIS/IMF – something about the appli-cant's total credit position, actual and potential, as affected by the commodities and manufactures he proposes to trade in. Surer access to ILLR could well be a 'carrot', persuading commercial banks to supply, and to seek, more such information.

Secondly, stricter supervision and surer ILLR, respectively, should stabilise the growth of lending in the 'euphoric' stage and minimise its contraction during more critical times. Sustained, possibly counter-cyclical flows would seem to be one of the most crucial likely achieve-ments of those mechanisms – if they can be properly specified. However, an ILLR with 'uncertainty' cannot be relied on to stabilise credit flows.

The third aspect of better lending, diversification, is also intimately linked to the availability of ILLR. We have pointed to the extreme concentration of bank credit expansion to developing countries in the 1970s on a handful of Latin American and Far Eastern countries. At the time, this concentration on a few apparently creditworthy middle-income lenders, plus neglect of almost all really poor coun-tries, seemed prudent to each bank and each syndicate. Each, however, by its own prudent concentration of extra lending, produced a somewhat imprudent concentration of the rapidly expanded volume of total lending. Prolonged recession, high interest and oil price gyrations then turned what was sound for each lender, and mildly imprudent for all lenders *ex ante*, into what seemed like disastrous imprudence after the event.

However, almost nobody was in 1973–4, or even 1978–80, pressing the banks not to recycle, or urging them to diversify their portfolios towards, say, Bangladesh or Mali. Probably it was felt that absolute risk (and lack of banking information) about low-income countries was so high, and their reliance on official flows (especially aid) so well-established, that the dangers and doubts about bank lending to these countries – not all of whom wanted bank money anyway – outweighed any possible gains from a better spread of risks.

Nevertheless, in retrospect (and for future reference!), greater diversity of customers among LDCs, to take in some low income countries (LICs), could have improved the safety of many banks' asset structures. So, perhaps, would a larger share of project lending, as against balance-of-payments lending. However, the gains from such shifts are available to bankers as a whole, if they move together; for any one bank, the shifts in some cases could increase risks, and would certainly increase information costs. In such circumstances, how can the authorities nudge banks in these directions? If ILLR obligations were made explicit by some group of central bankers, they could include – in the supervisory package that must be (as it is nationally) part of the quid pro quo for LLR support – appropriate pressures to induce all banks, participating in an assured ILLR facility, to move gradually towards such restructurings, as well as to obtain better information about creditor countries' total debt position and prospects, and to stabilise credit (including interbank) flows towards each borrowing country over time.

All this – even the last proposal – should not amount to pressure on individual banks to support particular countries. This 'interference with the market', indeed, has come, in practice, not from a carefully conceived ILLR/supervision package, but from the hasty cobbling together of rescheduling and new loan packages to specific countries, half-forced on numerous reluctant banks since late 1982 precisely because ILLR was and is inadequate.

How could improvements be brought about? In abandoning uncertainty as a way to raise costs of ILLR – because it defeats ILLR's very purposes – authorities can and should, we believe, replace it by adapting to the needs of today Bagehot's original concept of 'onerous terms': good collateral and the penal rate.

At first glance, this seems difficult. The only 'collateral' for sovereign debt is the willingness and ability of the governments to repay and service it, or to guarantee that the private sector does so. This collateral is by definition not very 'good' in hard times. Thus, if net capital inflows become severely negative alongside large trade deficits – as in much of Eastern Europe and Latin America since 1982 – the need to reschedule, even to go into arrears, merges imperceptibly into a temptation to default outright, as has reportedly been actively discussed in countries such as Brazil and Mexico (*The Economist*, May 1983; Whitley, 1983). Indeed, leading bankers argue that 'Poland, Mexico, Argentina, Brazil and now Romania have all unilaterally defaulted on their debts already' (Rohatyn, 1982).

What, then, can 'quality collateral' mean? And how high (and how self-defeating) would 'penal rates' be? There is not, as yet, a clear consensus among bankers about proposals for 'debt restructuring' (Avramovic, 1983; Guth, 1983; Rohatyn, 1982; ICIDI, 1983; compare, however, Lal, 1983; Taylor, 1983; McMahon, 1983).

Our suggestion is that such proposals be prepared in the form of a contingency plan, for use as part of an ILLR call when needed by a bank. Then, and only then, the ILLR would purchase some or all of the bank's claims upon sovereign debt at a substantial discount. This would impose a *de facto* 'penal rate', and turn large but doubtful claims on now insecure 'sovereign debt' into a smaller amount of 'good collateral' à la Bagehot. The private bank would thus suffer 'onerous terms' for using ILLR; but the private bank, its deposits, above all its capacity to lend, would survive.

Afterwards, the ILLR would negotiate with borrowers (e.g. developing countries) to recover the debt – presumably at a considerably lengthened maturity – at a rate above that implicit in the discount price paid to the commercial bank for the claim, but somewhat below the original rate due. The better maturity, and perhaps rate, would reduce constraints on the borrowing country's development; this would be 'traded in' by the new owner of the claim – the ILLR – against a firmer commitment by the borrowing country to ensure repayment. The more favourable conditions for LDCs would imply a less severe constraint on their future growth as well as a greater willingness by their governments to repay the debts.

Thus – 110 years later – Bagehot's proposals would again come into their own. Their two components for onerous terms – penal interest and good (in a sense) collateral – would have merged into one.

This proposal obviously raises problems too complex to consider in detail here. Valuing the discounted collateral could be difficult, where no markets are functioning at the time. Other holders of sovereign debt, who are not in need of LLR facilities, must be considered (though presumably they would, on balance, welcome a valuation). Terms must encourage neither debtor countries to seek them, nor banks to seek ILLR facilities. International arrangements – the role of IMF and BIS, the extent to which commercial banks pay a fee or contribute funds for ILLR access – need to be specified. The question of funding the operations of such an ILLR is of course crucial. However, we believe that these problems though difficult, are soluble; and that the proposal provides, by reviving truly 'onerous terms', a much better way than 'uncertainty' to overcome the moral hazard created by existing inadequate and crisis-prone ILLR arrangements.

This proposal would be complementary to the strengthening of international supervisory functions. Although much progress has been made, particularly since the 1975 Concordat, it is difficult to establish complementary and tightly coordinated international supervision. How can one resolve problems about differences in supervision procedures amongst industrialised countries, and – even more – problems with supervising banks in developing countries and offshore centres? Even if such 'piecemeal' difficulties can be overcome, what does an ILLR system with a supervision quid pro quo do about countries that opt out and allow international banks to operate from their territory? Such countries and banks may hope that the authorities will allow them to free-ride on the ILLR facility, and will regard the cost of not doing so, in an interlocked financial system, as socially unacceptable? Finally, how does one strike a balance which assures adequate supervision and control, but which does not imply excessive centralised overview or impose unacceptable quasi-governmental controls on private lending? In any case, the existence of a clearer ILLR must increase the leverage of existing supervisory authorities, allowing them more timely and appropriate control of lending, in so far as a condition for access to ILLR functions would be to have respected the rules agreed with the supervisory authorities.

We feel that our proposal does not create the problems; it merely makes them explicit. In fact they have become serious partly because

– in the interests of using 'uncertainty' to police commercial bank lending and to reduce moral hazard – the authorities have never clearly outlined and divided ILLR and supervisory responsibility, nor acquired the leverage to enforce what provisions do exist. Fundamentally such problems are always latent because of the complexity and internationalisation which now characterise banking.

As for the problem of 'free riders', if closer supervision accompanies clear-cut ILLR arrangements, each will reinforce the other. Rigorous supervision should become more acceptable to commercial banks, especially big international lenders, if accompanied by an explicit ILLR facility. On the other hand, an ILLR can work without excessive costs – whether from imprudent lending, or from the use of uncertainty to deter it – only with previous effective supervision. Both sides of the coin are currently somewhat tarnished, they need to be etched clearly – and simultaneously.

As we have discussed, the establishment (or otherwise) of an ILLR – together with more stringent supervision of bank lending – would affect the nature, level and distribution of private credit flows to different categories of developing countries. We have for example argued that the supervisory component could be used to improve the distribution, among LDCs, of commercial bank lending; it could be linked to achieving a more appropriate balance of different types of private loans (e.g. different maturities; project versus country loans; fixed versus variable interest) to LDCs.

Such matters inevitably have a major impact on the prospects of growth and development of the so-called Third World countries, who would borrow – or wish to do so – from the private capital markets; it would naturally also have a large impact on the interests of those developing-countries' governments who are major depositors in the private capital markets, such as the capital surplus oil-exporters. It would therefore seem appropriate that LDC governments should somehow be represented in the debate on the establishment of an ILLR and appropriate supervision. We are by no means suggesting incorporation of all or even many LDCs, as this would make any agreement infinitely more difficult; merely that the interests and concerns of the middle income and the poorest borrowers from – as well as the capital surplus lenders to – the international capital markets be clearly represented and considered.

Notes

1. Grubel (1971) derived the concept of 'moral hazard' from the economics of commerce, where it initially referred to the danger that persons would take greater risks because they were insured. Now it has acquired the more general definition used here and elsewhere (see IMF, 1983).
2. Namely control of each bank: for fraud; for overall lending, relative to cash and to capital; and for exposure to particular borrowers, or in particular countries or sectors.
3. The 1975 Concordat – sometimes wrongly thought to apply to ILLR – deals only with the separate, though linked, issue of bank supervision. In 1983 this Concordat was updated, again without explicit reference to International Lender of Last Resort.
4. Such cases have been examined in some detail (e.g. Spero, 1980).
5. Banco Ambrosiano Holdings was technically a holding company and not a bank, for whom neither authorities had accepted supervision or LLR responsibilities.
6. Ambrosiano's failure, however, was one of the main factors leading to a revision of the Basle Concordat on banking supervision (Hughes, 1983).
7. 'Not all countries have deposit insurance schemes and those that do offer widely differing coverage with respect to the size, type, currency denomination and status of deposits. In order to avert the danger that perceived differences in national protective arrangements could provoke destabilising capital movements in times of uncertainty, greater co-ordination in this area is desirable' (Dale, 1982, and IMF, 1983).

References

AVRAMOVIC, D. (1983) 'Bretton Woods II: an Agenda', SIFTS Background Paper No. 8, Commonwealth Secretariat.

BAGEHOT, W. (1873) *Lombard Street: A Description of the Money Market* (1873; reprint edition, London, John Murray, 1917).

BANK FOR INTERNATIONAL SETTLEMENTS (1981) *The Maturity Distribution of International Bank Lending*.

BANK FOR INTERNATIONAL SETTLEMENTS, *International Banking Developments*, several issues.

CARGILL, R. F. (1979) *Money, the Financial System and Monetary Policy* (Englewood Cliffs, N.J.: Prentice-Hall).

COOKE, P. W. (1983) 'The International Lending Scene: a Supervisory Perspective', *Bank of England Quarterly Bulletin*, March.

DALE, R. (1982) 'Bank Supervision around the World', Group of Thirty, New York.

The Economist, 30 April 1983: 'The International Debt Threat' and 'Latin America'; 7 May 1983: 'The Debt Bomb'.

FEDER, G. *et al.* (1979) 'Estimation of a Debt Service Capacity Index', (Washington, DC: World Bank).

FETTER, F. W. (1965) *Development of British Monetary Orthodoxy, 1797–1875* (Cambridge, Mass.: Harvard University Press).

GRIFFITH-JONES, S. (1980) 'The Growth of Multinational Banking, the Euro-currency Market and the Effects on Developing Countries', *Journal of Development Studies*, vol. 16, no. 2, June.

GRUBEL, M. (1971) Risk, Uncertainty and Moral Hazard, *Journal of Risk and Insurance*, vol. 38, March, pp. 99–106.

GUTH, W. (1983) 'The International Financial System and the Debt Crisis', Annual Meeting, Swedish National Committee of International Chamber of Commerce, mimeo, Stockholm, 23 March.

GUTTENTAG, J. and HERRING, R. (1981) 'The Lender of Last Resort Problem in an International Context', Rodney White Center for Financial Research, Wharton School, University of Pennsylvania.

HUGHES, M. (1983) 'BIS Code on Banking Supervision Revised', *Financial Times*, 10 May.

ICIDI (1983) 'Common Crisis', The Brandt Commission 1983 (London and Sydney: Pan Books).

INTERNATIONAL MONETARY FUND (1982) World Economic Outlook, Occasional Paper No. 9, Washington D.C., April. (1983) World Economic Outlook, Occasional Paper No. 21, Washington D.C., May.

INTERNATIONAL MONETARY FUND (1983) G. G. Johnson, with R. K. Abrams, 'Aspects of the International Safety Net', Occasional Paper No. 17, Washington D.C., March.

KINDLEBERGER, C. (1978) *Manias, Panics and Crashes: a History of Financial Crises*, Macmillan, USA and UK.

KINDLEBERGER, C. (1982) 'Distress in International Financial Markets', Lecture for the Swedish Economic Association, 15 December.

LAL, D. (1983) 'Time to Put the Third World Debt into Perspective', *The Times*, 6 May.

LIPTON, M. (1981) 'World Depression by Third World Default? *Bulletin of Institute of Development Studies*, 12, 2 April.

McMAHON, C. W. (1978) 'Central Banks as Regulators and Lenders of Last Resort in an International Context: a View from the United Kingdom', in *Key Issues in International Banking*, Federal Reserve Bank of Boston, Conference Series No. 18, pp. 102–110.

McMAHON, C. W. (1983) 'Bank of England Rejects Debt 'Lifeboat', Report by A. Friedman, *Financial Times*, 12 May.

McNAMARA, R. (1982) 'Economic Interdependence and Global Poverty: the Challenge of Our Time', the first Barbara Ward memorial lecture, Baltimore, Maryland, July.

MORGAN GUARANTY TRUST CO. (1983) *World Financial Markets*, February.

ROHATYN, F. (1982) 'The State of the Banks', *New York Review of Books*, November.

SPERO, J. E. (1980) *The Failure of the Franklin National Bank*, Columbia University Press (for Council on Foreign Relations).

TAYLOR, H. (1983) 'Loan Discounting: No Answer', World Banking I (Supplement to *Financial Times*), 9 May.

WALLICH, H. (1978) *Key Issues in International Banking*, Federal Reserve Bank of Boston, Conference Series No. 18.
WHITLEY, A. (1983) 'Brazil Recovery Doubts Raise Fears of Further Debt Crisis', *Financial Times*, 11 May.
WORLD BANK (1982) *World Development Report*, Washington, D.C.

Comment on 'International Lenders of Last Resort: Are Changes Required?'

K. Phylatkis

The authors focus on the need for an International Lender of Last Resort (ILLR). They see the main function of ILLR facilities as not being the protection of depositors but the maintenance of the capacity of the banking system to lend. In this way the debtor countries are assured of a steady, growing stream of flows. How will the ILLR help achieve that? ILLR will achieve that through better dissemination of information concerning lenders, by encouraging counter-cyclical flows and by obliging banks to diversify.

The question arises whether the above functions can be performed by arrangements other than an ILLR. The two other alternatives are private mechanisms and national LLRs. The authors conclude that these other alternatives are not suitable.

First of all, in a climate of financial unrest, the safeguarding of depositors is of paramount importance. In the case of the system being illiquid or of a bank being illiquid, that prevents the development of a 'domino process' which is perhaps more likely in international banking. In this way real financial crises are avoided. As Anna Schwartz says 'if defaults do result in bank failures, so long as the security of the private sector's deposits is assured, no financial crisis will ensue'.[1]

The authors have not stated the problem that necessitates the establishment of an ILLR. It is assumed that the current international debt problem is due to shortage of liquidity and not solvency. Thus the ILLR will ensure funds during this period and prevent illiquid but solvent institutions and countries to default.

If shortage of liquidity is really the problem then why should the private mechanism fail or why should the national LLR facilities be inadequate? One reason cited by the authors is that the national LLR may be unwilling to save a given bank from a liquidity crisis, because the domestic effects of inaction do not seem to be larger than the cost of support even though the world consequences may be. A clarification of this point would have been very helpful.

The efficiency of the private mechanism in conjunction with the Federal Board has been demonstrated recently when the Chicago bank Continental Illinois, ran into liquidity problems. A standby facility of $4.5 bn, the largest of its kind for an international bank, was quickly put together by America's sixteen biggest banks. It is worth bearing in mind that two-thirds of Continental Illinois deposits are provided by non-US sources.

It is not obvious how the 'life-boat' operation would have been better, had it been handled by an ILLR.

Unlike the authors, I do not think that the foreign debt problems faced by some Less Developed Countries (LDCs) are due to lack of liquidity.

These countries are having difficulties in meeting their obligations partly because they have mismanaged the funds borrowed from the international markets. They have used them for consumption and low yield investment projects. For example, Mexico invested in oil projects which were based on unrealistically high prices of oil. Brazil and Mexico and other Latin American countries have many price regulations and production subsidies which prevent the efficient use of resources. Brazil has invested in nuclear power to reduce energy imports.

At the same time other LDCs through good management have succeeded in staying out of trouble. For example, the Asian borrowers have low debt service burdens, no excess short-term debt and strong balance of payments positions. South Korea is often cited as an example of a country that used debt financing productively by investing in productive capital. These investments have produced a stream of income and exports sufficient to pay the interest and the principal.

If the international debt problem is not due to lack of liquidity then the ILLR will not be able to solve the problem. Furthermore, it is not clear to me how an ILLR will be more successful than the private banks in obliging the debtor countries to pursue good economic policies.

The establishment of an ILLR can be thought to be similar to the establishment of the IMF during the Bretton Woods era. One of the roles of the IMF was to provide assistance to countries during temporary balance of payments disequilibria and to permit countries to change the parity of their exchange rates in situations of fundamental disequilibrium. The system failed because the countries did not always take measures to put their house right. Secondly, they very rarely changed the parities of their currencies.

An ILLR will perform the same role. It will provide assistance to countries in trouble through the sustaining of bank lending without being in a strong position to oblige the countries to manage their affairs. I do not see how one can be talking about an ILLR without at least discussing issues like adequacy of resources and enforcement powers.

Note

1. Anna J. Schwartz, 'Real and Pseudo-Financial Crises', in F. Capie and G. E. Wood (eds), *Financial Crises and the World Banking System* (London: Macmillan, 1985).

10 The Theory of Last Resort Lending

Michael Beenstock

1 THE NEED FOR THEORY

One of the many by-products of the international debt crisis has been renewed interest in the role of lending for last resort. Indeed, this is evidenced by at least three of the chapters in this volume alone, not to mention the seemingly endless proliferation of proposals and suggestions that we have seen since the summer of 1982. These proposals are reviewed by Shelagh Heffernan in Chapter 8 and so will not be considered here. Instead, my objective is to stand back from the action and consider the theoretical underpinnings of lending for last resort (LLR). This is timely because recent debate has confounded numerous issues linked to LLR and the concept has been stretched beyond the limits of intellectual endurance. There is a clear need for a specification of the terms and conditions under which LLR is appropriate. LLR is a form of public sector intervention in the economy which is of a similar order to subsidisation. However, whereas the theory of public finance clearly defines the role of subsidies the theory of central banking is rather vague and even mysterious about the role of LLR. It is almost as if there is a mystique to banking and central banking which does not apply to, say, coal-mining and public finance. Texts on LLR such as Sayers (1967) usually refer with reverence to Bagehot's *Lombard Street*, accepting uncritically what the great man had to say. Indeed, it is rather surprising that there is no satisfactory theory of LLR.

The practical need for such a theory is important at the present time in two respects. First, there are many who argue that the IMF should become a LLR in the context of the international banking crisis. So far, this idea (thankfully) has progressed very little although the recent increase in SDR quotas may be interpreted as a step in this direction. There is a danger, prompted by influential groups such as the Brandt Commission, that we will build for ourselves international institutions that we will live to regret. Before we proceed any further down the road to the establishment of an international central bank we must ascertain the theoretical need for such an institution.

Secondly, domestic central banks have recently saved various banks in the name of LLR. In the US there has been the Continental Illinois affair and in the UK the Bank of England nationalised Johnson Matthey Bankers. No doubt central banks will continue to be tested in the future, not just in relation to banks but also in relation to non-bank financial intermediaries. It is as if central bankers find it difficult to draw the line between LLR and bale-outs. They hesitate and in many cases LLR is not appropriate and is a bale-out in disguise. A theory of LLR will help those lines to be drawn more sharply.

In this chapter a comprehensive theory of LLR is not developed partly because it is argued that in a rational society where information is fully disclosed and where insurance and capital markets are efficient the need for LLR vanishes. So if these conditions are met, LLR is not required. This argument has the corollary that the role of government in the banking system is to ensure that financial institutions fully disclose the necessary information while barriers are broken down that might inhibit the efficiency of insurance and capital markets. In particular markets in deposit insurance should be allowed to develop on a competitive basis. Under these conditions good banks, like good companies, will remain in business while bad banks, like bad companies, will go out of business. Banks are not a special case. Also, under these conditions the interbank market is not like a fragile pack of cards that needs kid-glove treatment. Nor will the public induce back runs through lack of confidence in the banking system.

If instead society is irrational then it is hardly surprising that the neoclassical analysis that is proposed suggests that there is an LLR role. This is always the case under such conditions – an external rational agency is required to protect society from itself. However, even under these conditions it turns out that LLR is redundant if labour and product markets are perfectly competitive. Another case for LLR arises in the event of certain catastrophes such as wars or large scale economic destruction.

2 INFORMATION AND INSTABILITY

Consider the case of bank X (or non-bank financial intermediary) which finds that its losses exceed its capital. The event might have been triggered by non-performing loans or by capital losses on a gilts portfolio; for the present the cause is not important. We shall assume that there is full disclosure of information applied to all companies including banks so that the market, subject to the usual uncertainties, is in a position to make a rational assessment of the stricken bank.

There are two basic assessments that might be made. In the first case the assessment might be favourable provided it is thought that the problem was simply due to bad luck and that the business is essentially sound. In an efficient capital market new equity capital will be forthcoming because the expected present value of the bank's profits is positive. Or it might be thought that various managerial changes are necessary to make the business viable. In cases such as this government intervention is not necessary, the capital market will ensure that the bank survives and its losses will be covered. Bygones are bygones.

In the second case the assessment is unfavourable. The business has no prospects, it is beyond resurrection and so it has no market value. In this case bygones are not bygones, the market will not come up with the necessary equity capital, either in terms of a rights issue or in terms of a merger or acquisition, and the bank will go out of business. In these respects a bank is no different from any other company. Provided that there is full disclosure of information and that the capital market is efficient a rational decision will be made, without central bank or government involvement, to save or close the bank.

If the loss in question happened because a sovereign loan to the Third World ceased to perform the same principles would apply. International debt is not a special case; either the capital market will save the bank or it will not according to rational assessment based on full disclosure of information.

Let us assume, for argument's sake, that the bank is beyond redemption and it is not saved. In this case, assuming that deposits are not insured, the depositors will receive their proportion of the equity capital. Say bank Y has inter-bank deposits with bank X – does this mean that bank Y will be the next domino to fall? The answer is certainly no if the losses of bank Y do not exceed its capital base. However, if these losses exceed the capital base and there is full disclosure of information the capital market will decide whether or not to save bank Y just as it did in the case of bank X; and so on for bank Z etc. Thus, one rotten apple does not spoil the barrel, each bank is judged on its own merits, the domino analogy is false. The entire banking system will collapse only if all banks are beyond redemption. Even if this remote contingency arose it would be unrelated to bank X's difficulties; the system would have collapsed in any case through lack of confidence.

Once again, in those respects banks are no different to companies. The logic of the interbank market no more implies that the international banking system is inherently unstable than does the logic of inter-industry transactions imply that if one company goes bankrupt so must all companies go bankrupt.

Similar considerations apply to the public. Depositors with bank X will suffer but should depositors with other banks panic and try to withdraw their money? It would be rational to do so if indeed they assessed that all banks were as beyond hope as bank X. But in view of what has already been said there would be no rational basis for such an assessment, so a panic would not spread. At most, it might be sensible to switch deposits to other banks (thus precipitating the closure of the weak banks) rather than seeking to convert deposits into cash.

Solow (1982) argues that 'any bank failure diminishes confidence in the whole system and brings stronger banks under increased pressure'. He goes on to say,

> The cumulative chain reaction is an important part of this argument. My goose-down business may suffer because of some events involving labour relations in the industry manufacturing cables that carry ski lifts, but hardly anyone would regard that complicated story as a case for indemnifying wholesalers of goose-down. The difference appears to be that the ski lift story is expected to damp quickly; the process is effectively stable, self-limiting. The financial panic is an unstable system; small differences in initial conditions lead to vast differences in the final outcome.

Familiar arguments such as these are based on the unstated assumption that while companies fully disclose information banks do not. If companies did not disclose information risk averse investors might reasonably think that if goose-down wholesalers were in trouble so might other companies be in trouble. The absence of adequate information prevents them from arriving at a rational assessment, idiosyncratic and market signals become difficult to distinguish, and just to be on the safe side tthere is a mass selling of shares and withdrawal of capital. The reason why the ski lift story dampens is that the proper disclosure of information enables investors to separate idiosyncratic from market developments. Rumours only spread when information is being withheld. It is for this reason that most governments insist on the proper disclosure of company accounts. In countries such as Kuwait where disclosure is inadequate the strengths of individual companies led to the belief that all companies were going to be more profitable and so the market boomed. But all this was reversed when the weakness of individual companies led to the collapse of the market as a whole.

Banking stories would also dampen if full information is disclosed. But if there is inadequate disclosure the wood cannot be seen for the trees and the difficulties of individual banks lead to the fear that all banks are in trouble. Risk averse investors and depositors would be rational to panic under such circumstances and bank runs are induced. It is at this point that the LLR issue is raised when in fact the obvious remedy is to insist on adequate disclosure of information. This indeed is the appropriate role for the authorities, not LLR.

Some of these arguments might be stated more formally. However, first we define the following glossary of terms:

D = deposits d = deposit withdrawals
K = capital k = new capital
A = loans a = loss provisions
R = reserves r = change in reserves

The balance sheet of a bank may be written as

$$D + K = A + R$$

The bank faces a liquidity problem when

$$d > R$$

i.e. withdrawals exceed reserves. Therefore, the condition for overcoming this problem is

$$r > d - R$$

The bank faces an insolvency crisis when

$$d + a > K$$

i.e. the capital base is insufficient to cover both loss provisions and withdrawals. The condition for overcoming this problem is

$$k > d + a - K$$

This condition will be met provided a rational assessment of the bank indicates that its expected net present value is positive. With the full disclosure of information the public can clearly distinguish liquidity from insolvency problems. With full disclosure the information available to the public may be denoted by I^* hence the measure of confidence in the bank may be written as

$$Z = G(I^*) \tag{1}$$

I^* will vary from bank to bank and so will Z. These Z scores are plotted in Figure 10.1 by the schedule *abc*. $\bar{Z}$ is a solvency threshold;

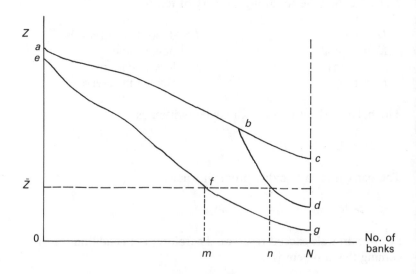

Figure 10.1

if Z falls below $\bar{Z}$ it goes out of business. In the initial situation all N banks meet this condition.

If new information becomes available such that the Z schedule becomes *abd*, nN of banks will become insolvent. Provided I^* is fully disclosed the remaining $0n$ banks are not affected. If, however, only $I < I^*$ is disclosed the public will rationally try to look to other indicators for guidance. In this case

$$Z = H(I,F) \tag{2}$$

where F includes the number of bank failures. In Figure 10.1 $F = nN$ in which case *abd* becomes *efg*. But this induces *mn* further bank failures. This will lower the Z schedule further thereby inducing further failures and so on until perhaps there has been a run on the whole banking system.

Thus, if equation (2) applies LLR is required in terms of either r or k in order to stabilise the system. However, the first best solution is to ensure that I^* is disseminated so that equation (1) rather than equation (2) operates.

3 DEPOSIT INSURANCE

Thus far we have assumed that deposits are not insured. Sharpe (1978) argues that there is a logical relationship between capital adequacy and the insurance premium on deposits. In fact, the two become synonymous in a competitive market because the premium should equal the present value of the underwriter's liability. The case made in Section 2 did not depend on the existence of deposit insurance, so it is not really necessary for our central thesis. Nevertheless, deposit insurance will make the system more robust. If deposits are insured, doubters about the health of their bank will sleep more easily because if the bank happens to fail they will benefit from the insurance fund. So if disclosure of information is not as complete as it should be deposit insurance will stabilise the system.

Indeed, Friedman (1959) has argued that under such circumstances the need for LLR disappears. Deposit insurance safeguards against bank runs and panics. This argument seems to confuse two things. As already argued deposit insurance will tend to make the system more robust assuming it is priced along the lines suggested by Sharpe. But a run on the banking system as a whole, as distinct to individual banks, is an uninsurable risk (assuming for argument's sake that such risks cannot be reinsured). A flight from deposits as a whole into cash would bankrupt the underwriters. Under such circumstances the only conceivable underwriter is the government itself that can print money to satisfy the demand for cash. This, of course, in Bagehot's classic LLR.

So Friedman is wrong to argue that deposit insurance obviates the need for LLR. However, it begs the question of what would induce a mass flight from deposits into cash in the first place. We have already answered this in the previous section; in a rational society with full disclosure of information and efficient capital markets there would never be a mass flight from deposits into cash. Correspondingly Bagehot's analysis, like Solow's, is based on unstated assumptions about the incompleteness of information, the inefficiency of capital markets or the irrationality of man. What is missing from Bagehot is a theory of panic and the causes of bank runs. *Lombard Street* in those respects reads like *Hamlet* without the Prince.

4 THEORY OF PANICS

There is no shortage of hypotheses about the determination of financial panics, none of which, however, seems very plausible. Perhaps the most influential of these has been proposed on several occasions by Minsky, e.g. Minsky (1982). Indeed, Minsky directly links his theory with the need for LLR and others such as Kindleberger (1978) have taken up Minsky's arguments in terms of the need for domestic and international LLR.

Minsky's thesis has several elements and stages:

(1) Displacement – an exogenous shock occurs, e.g. war or crop failure which is good for certain lines of business and bad for others. If the former are more numerous than the latter a boom will be triggered as financiers and businessmen take advantage of the new opportunities.
(2) Financial gearing – as the boom develops lines of credit are extended; the money supply expands and the boom is further reinforced. The structure of indebtedness becomes more labyrinthine and top heavy.
(3) Euphoria – the boom raises prices and the bears enter the market getting into debt in the process. Ponzi finance units emerge in

which 'payment commitments exceed anticipated cash receipts for all periods except some terminal periods'. This is sometimes referred to as over-trading. The euphoria causes people to over-estimate future profits.

(4) Swindling – out of desperation to keep the bubble inflated people turn to swindling and fraud. But in the end the crisis is precipitated by a bankruptcy, the fall in a price or even the revelation of a swindle. This leads to the final stage.

(5) Revulsion – the banks try to protect themselves and in the process pull the rug from under the debt pyramid. In the process they bankrupt themselves and the economy plunges into a headlong deflation. Buildings are left incomplete, projects are abandoned midstream; the economy is strewn with the debris of the collapse. Minsky suggests that LLR could prevent revulsion although he also suggests that the authorities should make sure that they do not fuel the euphoria while Ponzi finance should be resisted.

Minsky claims Keynes as his intellectual pedigree and no doubt populist Keynesians will feel sympathetic. However, the logic of his theory is vague; why do bankers pursue policies that they know will lead to disaster, why is the system stable in one case but not in another. On his definition every entrepreneur is engaged in Ponzi finance since cash flows are usually negative at first. It is more a jumble of assertions than a logically coherent theory of panic based on proper axioms. Further far-reaching criticisms may be found in the comments of Flemming, Goldsmith and Melitz that follow the cited reference.

A more coherent approach to the cause of panics lies in the application of catastrophe theory to bank runs, e.g. Ho and Saunders (1980). The basic insight here is that depending 'upon their relationship to each other, small changes in 'splitting variables' (e.g. news of bad debts) can cause large changes in depositors' responses. This implies that economic behaviour is best described by sudden non-linear responses which induce cusp catastrophes. Unfortunately, there is nothing in economic theory to suggest that our behaviour is cusp-like and catastrophe models are as arbitrary as loglinear models or any other mathematical form. In models of rational behaviour the mathematical form as far as stability analysis is concerned is usually unimportant and the catastrophes that occur in most catastrophe models is not because of the cusps *per se* but because of arbitrary and irrational assumptions about human behaviour. For example, in Ho and Saunders' model it is the unreasonable behaviour of the authorities that induces the cusp. In Zeeman (1974), one of the founders of catastrophe theory, it is the arbitrary assumption that investors do not make optimal predictions that induces the cusp. In short catastrophe theory, despite the obvious appeal in its name, offers few if any intellectual insights into the cause of bank runs and thus the theoretical underpinnings of LLR.

Blanchard and Watson (1982) explore the case for rational bubbles in terms of the non-uniqueness of rational expectations models that is induced by latent unstable roots. Usually these roots are ruled out by the boundary conditions which restrict prices to positive and finite values. However, the authors set up cases under which prices may deviate from their fundamental values even assuming rational behaviour. It turns out, however, that they merely redefine what is meant by fundamentals and that their bubbles do not relate to the proper interpretation. Not surprisingly, the rational expectations literature provides no theoretical insights into bubbles and the related issue of panics. A false alarm has been sounded.

In contrast, Batchelor (1983) sets out a rational theory of bank runs in which risk averse depositors withdraw their deposits from banks which they think are at risk. The central assumption is that depositors do not have full information about individual banks so that if one bank gets into difficulty they think that other banks may be affected by similar problems. It is this ignorance that generates the run and creates the need for LLR. But this brings us back to the arguments already stated, that the central problem is bank secrecy and the withholding of information so that a proper rational assessment cannot be made. LLR is redundant in rational societies with efficient capital markets and full information.

5   MARKET FAILURE

But what if society is irrational and we all suddenly think that everybody else is going to encash their bank deposits? This is an absurd question (it is like asking what if we all suddenly thought that everybody else was going to disregard the law or commit suicide for no apparent reason); nevertheless we shall address it. If the demand for bank deposits disappeared the demand for cash would rise by an equal and opposite amount. In the absence of LLR the quantity of cash would not alter, the banks would collapse and the money supply would consist only of cash. This would entail a drastic fall in the quantity of money. If wages and prices are perfectly flexible the aggregate price level would fall in proportion with the quantity of money. The real quantity of money would not alter and economic life would continue as before except without banks. All transactions would be in cash, there would be no deflation and LLR would be unnecessary. Of course, credit markets would cease to exist and there would be a real loss to the economy because we no longer trusted each other. On the other hand, we would not revert to barter because the real money supply is unchanged. Thus, for example, Solow's argument that there is a public good argument for LLR in order to avoid the threat of barter is invalid.

If instead wages and prices are sticky a flight from deposits into cash would be deflationary. The authorities could counteract the deflation by increasing the quantity of cash, however, they would have to reduce it again once confidence in the banking system was restored. This type of LLR is therefore inherently temporary and is an antidote to market imperfections that manifest in wage-price stickiness. Of course, LLR is a second best solution – the first best solution is to get rid of the imperfections that are inducing the stickiness.

Thus, the case for LLR hangs off too many unreasonable assumptions and even then it is a second best palliative.

6 CATASTROPHES

Under certain extreme circumstances, however, it might be rational for the public to seek *en masse* to encash their deposits. If they do so the entire banking system would collapse; catastrophic risks cannot be insured and LLR would be necessary to save the banking system. For example, when the First World War broke out there was a financial crisis in Britain because depositors feared for the solvency of their respective banks. This fear was prompted by several factors. First, loans to hostile countries were inevitably at risk. Secondly, loans to allied countries were more vulnerable; indeed, the Russians defaulted after the revolution. Thirdly, because of naval threats gold repayments to Britain were put at risk. All of those war induced risks affected the banking system as a whole and even in the absence of the full disclosure of information it was most probably rational for the public to react in the way they did.

LLR in such situations essentially underwrites all of these risks and the banking system will survive until hostilities have ceased. Once the dust has settled it becomes clear which banks have in fact suffered from the war. Those that lent to Russia will have lost out and certain banks might become insolvent. At this point the arguments presented in Section 2 apply – problem banks will be saved or not according to rational assessments based on full information.

In the face of such catastrophes, LLR essentially postpones the day of reckoning and in doing so fulfils a valid social function. It gives the financial system a breathing space until the dust of the war settles and the objective facts become known. Only the authorities can provide this kind of insurance since private markets cannot provide it. Indeed, most property insurance contracts cease to apply in the event of hostilities and other catastrophes such as earthquakes and floods. The insurance of deposits is no exception.

There are no social costs to such LLR because there is no social cost to the creation of base money. LLR is not inflationary because all that has happened is a change in the composition of the demand for money in favour of cash. The total demand for money is unaltered so that cash injections are not inflationary provided of course that they are withdrawn once the panic has subsided. Perhaps the only social cost is moral hazard – banks might expose themselves to political risks in the expectation that the authorities will eventually underwrite them. However, provided LLR facilities are appropriately priced those costs can be covered.

The catastrophes of which we speak must affect the financial system as a whole for LLR to be justified. For example, if hostilities break out in Latin America this does not affect the banking system as a whole but only those banks that have made loans to Latin America. The affected banks would be then assessed according to the criteria discussed in Section Z; LLR is not appropriate. Nor is LLR called for by the present debt crisis provided information is appropriately disclosed. The debt crisis is bad news for the banks that are extensively involved but it is not a catastrophe in the sense used here. Catastrophes do not discriminate between their victims.

From what has been said it should be clear that the catastrophic case for LLR is likely to be very rare. Apart from wars it is difficult to envisage other legitimate instances. Once possible candidate is a drought in a predominantly agrarian society.

7 THE LIFEBOAT MODEL

Thus far our consideration of LLR has related to the indemnity of the banking system as a whole by the central bank. In this process, however, support may be applied selectively in order to prevent weak banks from contaminating the banking system as a whole. An alternative to LLR is to set up a 'lifeboat' operation in which weak banks are supported by strong banks rather than by the central bank through LLR. This happened in the case of the secondary banking crisis in the UK in 1973–5, see Reid (1978), when a number of secondary banks were threatened with insolvency by the collapse of the property market. Deposits were being withdrawn from the secondary banks in favour of the primary banks which had access to the discount market. This was not a mass flight from deposits into cash but a switch in deposits from one part of the banking system to another.

The Bank of England sought to persuade the primary banks to support the ailing secondary banks by replacing the transferred deposits. This came to be known as a lifeboat operation. Although the Bank also contributed to the lifeboat operation, it essentially involved the primary banks rescuing the secondary banks.

Why did the primary banks agree to this? Two reasons suggest themselves; one sinister and the other enlightened. The sinister reason is that the primary banks feared that the Bank would penalise them if they refused to cooperate. No doubt there was much arm-twisting; the Bank has after all considerable feudal powers. The second reason is that it was in the enlightened self-interest of the primary banks since closures of secondary banks might undermine confidence in the primary banks themselves. In view of what has already been argued in Section 2 this dilemma only arises because there is insufficient disclosure of information. The public cannot be sure that the primary banks do not face the same problems as the secondary banks in which case it is in the interests of the primary banks to man the lifeboat. Thus the primary banks are prisoners of their own secrecy; with full disclosure they could have resisted the Governor's coercive efforts.

Let Z_1 and Z_2 denote the confidence indices for the primary and secondary banks respectively and let

$$u = u(\overset{+}{Z_1}, \bar{Y})$$

be the utility function of the primary banks where Y denotes their assistance to the secondary banks. Partial derivatives are shown over the respective variables. The secondary banks' confidence function is assumed to be

$$Z_2 = F(\overset{-}{X}, \overset{+}{Y})$$

where X denotes adverse news, e.g. property prices. Because of incomplete disclosure Z_1 is contaminated by Z_1 through the following contamination function

$$Z_1 = G(\overset{+}{Z}_2, \overset{+}{V})$$

where V denotes the adverse news that is specific to the primary banks.

The contamination function implies that in the event of bad news in terms of X it might pay the primary banks to support the secondary banks. The optimal size of the lifeboat which is in the collective self-interest of the secondary banks is the solution for Y generated by the following first order condition:

$$u_1^1(Z_1,Y)G_1^1(Z_2,V)F_2^1(X,Y) + u_2^1(Z_1,Y) = 0$$

which implies that the lifeboat is extended up to the point at which the marginal rate of substitution between confidence and income in the primary banking sector is equal to the marginal effect of support on primary bank confidence via its effects on confidence in the secondary banking sector. It may be shown that if $Y > 0$ then $dY/dX > 0$, i.e. the worse the secondary banking crisis the greater is the optimal lifeboat support.

It is clear from this analysis that in the absence of the contamination function $Y = 0$, i.e. it does not pay the primary banks to support the secondary banks. Thus if $G_1^1 = 0$, $Y = 0$. These conditions will be met in the case of full disclosure so that Z_2 does not affect Z_1. Z_1 and Z_2 might be correlated because X and V are correlated but this is an entirely different matter which has no analytical bearing upon the logic of lifeboat operations.

8 POLICY

The central policy recommendation is that banks should be required to disclose all the necessary information so that the public can arrive at an informed view about their payments. Honesty is the best policy otherwise rumour can quickly become the order of the day. Indeed, it is the lack of this disclosure and excessive secrecy by banks that creates the need for LLR.

Banks should disclose information on their lending by sector, country and maturity as well as providing details of bad debts and charge-offs in terms of these categories. They should also indicate their assets and liabilities in the interbank market. The central objective should be to make disclosure by financial corporations at least as effective as disclosure by nonfinancial corporations. In an efficient capital market it is this that removes the need for LLR (except in the case of catastrophes).

In practice the converse is true; the information published by financial corporations is unusually obscure. For example, in the 1982 report and accounts for Barclays Bank loans and write offs to the 'rest of the world' are lumped together without any indication of the sectors and maturities involved. Similar shortcomings exist in, for example, the case of the Swiss Bank Corporation in 1983. In contrast, Chase Manhattan now provide information on their loans by sector and country but not by maturity. They also provide a fairly detailed analysis of loss experience although this could be improved. Some of this greater disclosure has been prompted by the International Lending Supervision Act 1983 and the SEC.

Thus some countries are worse than others in terms of the disclosure of information and the British standard is quite poor. Disclosure of information is the best form of investor protection and the banks should be given, say, two years grace before they are required to achieve minimal standards of disclosure. The grace period will give them time to remove the skeletons from their closets which present arrangements enable and even encourage them to get away with. Moreover, information should be disclosed more frequently than annually – a year is a long time in a banking crisis. In this context the BIS or some similar body should keep a published monitor of the network of interbank transactions while domestic monetary authorities should monitor their domestic counterparts.

In this context, it is not necessary to disclose information on private clients so that the usual standards of confidentiality are preserved and respected. It is sometimes counter-argued that for a bank to disclose the nature of its portfolio is the equivalent in the financial sector of the disclosure of industrial secrets in the industrial sector. This implies that banks should be allowed to maintain secrecy in the same way that care manufacturers should be allowed to keep their new products secret. However, the analogy is false; it is more like suggesting that British Leyland need not divulge what part of the vehicles market in which it plans to operate. The only time the analogy holds is when the privacy of the individual is involved because it is only at this level that true portfolio secrecy is worth respecting.

It is perhaps worth asking why these policies have not already been enforced. Secrecy is not in the interests of healthy financial institutions since they have everything to lose by the contamination factor generated through the veil of ignorance. It pays to let the truth hang out. Lifeboat dilemmas only occur because of the veil of ignorance, so it is in the interest of strong banks to remove the veil as far as they can. However, the opposite applies in the case of the weak banks – it does not pay to let the truth hang out especially if there is a central bank to act as a dishonest broker. By withholding information the weak morally blackmail the strong. If the public suspect that one set of banks is withholding information the credibility of the other banks will be jeopardised. The contamination factor only ceases to apply when the public is confident that all banks are fully disclosing information. These externalities imply that complete disclosure is unlikely to be spontaneous and that a benign authority is required to enforce it.

It might be expected that the benign authority in question is the central bank acting on behalf of the government. The next question is therefore – why have central banks not insisted on full disclosure as a general rule? Most probably the answer is that they enjoy their LLR role; it makes them politically important. Hirsch (1977) believes that the arbitrary powers enjoyed by central banks are an undesirable but unavoidable consequence of LLR which in turn is unavoidable. Central bankers have a sectarian interest in perpetuating their LLR role. Despite their protests to the contrary, there can surely be nothing more exhilarating in a central banker's life than a financial crisis which he alone has powers to rectify. The same applies to generals in the case of wars. Thus Bagehot's Problem, as Hirsch has called it, is not a necessary evil but the result of central bankers' vested interests. The Problem would disappear if instead central bankers insisted on proper standards of disclosure, but this would undermine the foundations of their political power.

Instead, central bankers extend their power by the establishment of supervisory functions. But instead of publishing their supervisory reports they use them to exert pressure on various parts of the financial system. Most probably, an example of this is the case of Johnson Matthey Bankers in which the Bank of England advantaged by supervisory information has once again been coercing other banks to man the lifeboats. In addition, it has been using public resources to prevent the closure of a bank at a time when the government was insisting that public resources should not be used to prevent the closure of coal-pits.

References

BATCHELOR, R. (1983) 'The Avoidance of Catastrophe: two Nineteenth Century Banking Crises', in F. Capie and G. Wood (eds), *Financial Crises and the World Banking System* (London: Macmillan, 1986).

BLANCHARD, O. J. and WATSON, M. W. (1982) 'Bubbles, Rational Expectations and Financial Markets', in P. Wachtel (ed.), *Crisis in the Economic and Financial Structure* (Lexington Books).

FRIEDMAN, M. (1959) *A Program for Monetary Stability* (New York: Fordham University Press).

HIRSCH, F. (1977) 'The Bagehot Problem', *Manchester School of Economic and Social Studies*, pp. 241–57.

HO, T. and SAUNDERS, A. (1980) 'A Catastrophe Model of Bank Failure', *Journal of Finance*, December.

KINDLEBERGER, C. P. (1978) *Manias, Panics and Crushes* (London: Macmillan).

MINSKY, H. P. (1982) 'The Financial – Instability Hypothesis: Capitalist Processes and the Behaviour of the Economy', in C. P. Kindleberger and J. P. Laffague (eds), *Financial Crises* (Cambridge University Press).

REID, M. (1978) *The Secondary Banking Crisis, 1973–75* (London: Macmillan).

SAYERS, R. S. (1967) *Modern Banking*, seventh edn (Oxford: Clarendon Press).

SHARPE, W. F. (1978) 'Bank Capital Adequacy, Deposit Insurance and Security Values', *Journal of Financial and Quantitative Analysis*, November, 1978.

SOLOW, R. M. (1982) 'On the Lender of Last Resort', in C. P. Kindleberger and J. P. Laffargue (eds), *Financial Crises* (Cambridge University Press).

ZEEMAN, E. C. (1974) 'On the Unstable Behaviour of Stock Exchanges', *Journal of Mathematical Economics*, pp. 39–49.

Comment on 'The Theory of Last Resort Lending'

Lionel D. Price

The central proposition of Beenstock's chapter is stated succinctly at the end of Section 4. It is that last resort lending 'is redundant in rational societies with efficient capital markets and full information'. Later, in Section 8, he asserts that it is the lack of 'disclosure and excessive secrecy by banks that creates the need for LLR'. This need would disappear if banks were 'required to disclose all the necessary information so that the public can arrive at an informed view about their payments'.

The first question we need to address is how much information is theoretically necessary for the public to arrive at a view sufficiently well-informed for their actions – in terms of placing and withdrawing deposits, and providing capital to banks – to maximise social welfare (at least in the sense of achieving a Pareto-optimum). Beenstock appears to believe that 'efficient capital markets' will produce such an optimal result. But for this proposition to be demonstrably true, the notion of efficient markets has to be extended well beyond the usual requirement that specific markets make proper use of all *available* information. In an uncertain world we cannot be sure that competitive markets will deliver a Pareto-optimum unless such markets exist in each and every one of Arrow and Debreu's state-contingent commodities.

In Beenstock's world, full disclosure would enable depositors and investors to distinguish between banks which are sound and those which are not, and an efficient capital market would ensure that the sound banks survived. But for us to be sure that the capital market would achieve this satisfactory outcome, either the disclosure envisaged would have to be sufficiently full to eliminate all uncertainty, or spot and futures markets would have to exist in all the various assets held by banks; moreover there would have to be sets of such futures markets contingent on the state of the world at each future date. In other words, 'full disclosure' would mean a full description of the value of each loan at every future date in each possible state of the world – a daunting task!

In Section 2 of his chapter, Beenstock seems to define a less ambitious concept of full disclosure, being that set of facts sufficiently large to ensure that depositors take no account of the number of bank failures in assessing the viability of remaining banks. But what is this full set of facts? If we do not know what it comprises, we are in danger of producing a tautology whereby the lender of last resort function can be obviated by disclosing an amount of information sufficient to ensure that last resort lending can produce no improvement in social welfare.

On a more practical plane, Beenstock offers in Section 8 specific suggestions envisaging that banks should disclose information on their lending by sector, country and maturity. (He acknowledges that there are ultimately difficulties in banks providing details of individual accounts.) But is such disclosure sufficient for the market to reach a proper view of the solvency of individual banks, or of the extent of any risk that they might be unable to meet their obligations? At a theoretical level, it certainly falls a long way short of Arrow and Debreu's requirements, and in practice it is evident that even with such information available, considerable uncertainty about the net worth of a bank at any moment in time will remain.

It is the uncertainty about the net worth of a bank which lies at the heart of the problem. We have so far concentrated on the lack of complete (state-contingent) markets in banks' assets, but even if it were possible to have such full information, there would still remain a problem of 'market failure' relating to banks' liabilities. As long as a bank is sufficiently well-capitalised that the prospect of bankruptcy is negligible, then depositors hold an asset which is virtually capital-certain in money terms, leaving shareholders to bear the risks of any changes in net worth. But if a contingency arises that raises the probability of bankruptcy to some non-negligible level, then depositors face some risk of capital loss. There is, however, no market mechanism by which the value of all deposits is discounted by the same percentage to reflect the possibility of bankruptcy (as would be the case with a unit trust, for example). Depositors who withdraw their funds early will receive full value for their deposits. The remaining depositors will face an increased risk, not just because of the consequential lower gearing of the bank's capital, but also because continuing withdrawals are likely to force the bank to have to realise less and less liquid assets at a discount on the price that could be obtained given more time and a less desperate need for cash. (Alternatively, the bank could try to redress the perceived riskiness of its deposits by offering a higher interest rate, but the higher cost of deposits would itself be likely to damage the bank's financial position.) In such circumstances a rational depositor will wish to be first in line to withdraw his deposit from the possibly failing bank. There may be instances where the provision of fuller information than was at first available to a bank's depositors would reduce their perceptions of the probability of bankruptcy back to a negligible level, so that the run could be averted; but as long as the future is uncertain – as it surely must be – then there are bound to be instances when even possession of all conceivable presently knowable information will leave significant possibility of bankruptcy and the run on deposits will proceed even though the mean expectation is that the bank is solvent. In instances such as this, the provision of last resort lending, or even the knowledge that it is available, can prevent a bank which ultimately proves to be sound failing because of uncertainty – an uncertainty generated not by a failure to provide information which is available, but because the required information simply does not exist.

Beenstock in fact offers an example from 1914 of 'certain extreme circumstances' in which the banking system faces such catastrophic risks that last resort lending would be necessary to save the banking system. In such cases, he sees last resort lending as fulfilling a valid social function by providing 'a breathing space until . . . the objective facts become known'. In fact, the circumstances of 1914 were so catastrophic that many of the financial institutions involved faced such heavy write-offs of their overseas claims that there was little chance that they were still solvent. The authorities' response on that occasion was not lending by the central bank but effectively a capital injection by Government, which itself agreed to meet the financial losses that were likely to have been suffered. The Bank stood ready to buy at full value (and without recourse to the seller) even probably worthless bills drawn on overseas creditors, with the Government undertaking the very substantial financial risk. Last resort lending would *not* have been appropriate in this case; indeed it would have been of no use for it would not have restored the solvency of the institutions in question.

11 Country Risk: A Model for Predicting Debt Servicing Problems in Developing Countries

R. J. Taffler and B. Abassi

1 INTRODUCTION

1.1 Default in international markets

Recent events in the international capital markets with more than thirty countries in the last two years unable to meet their debt service obligations have focused attention on the method of country risk analysis used by international banks and financial agencies.

Unlike corporate borrowers, countries do not disappear into bankruptcy when they are unable to meet their financial commitments nor are lenders able to seize country assets in lieu. None the less it is virtually inconceivable today, unlike in the 1930s, that any sovereign borrower would default formally in the sense of repudiating its outstanding obligations as this would deny it access to credit markets and call into question its trade relationships with the international community subsequently. In addition banks have strong incentives to avoid default if only to avoid the impact of large asset write-offs on their balance sheets. Instead countries with debt service problems negotiate rescheduling agreements with their main commercial bank creditors or their aid consortia directly and through the so-called 'Paris Club', consisting of the 17 members of the Development Assistance Committee of the OECD. Frequently such agreements, which are renegotiated annually in some cases, are associated with International Monetary Fund assistance conditional on debtor countries meeting IMF policy prescriptions for the adjustment of their balance of payments, the basis on which the Fund itself disburses assistance to member countries.

1.2 Objectives and plan of the chapter

Country risk analysis, the concern of this study, seeks to identify in advance those countries which will be unable to meet their commitments on external debt. This latter is defined as debt owed to non-residents with an original or extended maturity of greater than one year, repayable in foreign currency, goods and services. It may be divided into two categories, namely sovereign debt, foreign loans made to the public sector or private sector with repayment guaranteed by the national government, and non-publicly guaranteed private external debt. We are here concerned with the former category – loans made directly or indirectly to the government of a sovereign nation.

This chapter has three main thrusts, first it describes the development of an operational discriminant model of country risk and economic performance in current use by practitioners. Secondly it examines the true *ex ante* predictive ability of the function over the period 1979 to 1983 inclusive subsequent to it development. Emphasis is placed on the degree of robustness of such models outside the original sample time frame particularly when the economic environment to which they are applied changes substantially. The final strand is a comparison of the model results with those provided by a consensus view of barker judgement as measured by the *Institutional Investor* (II) credit risk index – the question of interest is whether bankers appear to know better.

Section 2 describes existing methods of country risk analysis used by bankers and provides a literature review of relevant empirical work. This is following by a description of the database and variables used in this study and Section 4 discusses the development of the model itself, statistical tests of its efficiency and provides a justification and interpretation of its component measures. In Section 5 the performance of the discriminant model in practice is assessed in some detail and Section 6 gives comparative prediction results for the II credit ratings. Some reasons for the differences in results are suggested. The chapter concludes with a summary and some remarks.

2 LITERATURE SURVEY

2.1 How banks assess country risk

Substantial resources are expended in sovereign credit risk analysis in most international banks due to the large share developing country credits account for in their loan portfolios. Goodman (1977) reports on a survey of country risk appraisal methods conducted by the US Export-Import Bank (Eximbank) covering 37 US banks accounting for well over half the US banking system's total international loans. Goodman divides the systems of appraisal in use into four types: fully qualitative, where emphasis is placed on a country report with structure and format differing between countries and evaluation is subjective, structured qualitative where the country report is prepared to a standardised format and some statistical analysis or summary is generally included, the weighted checklist approach where a set of variables are scored and aggregated into a summary country rating using subjectively determined weights, and other quantitative–multivariate and econometric techniques generally.

Of the banks surveyed, 5 (14 per cent) used no systematic system, analysing country risk on an *ad hoc* basis only when required by a loan application. For (11 per cent) took a fully qualitative approach, 23 (62 per cent) a structured qualitative approach, 4 (11 per cent) used a structured qualitative approach together with a checklist and one bank used a checklist and other quantitative methods. Eight of the 27 banks using a structured qualitative approach translated the evaluation into a country rating, usually an A–E letter system. Goodman was surprised to find that only one bank had tested the results of its evaluation system. The weighted checklist system in question was compared with subsequent repayment experience and was found to be a poor predictor. As a result, this bank was stated to be developing statistically more sophisticated techniques.

The country evaluation systems were used primarily to help in setting overall country exposure ceilings but also to assist in analysing loan portfolio quality. It is interesting to note not one of the banks used the results to help fix interest rates or fees with regard to a loan whereas the margin above LIBOR (London Interbank Offer Rate) negotiated is generally viewed as a risk premium.

In a later survey of 25 international private sector banks undertaken in 1980, of which only 11 were US based, Burton and Inoue (1983) found some evidence of a trend towards greater sophistication in country risk analysis, particularly in US banks, and towards more systematic and less subjective methods of analysis. However, they comment that even by the time of the survey some large non-US banks had yet to introduce systematic analysis relying instead on 'hunch, guesswork and rule of thumb'. They attribute the generally more complex assessment procedures employed by US banks both to their greater experience in international lending and also the importance given to the degree of sophistication of evaluation methods used in the regular bank inspections by the Office of the Controller of the Currency and the Federal Reserve Board. The authors note that there is clearly far less enthusiasm among non-US banks, and especially British banks, for systematic country risk analysis and a greater scepticism of quantitative methods. Merrill (1982) provides a case study of how a large international US bank is currently conducting country risk analysis.

Checklist systems are the main formal computational approaches to risk assessment used by international banks and are the techniques with which bank economists in general tend to feel happiest. This is also confirmed by the many normative linear additive models based on judgementally determined and intuitively weighted variables proposed by practitioners (e.g. Nagy, 1979; Robinson, 1981; Thompson, 1981) and used in commercial subscription services such as FORELEND of BERI S.A. However, tests of the operational efficiency of such approaches invariably are not provided by their authors. Certainly in the absence of such tests and the difficulty of testing intuitively determined categories of risk which do not relate clearly to a measurable dependent variable or outcome, we must remain somewhat sceptical of their operational utility in general. Blask (1978), in fact, tested the five checklists used by banks in the Goodman survey together with two others on the basis of their ability to predict multilateral debt reschedulings and found six of the seven to perform poorly. Some other problems with the checklist approach relate to the way in which component variables, which are often very large in number, are selected, how the weights are determined, what the variables are actually measuring and their logical relationship with the predicted variable of interest etc. None the less it should be stressed that almost any form of systematic analysis is likely to provide a better understanding of country risk than a pure 'seat-of-the-pants' approach.

Finally, it is of interest to consider the approaches advocated by two international banking magazines, *Euromoney* and the *Insti-*

tutional Investor (II). The Euromoney Country Risk League Table
(Bance, 1978) is produced by ranking countries which have borrowed
on the Eurocurrency market, on the basis of the weighted average
spread (i.e. margin above LIBOR) they were able to obtain. This
'market knows best' approach is viewed as providing a valid predictor
of country risk. However, whereas the average spread *may* reflect
the market view of the standing of an individual country, this cannot
be accepted directly as a true assessment of country risk as *inter alia*
the key relationship between the published spread figure and risk of
default (which is the prime concern in risk assessment) has not been
empirically established. There are also a number of practical issues
which call into question the value of the measure even for other
purposes. There are computational problems (*Euromoney*, April
1980, pp. 7–10), a country can be rated only if it borrows on the
Eurocurrency market and then only on the basis of the loan it has
negotiated, and also the timing of the loan is critical since when
average spreads change, the ranking system is biased by when the
loan actually took place. A further important point is that front end
commitment, service and management fees, which may be substantial, are generally not published and may be loaded to reduce the
published spread figure.

None the less there may be some information content, with regard
to country risk, albeit small, conveyed by the terms of the loan.
Following detailed econometric analysis Feder and Just (1980,
p. 137) conclude 'In summary, it appears that fairly precise estimates
of default probabilities, as perceived by lenders, are possible under
competition using only the terms of the loan if loss rate for the event
of default can be determined (estimated)'.

The *Institutional Investor* Credit Rating System, which has been
in operation since September 1979, involves the participation of
75–100 banks. Each banker grades the creditworthiness or chance
of default of each country on a scale 0–100 (certain default – no
chance of default). The individual responses are then weighted
according to an undisclosed formula that '. . . properly gives more
weight to responses from banks with the largest worldwide lending
exposure and the most sophisticated country analysis systems' (II,
September 1983, p. 240). The ranking includes developed countries
and also those which have not borrowed on the Eurocurrency
market. Currently 107 countries are being rated and updated
rankings appear biannually in March and September issues. Feder
and Ross (1982) show that the survey can be used empirically to

provide an assessment of the general consensus view on the relative credit risks and perceived default probabilities of countries.

In the Angeloni and Short (1980) regression studies into the determinants of Eurocurrency spread in 1978 and 1979, the II rating was consistently the most significant variable. However, the authors point out that both the rating index and the interest spread may be being jointly determined by related banking opinions rather than objective measures of creditworthiness. Feder and Ross (1982), in fact, find a correlation between spread charged in a sample of 78 loan transactions and the contemporaneous II scores of −0.71 and after further work conclude (p. 689) that 'credit pricing in the market is generally consistent with lenders' risk perceptions' (as measured by the *Institutional Investor* index). However, they do point out that 'judgment regarding the appropriateness of credit pricing will need to focus on the quality of country risk analyses performed by lenders'.

To test the validity of the Institutional Investor rating system, which we may term the 'bankers know best' approach in line with the 'market knows best' arguments discussed above, a comparison of rescheduling experience with the respective country ratings (predictions) prior to the event is necessary. This is undertaken in Section 6 of this chapter and the results compared with those of the discriminant function described below.

2.2 Related empirical work

Frank and Cline (1971) provide the germinal study in this area. They used a data sample of 26 countries covering the period 1960–68 with 13 rescheduling country-year (RC) cases and 132 non-rescheduling country-year (NRC) cases and both linear and quadratic discriminant methodologies. Three ratios were found significant, the debt service/exports ratio (DSR), amortisation/total outstanding debt (A/D) and imports/reserves (M/R).

Whereas, as inevitably with an early study, there are a number of statistical problems, perhaps a more interesting issue relates to the positing of a causal relationship between the maturity term (A/D) and rescheduling. In the case of rescheduling countries this ratio *reflects* the result of the exercise in the form of longer maturities although certainly prior to rescheduling its use avoids the difficulties inherent in the use of the DSR in the case of bunching of maturities. Another qualification is that made by Feder and Just (1977, p. 32): 'It may well be that the loan maturity allowed by the lender depends on the country's debt servicing capacity; hence, the amortisation/ debt ratio may be highly correlated with defaults . . .' That is, when bankers perceive country risk as likely to increase over time their first reaction will normally be to reduce the length of loan they are prepared to make. However, if the country cannot meet its immediate obligations and rescheduling occurs then maturities are lengthened which may be misinterpreted as increased confidence in the LDC.

Feder and Just (1977) use logit analysis for assessing the probability of rescheduling. Five variables were found significant, namely, DSR, GNP per capita, imports/reserves, export growth and capital inflows/ debt service and their cases related to 21 rescheduling years for 11 countries and 217 NRC cases drawn from 1965–75. Data for the rescheduling countries for two years prior to rescheduling was excluded from the non-rescheduling sample. RC debt service payments were scaled up by 25 per cent when the due amount (as opposed to the amount actually paid) was not known. *Ad hoc* amortisation estimates were also made in the computation of their A/D ratio which was not found significant.

Both of these studies drew on the conceptual approach to debt servicing capacity of Avramovic *et al.* (1964) of the World Bank. Sargen's (1977) discriminant study was the first to treat rescheduling also as a monetary phenomenon and to incorporate indicators of monetary policy. His data, drawn from the period of 1960–75, consisted of 24 RC and 442 NRC cases. Variables were computed on a three year average basis and both inflation (or money supply growth when inflation was excluded from the model) and the DSR (again 'schedule' not actual) were important measures in the fitted models.

Mayo and Barrett (1978) at the Export-Import Bank (EXIM-BANK) applied logit analysis to a sample of 48 countries for the period 1960–75, with 28 instances of formal multilateral reschedulings in 11 countries. Their final model briefly reported contained six variables, namely, debt/exports, reserves/imports, gross fixed capital formation/GDP, imports/GDP, IMF reserve position/imports and rate of increase in consumer prices. This study is the first to report poor predictive ability and unstable performance for the DSR. Their rescheduling group was defined so as to include 'a rescheduling up to five years hence'. As such their reported misclassification error rates are not comparable to those of the previous studies.

Saini and Bates (1978) in a very carefully considered paper review problems in the extant studies in detail. Drawing on this analysis they test empirically (i) different definitions of the dependent variable, (ii) the hypothesis that the statistical significance of the DSR in earlier studies might have been due to the authors' adjustments alone, (iii) the benefits of adopting a logit approach as opposed to conventional discriminant analysis and (iv) the degree of structural shifts in parameter estimates over time.

Their sample contained data on 20 countries for the period 1960–77 with up to 23 rescheduling cases depending on definition. Observations for the year of rescheduling and the following year were omitted. Functions fitted varied in number of dependent measures. Based on their results Saini and Bates argued the case for a dependent variable definition that comprised only 'involuntary' debt reschedulings but including balance of payment support loans etc., found (p. 15) that 'the debt service ratio without adjustment is virtually useless in isolating debt servicing problems', discovered no material difference in results using the different statistical methodologies and met some differences between sub-periods.

The most recent paper of relevance, Feder *et al.* (1981), reworks the earlier Feder and Just study. It is of interest both in terms of the more refined data used which included private (non-guaranteed) external debt information, via access to World Bank files, and a number of issues relating to the methodological approach. Their model was developed ostensibly to provide a framework to facilitate forecasting. The sample data, 580 observations, of which 40 related to cases of debt rescheduling, or proxies thereof, were drawn from the period 1965–76 and covered 56 LDCs. Six variables somewhat related to those found useful in the earlier study were used although two required non-publicly available capital flow data. The debt service ratio included service on long-term private debt in the numerator where available and was also adjusted to reflect 'originally due' figures. Regional dummies were introduced. Sargen's (1977) arguments regarding the need to include monetary policy indicators were rejected as difficult to project.

With regard to the dependent variable, if a rescheduling request was viewed by the authors as being made in anticipation of economic circumstances in the following year then the latter was classed as the year of rescheduling. Ten of the 40 'rescheduling' cases were identified by access to private World Bank files and related to serious debt arrears and little documented private lender reschedulings which were viewed as surrogates.

The study is interesting. However, the restricted set of variables considered will be noted as will the definitional problems relating to what is or is not a 'true' rescheduling or a valid proxy and also when a country should be considered as a rescheduling case particularly *ex ante* in practical application of the model. In addition there are difficulties in determining, again on an *ex ante* basis, what the DSR should be.

Two comparative methodological avenues are those of Fisk and Rimlinger (1979), who provide an original non-parametric approach where the prediction of rescheduling is based on the search for similarity with historical precedents and Abbassi and Russell (1980) who adopt a mixed integer programming approach.

3. THE DATA

3.1 The country data

The World Bank World Debt Tables and the International Monetary Fund International Financial Statistics (IFS) were the main data sources used in the development of the model. The former provide data on external and publicly guaranteed debt of more than one year maturity and the latter, available on magnetic tape, contains data relating to current account balance of payments, national account, external trade and government spending statistics, etc. A database of economic information for 95 developing countries was compiled for the 12-year period to 1978, the latest year for which data was available when model development commenced. Data from 1967 to 1977 was used for fitting the model which was initially tested, using the 1978 data, to identify likely rescheduling countries in 1979. The statistical unit was the country-year and all told there were 1140 (12 × 95) cases.

The model of debt servicing capacity is derived from fitting a discriminant function to data from two populations. In corporate failure studies (e.g. Altman, 1983; Taffler, 1982) the criterion for classification is whether a company is bankrupt or not. In the case of LDCs, debt rescheduling is the nearest state to default, defined as unwillingness or inability on the part of a government to honour contractual obligations to foreign debtors, on both private and publicly guaranteed debt, which developing countries strive to avoid at all costs. In fact, the only documented case of outright default in the last thirty years appears to be Cuba after the Bay of Pigs episode in 1961, although a number of countries have come quite close. Thus, two groups were formed on the basis of whether a given country for a particular year was reported as having been obliged to seek a rescheduling of part or the totality of its debt on a bilateral or multilateral basis. No attempt was made to separate out 'voluntary' reschedulings or use proxies for the event because of the potential bias arising in identification.

Fourteen countries could be identified clearly as having rescheduled their debt between 1968 and 1978 at least once making 55 such country-year cases. Each rescheduling was treated as an independent case since it is usually considered as such by the bankers who agree to it on its own merit. To capture the conditions conducive to rescheduling, data for the year prior to rescheduling was employed. However, in discriminant analysis it is necessary to ensure the groups are distinct and cases which are members simultaneously of more than one group should be discarded. The simulation studies of Lachenbruch (1974) in fact demonstrate how with incorrect assignment of sample observations to groups in a non-random fashion, as in the case of interest here, apparent error rates are likely to be substantially affected. Hence country-year cases for up to three years before or after a rescheduling termed 'weak years' were omitted from the NRC group since they may have still contained RC characteristics. For related reasons, countries experiencing serious economic or financial difficulties, even though this may not have resulted in rescheduling *per se*, were also excluded. Thus leaving out of consideration 305 cases where data for at least one variable in the final discriminant function was missing, the NRC group was of size 660 and there were 120 weak year country cases. An average of 72 countries were used in the analysis each year, making the database employed apparently the most extensive, up to now, in published studies of debt servicing capacity.

3.2 The variables

To derive a comprehensive and defensible set of explanatory variables a detailed review was first undertaken of the measures found useful in the earlier multivariate studies discussed above. This was augmented by the set of indicators of potential relevance to the debt problem provided by the OECD (1974) as well as various ratios quoted by bankers or economists in the specialised literature. Others were synthesised on the basis of theoretical considerations. The general guideline adopted was that the measures selected should have some relevance to the foreign exchange sector, country debt or the domestic economic situation and particularly that each should be logically defensible on theoretical grounds. An initial set of 60 was established. However, because of consistently missing values for certain basic indicators it was not possible to derive all the desired ratios in all cases. As such final analysis focused on the variable set of 42 ratios or rate of growth measures of Table 11.1.

3.3 Data transformation

Multiple discriminant analysis is based on the underlying assumption of separate multivariate normality and equality of the dispersion matrices of each of the constituent groups. However, these conditions are unlikely to be met in practical application of the technique with data of the nature used in this study. Although marginal (i.e. individual variable) normality is a necessary but not sufficient condition for multivariate normality it is generally accepted that constituent model variables be bounded and transformed to approximate normality (e.g. Lachenbruch et al., 1973) prior to fitting the model. To reduce the degree of skewness and kurtosis inevitable in ratio data and the number of outlier observations, logarithmic, square root and reciprocal transforms were applied to each of the 42 measures. Coefficients of skewness and kurtosis were then calculated for the untransformed and transformed variables for the RC and NRC groups separately to indicate the appropriate transformation (if any) for each variable. After transformation any outlying observations in each group were winsorised, i.e. replaced by limiting values 2.5 standard deviations from the mean of the other observations calculated on the basis of the remaining cases.

3.4 Data dimensionality

Multicollinearity constitutes a potentially serious problem in the practical application of discriminant analysis (Pinches, 1980; Taffler, 1982) and any large number of ratios computed from a smaller set of indicators is liable to contain highly correlated subsets. To identify the degree of intercorrelation among the variables, ensure that serious collinearity was avoided in the development of the discriminant function and understand better the salient characteristics of

Table 11.1   Variables employed in the analysis

List of variables

1. A	15. DIS	29. M
2. B/M	16. DS	30. Ml
3. B/R	17. DSR	31. M°
4. B/X	18. D/GDP	32. Ml°
5. B3/M	19. D/Ml	33. M/GDP
6. B3/R	20. D/POP	34. Ml/GDP
7. B3/X	21. D/X	35. NF
8. C	22. DC/GDP	36. NF/M
9. C/GDP	23. DIS/M	37. POP
10. C/POP	24. GDP	38. R
11. D	25. GDP°	39. R/M
12. DB	26. GDP/POP	40. R°
13. DC	27. I	41. X°
14. DC°	28. INF	42. X/GDP

Key to abbreviations

A   Amortisation of debt.
B   Trade balance $(X - M)$.
B3   3 years cumulative B.
C   Loan commitment (debt contracted during the year).
D   Debt, disbursed only.
DB   Debt owed to private banks.
DC   Domestic credit.
DIS   Debt disbursed in the current year.
DS   Debt service: amortisation and interest.
DSR   Debt service ratio (DS/X).
GDP   Gross domestic product.
I   Annual interest payment.
INF   Geometric mean rate of change of the consumer price index.
M   Imports of goods CIF.
Ml   Money supply.
NF   Net financial flow $(DIS - DS)$.
POP   Population.
R   International reserves including gold at market price.
X   Exports of goods FOB.

Notes:
 (i) (°) denotes geometric mean rate of change over three years.
(ii) The World Bank definitions are used for all debt items.

country economic performance being measured, a varimax rotated principal component analysis (PCA) was conducted on the entire data set. PCA projects the original variable set into new axes such that the new variables (components) are orthogonal (uncorrelated) to each other. Variables that are highly loaded on (correlated with) the same component can be considered to be measuring a similar aspect (dimension) of the data. Components that explain little of the variance in (information conveyed by) the original data set can simply be discarded. Varimax rotation keeps the retained component set orthogonal but rotates it such that the correlations of the original variables (in our case ratios) with the derived components tend towards 0 or ±1 thereby aiding interpretation.

Table 11.2 provides the results of the varimax rotated PCA for the measures used in this study, transformed as appropriate and calculated where possible for the full 1235 cases. Absolute loadings above 0.4 are indicated. It will be seen that ten statistically distinct components with eigenvalues greater than 1 accounted for 84 per cent of the variance in the data set. Reification indicates these to be measuring an LDCs size, degree of external indebtedness, trade balance, wealth, growth, debt service, external trade, trade balance to exports, monetary policy and level of reserves.

4 THE DISCRIMINANT ANALYSIS

4.1 Discriminant analysis versus logit analysis

In this study a two-group linear discriminant approach is adopted in preference to logit analysis. There is currently some debate in the literature about which of the two techniques to use. The logit regression model is formulated through the logistic cumulative density functional form and in our case assumes the probability of country i rescheduling is related to its vector of economic and associated variables x_i via

$$\Pr(y_i = 1|x_i) = (1 + e^{-\lambda_i})^{-1}$$

where $y_i = 1$ for rescheduling cases and 0 otherwise, and λ_i is a linear combination of m explanatory variables given by $\lambda_i = \beta_0 + \sum_{j=1}^{m} \beta_j x_{ij}$, and β is the coefficient vector to be estimated. The rationale for the use of the logit model is that it does not depend on assumption of multivariate normality and equality of covariance matrices (e.g. Press and Wilson, 1978) and as such, for example, is robust to the use of binary independent variables (as with Feder et al., 1981).

Table 11.2 Varimax rotated principal component analysis, loadings >0.4 with signs omitted

Description					Component					
	1	2	3	4	5	6	7	8	9	10
GDP	0.895									
D	0.895									
M1	0.887									
DIS	0.860									
DC	0.858									
C	0.836									
NF	0.823									
M	0.817									
R	0.692									
POP	0.624			0.431						
DB	0.568			0.453						
D/GDP		0.870								
NF/M		0.830								
DIS/M		0.803								
D/MI		0.797								
C/GDP		0.743							0.496	
D/X		0.731								
DSR		0.526				0.530				
B3/R			0.934							
B/M			0.833							
B/R			0.925							
B3/M			0.820							

Braces: column 1 group (GDP–DB) = country size; column 2 group (D/GDP–DSR) = external indebtedness; column 3 group (B3/R–B3/M) = trade balance

	Component										
Description	1	2	3	4	5	6	7	8	9	10	
GDP/POP				0.862							} wealth
D/POP		0.406		0.833							
C/POP		0.428		0.742							
GDP°					0.875						} growth
MI°					0.863						
M°					0.776						
X°					0.665						
DC°					0.638					0.508	
DS						0.927					} debt service
A						0.923					
I						0.890					
M/GDP							0.730				} external trade
X/GDP							0.718				
INF							0.518				
B/X								0.965			} trade balance to exports
B3/X								0.960			
MI/GDP			0.413						0.882		} monetary policy
DC/GDP				0.441					0.490		
R°										0.815	} level of reserves
R/M									0.451	0.636	
% Variance	24.0	13.2	12.8	10.4	5.3	4.9	4.1	3.6	3.1	2.7	
Cumulative %	24.0	37.2	50.0	60.4	65.7	70.6	74.7	78.3	81.4	84.1	

However there is little evidence in the literature of the superiority of such techniques compared with conventional discriminant analysis particulary with continuous explanatory variables and where the groups are well separated. Efron (1975), for example, shows that if the data satisfy conventional normality and common covariance assumptions, the logistic approach could lead to a substantial loss in efficiency particularly with well separated groups. O'Neill (1980) found this result also held under other distributional forms.

Press and Wilson (1978) compare the performance of logistic regression and discriminant analysis in two classification problems both using binary independent variables and find only a marginal difference in classification rates particularly for the validation samples. They conclude that generally 'It is unlikely that the two methods will give markedly different results, or yield substantially different linear functions . . .' (p. 705) but advocate the use of the logistic regression model particularly when a number of the variables are qualitative. Ball and Tschoegl (1982) in a study into the foreign direct investment behaviour of international banks using non-continuous measures, provide similar results. However, of most direct relevance to the present study are the several comparative results reported by Saini and Bates (1978) who using continuous independent variables conclude (p. 15): 'we do not observe any material difference between the discriminant and logistic analyses in their ability to isolate cases of debt servicing difficulties'. As such since there would appear to be few benefits in practice, as opposed to theory, in adopting the logit approach and the probability form of the logit function can be matched by the appropriate transformation of the discriminant score z via $\Pr(\text{NRC}) = (1 - e^{-z})^{-1}$ allowing an equivalent interpretation, if required, linear discriminant analysis was adopted in this study.

4.2 The statistical methodology

Discriminant analysis can be viewed as a classification technique based on the computation of a similarity profile. The 2-group linear formulation $z = w_0 + \Sigma_{j=1}^{m} w_j x_j$, where w are the discriminant weights and x the m variable set, is theoretically justified only if certain statistical assumptions are met, namely, distinct groups, separate multivariate normality for the populations in the analysis and equality of dispersion matrices. However, the technique is quite robust with large samples, as used in this research (Pinches, 1980; Taffler, 1982).

Taffler (1982, pp. 350–51) points out how although in theory unequal covariance matrices indicate a quadratic formulation, a quadratic approach cannot normally be defended in practical application. None the less, because the database is a pooled cross-section and time series the problem of serial correlation may arise (Sargen, 1977, footnote 20). To correct for this and obtain an unbiased estimate of the true classification error rate the fitted model was derived in three stages using a jack-knife approach.

Jack-knife analysis is a method for reducing bias in an estimator by means of sample reuse and provides not just an unbiased, or nearly unbiased estimator, but also a measure of its variance. It also has the advantage of removing serial correlation. Miller (1974) provides a good review of the general approach. The three stages were as follows:

Stage 1: A stepwise Fisher linear discriminant approach was used to select the constituent model variables according to different criteria, discussed below, and to estimate the overall coefficient set $\{\bar{w}_j\}$.

Stage 2: An almost unbiased estimate of the true error rate was next determined via the hold-out procedure (U-method) of Lachenbruch (1967) and m (= total number of cases) jack-knifed coefficient sets $\{w_{-i,j}\}$ known as pseudo-values calculated where $-i$ denotes the deletion of the ith case.

Stage 3: The first order jack-knife coefficients were then finally estimated to provide the operational model by

$$\hat{w}_j = m\bar{w}_j - \frac{m-1}{m} \sum_{i=1}^{m} w_{-i,j}$$

The statistical significance of the jack-knifed coefficients is tested from the pseudo-values in the conventional manner using the Student t test with $m-1$ degrees of freedom.

4.3 Fitting the model

To arrive at a defensible and parsimonious set of measures to be used in stages 2 and 3 for the derivation of a final model, many different discriminant runs were undertaken. Concern was both with the selection of variables with appropriate discriminatory and statistical properties and also whether these measures were meaningful within the context of the exercise. The reification of the economic dimensions identified by the PCA was of particular value.

Initial analysis focused on identifying potential predictor variables. Forward and backward discriminant analysis was conducted on a large number of small arbitrarily drawn subsamples of the full RC and NRC data set to provide a list of discriminant measures to be used subsequently. Nineteen different variables with minimal missing data items appeared at least once in one of the models. Table 11.3 lists these together with their PCA classification from Table 11.2.

Table 11.3 Preliminary variable selection

PCA component	Variables
External indebtedness	D/GDP, NF/M,* C/GDP, D/X, DSR
Trade balance	B3/R, B3/M
Wealth	GDP/POP, D/POP, C/POP
Growth	GDP°, X°, DC°
External trade	M/GDP, X/GDP, INF
Monetary policy	DC/GDP
Level of reserves	R°, R/M

* Ringed variables are retained for detailed analysis, see text.

The problems of multicollinearity are often overlooked in discriminant analysis. When this exists between variables both the signs and the stability of the coefficients are suspect and there may be potential problems of sample bias arising (Pinches, 1980; Taffler, 1982). This motivated the retention of only relatively uncorrelated measures from Table 11.3 for further analysis and theoretical considerations led to the selection of the eight variables ringed in Table 11.3. The final variable selection decision was then made on the basis of the stability of discriminant weights, correctness of signs, variable contribution to the discriminatory power of the derived function, low level of Type I error (misclassification of an RC as an NRC), because of the differential error costs, and economic defensibility.

Coefficient stability was assessed by deriving different discriminant functions for different subsets of the eight variables over 13 different samples, each consisting of the rescheduling cases together with an equal size random sample of non-rescheduling countries. Standardised weights were examined and their coefficients of variation computed across the samples for each variable in each subset separately. It was conjectured that low stability, represented by a large coefficient of variation, might lead to poor outside sample performance of that variable, and thus was taken to justify, together with other considerations, exclusion of the measure from further analysis. A substantial and balanced (fairly equal) contribution of the individual variables to the discriminatory power of the function was also sought. Different methods are suggested in the literature for measuring this. Of these standardised coefficients, Mosteller–Wallace variable contributions, which represent the proportion of the Mahalanobis D^2 – distance between group centroids accounted for by each variable (see Taffler, 1982 for a discussion) and conditional-deletion F-values were computed for each of the different models derived. Variables with consistently low levels of discriminatory power were eliminated.

The final variable set consisted of four measures, namely, commitments per capita (C/POP), debt/exports (D/X), rate of change of inflation (INF) and domestic credit/gross domestic product (DC/GDP). The relative discriminatory importance of each of these variables to the power of the Fisher linear discriminant function derived from the complete RC and NRC samples is provided in Table 11.4, together with the coefficients of variation previously discussed. With the completion of stage 1 of the analysis, the Lachenbruch estimation procedure of stage 2 could be undertaken and the first order jack-knifed coefficient set finally determined to provide the operational model in stage 3. Each of these coefficients had calculated t statistics of >100 and differed little from the Fisher coefficients derived. Taffler (1984), adopting a similar jack-knife approach in the corporate bankruptcy area, also found similar results.

Because of the differential prior probabilities of group membership and the differential costs associated with the Type I and Type II errors (classifying a rescheduling country as non-rescheduling and vice versa) explicit consideration of both factors is necessary in deriving a classification decision rule. Based on the probability–cost (likelihood) ratio given by

$$l = \frac{p_1}{p_2} \times \frac{c_{12}}{c_{21}}$$

Table 11.4 The relative importance of the constituent model ratios

Ratio*	PCA dimension represented	Fisher standardised coefficients {$\bar{w}_i$}	Mosteller –Wallace contribution†	Conditional deletion F-value‡	Coefficient of variation of the standardised coefficients
C/POP	Wealth§	+0.801	20.7%	101.48	0.170
D/X	External indebtedness	+0.695	43.6%	97.374	0.063
INF	Inflation	−0.555	24.2%	54.433	0.079
DC/GDP	Monetary policy indicator	+0.397	11.5%	27.057	0.106

* The ratio transformations used in the model are respectively $\ln(1 + C/POP)$, $(1 + D/X)^{-1}$, $(CPT_t/CPI_{t-3}) − 1$, where CPI_t denotes the consumer price index in year t, and $(1 + DC/GDP)^{-1}$.
† The jack-knifed contribution figures were almost identical.
‡ All significant at $\infty < 0.001$.
§ This is also interpreted as the subjective assessment made by foreign lenders of a country's capacity to service debt (see text).

where p_1 and p_2 denote *a priori* determined probabilities of belonging to the RC and NRC groups respectively, c_{12} is the cost of misclassifying an RC as an NRC (Type I error) and c_{21} is the cost of misclassifying an NRC as an RC (Type II error), a Bayesian procedure provides for the determination of a cut-off point given by the distance from the midpoint between group centroids.

Since the main objective of the derived model is to measure economic performance, the weak year cases were added to the RC group to determine the *a priori* group membership probabilities. On this basis the odds ratio becomes 0.2:0.8 = 1:4, i.e. 20 per cent of country-year cases in the sample belonged to the rescheduling group, or were reported in the economic press as experiencing financial difficulties. Following Sargen (1977), a cost ratio of 3:1 is employed, resulting in

$$l = \frac{1}{4} \times \frac{3}{1} = \frac{3}{4}$$

and $\ln l = -0.288$. For operational convenience the discriminant function constant w_0 was then adjusted to incorporate this figure to provide a cut-off of zero.

4.4 Preliminary validation results

The unbiased classification matrix derived from applying the first order jack-knifed discriminant function on the basis of the above decision rule to the full data set is provided in Figure 11.1. Type I errors are 10 per cent and Type II errors 8.9 per cent. (Applying the Lachenbruch U-test to the original Fisher function of stage 1 resulted in an unchanged Type I error rate and two fewer Type II

		Classified as:		
		NRC	RC	Total
	NRC	575 (91.1%)	56 (8.9%)	631
Actual group membership:	RC	5 (10.0%)	45 (90.0%)	50

Figure 11.1   Unbiased classification matrix

errors.) These results compare favourably with those of earlier studies as summarised in Table 3 of Saini and Bates (1978). However, it should be noted that none of these report such 'almost unbiased' tests and more importantly, the key issue of interest is how well such models predict *future* reschedulings.

Considering the critical cut-off as a solvency threshold and applying the derived model *ex post* to all the available cases for each year between 1967 and 1978 indicates an average of 19.25 per cent of countries possessing an economic profile similar to the rescheduling sample. Such a similarity pattern can be interpreted as a necessary but not sufficient condition for overt financial difficulties when the probability–cost ratio is taken into account. As such the function can be viewed as an 'early warning' model (EWM), a description used from now on.

4.5 Interpretation of the early warning model

The variables included in the model can best be interpreted with respect to the principal component analysis results of Table 11.2. If the constituent elements of these measures are examined, it can be seen that seven different aggregates are present, namely, domestic credit, inflation rate, loan commitments, external (disbursed) debt, exports, gross domestic product and population. Considering the model variables in the order of Table 11.4 it will be noted first that commitments per capita (C/POP) is positively correlated with the wealth factor so labelled because of its highest loaded ratio (GDP/ POP). The other ratio highly correlated (positively) with this dimension is external debt per capita (D/POP) and this suggests, not surprisingly, that it is the richer countries that are able to borrow more. We thus have the proposition that the ratio C/POP may well be reflecting international banking sentiment about a country.

The debt to exports ratio (D/X) is loaded on the external indebtedness dimension on which the classical debt service ratio (DSR) is also partially loaded, although at a relatively low level. The importance of the debt to exports ratio in the model clearly indicates, probably not unexpectedly, that the risk of rescheduling is positively associated with the level of external borrowing. When borrowings increase, the higher proportion of non-concessional debt in the total leads to heavier debt service through increased interest charges and amortisation absorbing a greater share of export revenues. The ratio of domestic credit to gross domestic product (DC/GDP) is correlated with the monetary policy factor on which the ratio of money supply (Ml) to GDP has the highest loading. Both DC/GDP and the domestic price rate of change measure (INF), are positively correlated with rescheduling. This result confirms Brittain's (1977) finding that a high level of domestic credit is a source of overall external deficit.

It is interesting to consider why the DSR performed poorly in our study, a result which although paralleled by Mayo and Barrett (1978), who also found the D/X ratio superior, was not consistent with other researchers. Saini and Bates (1978) show that the statistical significance of the DSR in earlier studies might well have been due to their authors' upward adjustments of the numerator in rescheduling cases in an attempt to estimate *scheduled* debt service payments rather than actual payments. This they point out is not only likely to bias their results, but appears unwarranted in most cases as lagged explanatory variables are being used (footnote 14). Another reason for the ratio's lack of importance may relate to problems with the restriction of the numerator to debt service on long and medium-term public and publicly guaranteed debt alone through lack of data.

To summarise it can be seen that the model of country risk described here both assesses economic performance as reflected in monetary policy indicators (DC/GDP and INF) and debt servicing capacity as measured by the relative level of debt (D/X) and the capacity to secure new borrowings (C/POP). The measures of relative importance provided in Table 11.4, despite lack of consistency between the three methods used, indicate that the debt servicing capacity ratios make a greater contribution to the model than the monetary indicators.

5 TESTS OF THE EARLY WARNING MODEL

5.1 Data limitations

Unlike with corporate data, the quality of much of both debt related and non-debt LDC statistics is poor and as such the potential limitations of any models developed need to be recognised explicitly. To start with the available statistics on external debt are incomplete. The main source of debt data used to develop the model, the World Bank World Debt Tables, provide data, and commitment and debt service information relating only to public and public guaranteed debt with original maturity greater than one year with a lag of around 18 months. Whereas the Bank of International Settlements (BIS) series of external positions of international banks publishes short-term and private debt data with minimal lag such information is not a good proxy for external indebtedness of this nature for all LDCs as coverage is incomplete. Turning to non-debt data, we have already noted how our original variable set of 60, in the end, had to be restricted to 42 because of major gaps in data availability particularly among the smaller and poorer LDCs. In addition much of the non-debt data is subject to constant revision for some countries and may also be delayed. Potential comparability difficulties can also exist through definitional problems in certain instances (Saini and Bates, 1978, p. 7).

The International Economic Appraisal Service (IEAS) of The Economist Intelligence Unit Ltd (EIU) *inter alia* provides a large and timely standardised database of economic and financial information relating to most LDCs. It provides an extensive list of indicators, key statistics and ratios with series commencing in 1970 and is compiled by a team of professional economists and statisticians from private national as well as official and semi-official international sources. Where data is not available EIU staff estimates are provided. The database is continuously updated and would appear to be both more accurate and more timely than official sources. Care is also taken to ensure standardisation of data across countries in line with IFS and World Bank definitions etc. Also of particular relevance to us here is that short-term (one year) forecasts are made of key variables such as those used in the Early Warning Model.

Access to the IEAS database provides a reliable data source as a starting point with which to test the true *ex ante* predictive ability of the EWM and also to generate forecasts of debt servicing problems. However, it should be noted that in effect we are testing a joint hypothesis. This is both that the EWM has predictive ability *and* that the EIU generated statistics are an accurate assessment of the figures ultimately reported in the IFS and World Debt Tables, the basis on which the model was developed. Strictly speaking there is also the additional problem that since country variables are updated as better information becomes available there is difficulty in reconstructing the true foresightful position for earlier years. For example, the first EIU short-term estimates of data for 1982 used to assess the likelihood of rescheduling in 1983 were available at the end of 1981 and these will have been modified throughout 1982 and into 1983.

The question is, which set of estimates should be used? Tests below draw on the IEAS database as at the end of 1983 on the basis that in practice the EIU estimates halfway into the year being forecast appear to match fairly closely the official statistics eventually appearing up to two years later.

5.2 Tests of model performance

The ultimate test of such a model as derived here is its ability to predict subsequent cases of formal rescheduling. Of particular interest is how well the function works outside the original set from which it was developed and particularly its robustness to the changes in the economic environment since it was developed. Although as we have seen Saini and Bates (1978) and Feder *et al.* (1981) argue that options other than a formal rescheduling may be available to countries facing severe debt service problems which serve as proxies and also some reschedulings may be 'voluntary' in nature and not for balance of payment reasons, the event predicted by the EWM was formal rescheduling. This was both because of the problems in identifying such situations without bias and also because formal rescheduling was the definition of the dependent variable used to develop the model.

The predictive ability of the model was tested with respect to all cases of formal rescheduling that could be identified as taking place between the beginning of 1979 and the end of 1983 among the 78 LDCs followed by the EIU. Countries with negative z-scores in year t, termed as possessing an 'at risk' profile, which rescheduled in year $t + 1$ were correct classifications, those which did not apparently reschedule were Type II errors and countries rescheduling in year $t + 1$ without a negative z-score in year t, i.e. not considered at risk, were our Type I errors. All told there were $78 \times 5 = 390$ case years. Seventy-three rescheduling cases were identified during the five-year period with 64 per cent occurring in 1982 and 1983. Table 11.4 lists summary results by year and all cases are provided in the appendix with sources together with an indication of whether the model correctly assessed such rescheduling propensities in advance or not. In total 50 of the rescheduling cases (69 per cent) were correctly predicted, which contrasts with the 90 per cent within sample hit rate of Figure 11.1, a not unsatisfactory performance considering the lack of population stationarity since 1978. Interestingly enough Table 11.5

Table 11.5 Early warning model prediction results by year

Year of rescheduling	1979	1980	1981	1982	1983	Total
Correct predictions	4	5	7	17	17	50
Type I errors	3	2	5	7	6	23
Type II errors	16	17	15	15	20	83
Total cases	78	78	78	78	78	390

provides little evidence to suggest the model performs less well further away from the time frame of the original sample.

In practical application the utility of the EWM z-scores is enhanced by ranking to monitor relative country performance over time in the manner of Taffler (1984) with corporate data. In addition, deciles of the population in which a country's constituent ratios lie in each year separately are used to construct a financial 'strengths and weaknesses' profile to highlight its salient characteristics.

5.3 The statistical significance of the model

To test whether the EWM has true predictive ability the standard significance test for sample proportions is used, namely, $z = (p - \pi)/\sqrt{[\pi(1 - \pi)/n]}$, where z is the standardised normal deviate, p the sample proportion and π the probability of chance classification. Considering Table 11.5 and pooling the five-year results let the rescheduling event be denoted by R and an at risk profile by AR. The $\Pr(R_{t+1}/AR_t) = p_1 = 0.38$ and $\Pr(\bar{R}_{t+1}/\bar{A}\bar{R}_t) = P_2 = 0.91$. The respective chance classification probabilities π_1 and π_2 are 0.19 and 0.81. Then testing the null hypotheses: $p_1 = \pi_1$ and $p_2 = \pi_2$ against the alternate hypotheses $p_1 > \pi_1$ and $p_2 > \pi_2$ with $n_1 = 133$ and $n_2 = 257$, we are forced to reject the null hypotheses at $\alpha = 0.001$ with $z_1 = 5.59$ and $z_2 = 4.09$. $\Pr(z > 3.3) < 0.001$, one-tailed test. Thus we may conclude the Early Warning Model has true *ex ante* predictive ability and inter-temporal validity well outside its training sample time frame despite the major shocks to the international economic system since its development.

5.4 Discussion of the error cases

Five countries appear more than once as Type I errors: Ecuador, Guyana, Liberia, Senegal and Venezuela. Ecuador and Venezuela, both rescheduling in 1982 and 1983, are substantial oil producers and have been badly hit by falling oil revenues. Liberia had a coup in 1980 and as a result loan commitments by international lenders dried up leading to short-term liquidty problems and the continuous rescheduling between 1980 and 1983. In this case also the quality of the monetary aggregates reported may be questionable because of the use of the dollar as the main currency. In the case of Senegal the high z-scores in 1980 and 1981 may again reflect a measure of doubt about the validity of the monetary variables given its unexpectedly low inflation rates and substantial receipts of bilateral aid. However, the risk rating based on 1982 data did herald the 1983 rescheduling. All other countries provided single Type I errors. Errors of note are Mexico in 1982, although the Early Warning Model was in good company(!) and its 1982 and 1983 z-scores are substantially at risk, and Nigeria, both major oil producers. It is probably fair comment that the model has difficulty in handling particularly oil-based and generally single commodity dependent economies where volatile world prices can lead to serious financial problems within a very short period. In addition, we may speculate that the performance of the model might be improved were short-term and private debt information available.

Turning to the 83 Type II errors, countries with rescheduling profiles that did not reschedule, three fairly arbitrary groups can be identified, namely: (1) countries predominantly dependent on foreign aid and concessional lending at low interest rates and long maturities: Bangladesh, Burma, Egypt, Ethiopia, Ghana, India, Israel, Nepal, Pakistan and Tarzania, which in total account for 38 cases. (2) 'Over-extended economies': Argentina, Brazil, Chile, Panama, Peru, Portugal, Uruguay, Yugoslavia. These countries had almost continuous access to new loans over the period resulting in a rapid increase in foreign debt and/or had made use of IMF standby facilities. The eventual need for formal rescheduling was generally only postponed as the entries of most of these countries in the appendix at some stage highlights. These countries account for a further 21 Type II errors. (3) Countries characterised by political instability, coups, etc.: Ghana, Iran, Syrian Arab Republic and Uganda. However, Iran is a distinct case as although arrears in debt occurred immediately after the coup, reserves were adequate eventually to cover all debt service payments.

6   A COMPARISON WITH BANKER JUDGEMENT

6.1   The 'bankers know best' approach

Results for the comparative performance of the systems operated by commercial banks are not available. However, a good proxy for banker judgement is provided by the *Institutional Investor* country credit inex described in Section 2.1 above (Feder and Ross, 1982). The II credit ratings are provided on a scale of 0–100 but they cannot be used directly as no *explicit* association with any predicted event is drawn. Thus to test the ability of the index to predict rescheduling, the event of interest and used as a proxy for default, compared with the EWM, the following procedure was adopted:

Stage 1: Countries common to both databases were identified (II ranks developed Western economies, Comecon members and Middle Eastern oil producers as well).

Stage 2: The September 1979 and September 1980 II credit rating scores were used in conjunction with the list of 1980 and 1981 rescheduling cases of the appendix to determine an appropriate cut-off.

Stage 3: This threshold was then employed to predict 1982 and 1983 reschedulings on the basis of the September 1981 and September 1982 II scores.

Stage 4: The results were compared with the performance of the EWM on the same restricted country set.

The September ratings are used as these are the last scores available to external analysts before the beginning of the year for which 'predictions' are made even though banking respondents are surveyed in the two previous months. As such it should be noted the opinions surveyed may be formed up to six months before the start of the year in question.

6.2   Test results

Examination of the six 1980 and ten 1981 rescheduling country credit rating scores provided by the II in its preceding September issues shows a distinct cut-off at a value of 30.0 pooling all 111 country scores. On this basis Type I errors are minimised at 12.5 per cent (two cases) for a relatively small number of Type II errors (17). Table 11.6 shows the prediction results for 1982 and 1983 using this

Table 11.6   Performance comparison of the II credit worthiness index and EWM

	1980†	*1981†*	*1982*	*1983*	*Total*
		Rescheduling year t*			
Correct predictions					
II	4	10	13	10	37 (64%)
EWM	4	7	15	15	41 (71%)
Type I errors					
II	2	—	8	11	21 (36%)
EWM	2	3	6	6	17 (29%)
Type II errors					
II	10	7	11	16	44 (54%)
EWM	15	12	10	15	52 (56%)
Sample size	55	56	61	64	236

Notes:
* Prediction of rescheduling in year t is made on the basis of year $t - 1$ data
† The 1980 and 1981 II results are fitted to minimise the Type I and Type II errors.

threshold value with the EWM results for the same sample of countries provided for comparison purposes.

Whereas the II results for 1980 and 1981 used to fit the threshold dominate the EWM results this position is reversed in 1982 and 1983 when the two approaches to country risk analysis are compared on equal terms. Pooling all the four year results the EWM has a correct hit rate of 71 per cent compared with 64 per cent for the II index. Restricting the results to 1982 and 1983 alone provides percentages of 71 per cent and 55 per cent respectively. Similarly, considering the Type II error rates, an important consideration in the practical application of such approaches, the overall 56 per cent figure for the EWM falls to 46 per cent considering 1982 and 1983 alone whereas the II percentage stays at 54 per cent.

When the 1982 and 1983 March II ratings for the rescheduling year are substituted for those of the previous September to allow for revision of interviewee judgements, the II results are virtually unchanged with the only difference one less Type I error in 1982 (Costa Rica).

6.3   Discussion of results

Table 11.7 lists the respective Type I errors of the II index and EWM applied to the same data set and shows some lack of agreement with only 9 out of the 29 country year cases in the table misclassified by one or other or both of the approaches common. Of note both the II index and EWM were unable to forecast the recent major reschedulings by Mexico, Nigeria and Venezuela. Conversely the II credit worthiness index was able to pick up Liberia in three years out of four, missed in all years by the discriminant model. On the other hand, the II index did not predict many of the recent large Latin American reschedulings forecast by the EWM, namely: Argentina (twice), Brazil (twice), Chile, Costa Rica, Peru (twice) and Uruguay. Other recent reschedulings of note similarly missed are the Philippines and Yugoslavia.

In fact in some cases the II rating remains quite robust even to the event of rescheduling itself, for example Venezuela was ranked 6th out of 61 countries in September 1981, 5th out of 64 in both September 1982 and in March 1983 and only fell to 15th position out of 64 in September 1983 with a score of 43.4, well above the threshold of 30.0. In this case it should be noted similar behaviour was also exhibited by the EWM. However, this latter does not apply to Brazil, which was ranked 19th in September 1981, 14th in September 1982 and 18th in September 1983, nor Argentina which was ranked 14th in September 1981, 29th in September 1982 and its rating only went below the cut-off in September 1983. Likewise the major Mexico rescheduling commencing in August 1982 appeared to take the banking community by surprise on the basis of the II ratings, in September 1982 it was still ranked 11th with a healthy score of 54.7, although its rating fell to 36.9 in March 1983 with ranked position 24, albeit still quite well above the threshold value of 30.0.

The relative performance of the two approaches to country risk analysis is somewhat unexpected. *A priori* it is surprising that a simple four variable discriminant model derived from economic data of arguable quality should demonstrate good predictive ability several years after it was developed despite the major structural changes occurring in the environment in which it is applied. Secondly it is possibly even more interesting that a rating system based on the pooled knowledge, up-to-date information and collective wisdom of up to 100 banks does not appear able to outperform the statistical approach.

Table 11.7 Comparison of II and EWM Type I errors

Rescheduling year

1980		1981		1982		1983	
II	EWM	II	EWM	II	EWM	II	EWM
Liberia	Liberia	—	Bolivia	Argentina	—	Argentina	—
—	Sierra Leone	—	Liberia	Brazil	—	Brazil	—
Yugoslavia		—	Senegal	Costa Rica	—	Chile	—
				Ecuador	Ecuador	Ecuador	Ecuador
				—	Honduras	Ivory Coast	Ivory Coast
				—	Liberia	—	Liberia
				Mexico	Mexico	Morocco	Morocco
				Peru	—	Nigeria	Nigeria
				—	Senegal	Peru	—
				Uruguay	—	Philippines	—
				Venezuela	Venezuela	Venezuela	Venezuela
						Yugoslavia	Yugoslavia

However, perhaps such results may be less unexpected than they at first appear. Firstly there is considerable evidence in related decision areas such as corporate bankruptcy prediction (Taffler, 1982; Altman, 1983, ch. 4) that appropriately developed discriminant models *can* maintain their predictive ability for many years subsequent to their development despite substantial changes in the environment in which they are applied. This empirical observation may partly reflect the 'holistic' nature of multivariate statistical models as a class. In addition what we may have been finding is not that the model variables taken together become less important discriminators *per se* but that their distributions change leading to lower z-scores and more countries at risk (and rescheduling) as the economic environment worsens.

On the other hand, there is an extensive literature (surveyed in for example, Wright 1980; Taffler, 1981) explaining why the subjective judgements of decision-makers acting as 'intuitive statisticians' may be problematical and potentially subject to bias. This tendency may be somewhat reduced by using a consensus judgement (Goldberg, 1970) as in the II case, but difficulties can still arise. In addition, such opinions and feelings may not be in accord with what bankers actually do.

We must also consider that the *Institutional Investor* rating system might actually be measuring something else than banker views on a country's creditworthiness, namely: 'banking sentiment' about a particular country which may be related to other factors than likelihood of rescheduling. The high ratings given to Latin American countries in many cases, for example, may reflect more familiarity through geographical and ethnocentric association with the United States, and the large sums already lent, rather than their intrinsic creditworthiness *per se*.

7   SUMMARY AND REMARKS

This chapter reviews an 'early warning' discriminant model (EWM) to evaluate country risk and highlight rescheduling propensity that is in operational use. The function derived consists of four variables, too measuring debt servicing capacity directly and the other two monetary policy indicators. Adopting 'a proof of the pudding is in the eating' approach performance was evaluated across the five-year period (1979–83) subsequent to the development of the EWM. This was found to exhibit true *ex ante* predictive ability in a statistical sense and 69 per cent of the 73 rescheduling cases in this period were correctly anticipated at a cost of a very manageable number of Type II cases. A large number of the latter were found to be countries dependent on international aid to avoid forced rescheduling. The model appeared quite robust to the major structural changes in the economic environment since it was developed.

Whereas the function appeared relevant to most LDCs its use in practice indicated problems with certain oil producers and some countries experiencing predominantly short-term debt problems. To some extent, also, rescheduling by single commodity based economies where a collapse in world price levels often leads to immediate economic difficulties proved less predictable than in other cases. In addition, it should be noted the EWM is not designed to predict the effects of political coups which are often followed by a meeting of the Paris Club (Hardy, 1981, p. 34). Because of the nature of its component variables the model can best be viewed as measuring a country's underlying solvency more than its short-term liquidity position.

Methods used by bankers to assess country risk were reviewed and attention drawn to their preference for qualitative and judgemental checklist systems. In an attempt to assess the predictive ability of conventional approaches the widely respected *Institutional Investor* credit rating index which provides a consensus measure of banker views on the creditworthiness of countries was used. Results were, however, disappointing with unexpectedly high prediction error rates and the good credit ratings of many countries unaffected even by the rescheduling event itself.

None the less it should be noted that despite the superficial attractions of basing a decision on mechanical application of such a model, the real benefits of such a systematic evaluative tool come not from its being a substitute for the skills and long experience of the loan officer but only as another input into his very complex, judgemental task. We may also speculate on the benefits of using a measure of banker judgement such as the *Institutional Investor* index as a variable in such discriminant models in future.

One final point relates to the nature of the EWM which is essentially a short-term prediction tool based on a pattern similarity approach. If it were possible to forecast the component measures accurately beyond a one year time horizon then its operational utility could be enhanced correspondingly.

ACKNOWLEDGEMENT

The authors wish to thank Philip Robbins, consultant, The Economist Intelligence Unit Ltd, for his help with testing the model and Dr Derek Kent-Smith, director, for allowing access to the IEAS database.

APPENDIX

Less developed country reschedulings 1979–83

1979	1980	1981	1982	1983
Guyana*	Liberia*	Bolivia*	Argentina	Argentina
Jamaica*	Nicaragua	Jamaica	Bolivia	Bolivia
Peru	Sierra Leone*	Liberia*	Brazil	Brazil
Sudan	Togo	Madagascar*	Costa Rice	Chile
Togo*	Turkey	Nicaragua	Ecuador*	Costa Rica
Turkey	Yugoslavia	Pakistan	Guyana*	Ecuador*
Zaire	Zaire	Senegal*	Hondurus*	Guyana
		Sudan	Liberia*	Ivory Coast*
		Togo*	Madagascar	Jamaica
		Turkey	Malawi	Liberia*
		Uganda	Mexico*	Malawi
		Zaire	Nicaragua	Morocco*
		Zambia	Pakistan	Nicarague
			Peru	Nigeria*
			Senegal*	Peru
			Sierra Leone	Philippines
			Sudan	Senegal
			Togo	Sudan
			Turkey	Togo
			Uganda	Venezuela*
			Uruguay	Yugoslavia
			Venezuela*	Zaire
			Zaire	Zambia
			Zambia	

Notes:
(i) * Denotes misclassification by model.
(ii) The only other non-Communist bloc country identified as rescheduling during the period was C.A.R. in 1981 and 1982. Lack of data precluded its coverage.

Sources:
Euromoney (August 1982), p. 21. *World Debt Tables* (World Bank, 1982), p. viii. *External Debt of Developing Countries* (OECD, 1982). Quarterly Economic Reviews (*Economist Intelligence Unit*, London), various issues. Press comment.

References

ABBASSI, B. and RUSSELL, A. H. (1980) 'A Mathematical Programming Method of Discriminant Analysis', City University Business School, Working Paper No. 19.

ALTMAN, E. I. (1983) *Corporate Financial Distress* (New York: John Wiley % Sons).

ANGELONI, I. and SHORT, B. K. (1980) 'The Impact of Country Risk Assessment on Eurocurrency Interest Spreads: a Cross section Analysis', International Monetary Fund, document DM/80/35.

AVRAMOVIC, D. *et al.* (1964) *Economic Growth and External Debt* (Baltimore: Johns Hopkins Press).

BALL, C. A. and TSCHOEGL, A. E. (1982) 'The Decision to Establish a Foreign Branch Bank or Subsidiary: an Application of Binary Classification Procedures', *Journal of Financial and Quantitative Analysis*, vol. 17, pp. 411–424.

BANCE, N. (1978) 'How Our New Rating System Works', *Euromoney*, October, pp. 129–31.

BLASK, J. K. (1978) 'A Survey of Country Evaluation Systems in Use', in S. H. Goodman (ed.), *Financing and Risk in Developing Countries*, pp. 65–70 (New York: Praeger Publishers).

BRITTAIN, W. H. B. (1977) 'Developing Countries' External Debt and the Private Banks, *Banca Nazionale del Lavoro Quarterly Review*, December, pp. 365–80.

BURTON, F. N. and INOUE, H. (1983) 'Country Risk Evaluation Methods: a Survey of Systems in Use', *The Banker*, January, pp. 41–43.

EFRON, B. (1975) 'The Efficiency of Logistic Regression Compared to Normal Discriminant Analysis', *Journal of the American Statistical Association*, vol. 70, pp. 892–8.

FEDER, G. and JUST, R. (1977) A Study of Debt Servicing Capacity Applying Logit Analysis', *Journal of Development Economics*, vol. 4, pp. 25–39.

FEDER, G. and Just, R. (1980) 'A Model for Analysing Lenders' Perceived Default Risk', *Applied Economics*, vol. 12, pp. 125–44.

FEDER, G., JUST, R. and ROSS, K. (1981) 'Projecting Debt Servicing Capacity of Developing Countries', *Journal of Financial and Quantitative Analysis*, vol. 16, 651–70.

FEDER, G. and ROSS, K. (1982) 'Risk Assessments and Risk Premiums in the Eurodollar Market', *Journal of Finance*, vol. 37, pp. 679–91.

FISK, C. and RIMLINGER, F. (1979) 'Nonparametric Estimates of LDC Repayment Prospects', *Journal of Finance*, vol. 34, pp. 429–35.

FRANK, C. R. Jr. and CLINE, R. (1971) 'Measuring Debt Servicing Capacity: An Application of Discriminant Analysis', *Journal of International Economics*, vol. 1, pp. 327–44.

GOLDBERG, L. R. (1970) 'Man versus Model of Man: a Rationale, plus some Evidence for a Method of Improving on Clinical Inferences', *Psychological Bulletin*, vol. 73, pp. 422–32.

GOODMAN, S. H. (1977) 'How the Big US Banks Really Evaluate Sovereign Risks', *Euromoney*, February, pp. 105–110.

HARDY, G. (1981) 'Rescheduling Developing Country Debts', *The Banker*, July, pp. 33–8.

LACHENBRUCH, P. A. (1967) 'An Almost Unbiased Method of Obtaining Confidence Intervals for the Probability of Misclassification in Discriminant Analysis', *Biometrics*, vol. 23, pp. 639–45.

LACHENBRUCH, P. A. (1974) 'Discriminant Analysis when the Initial Samples are Misclassified. II: Non-random Misclassification Models,' *Technometrics*, vol. 16, pp. 419–24.

LACHENBRUCH, P. A., SNEERINGER, C. A. and REVO, L. T. (1973) 'Robustness of the Linear and Quadratic Discriminant Function to Certain Types of Non-normality', *Communications in Statistics*, vol. 1, pp. 39–56.

MAYO, A. L. and BARRETT, A. G. (1978) 'An Early Warning Model for Assessing Developing Country Risk', in S. H. Goodman (ed.), *Financing and Risk in Developing Countries*, pp. 81–7. (New York: Praeger Publishers).

MERRILL, J. (1982) 'Country Risk Analysis', *Columbia Journal of World Business*, vol. 17, no. 1, pp. 88–91.

MILLER, R. G. (1974) 'The Jack-knife – a Review', *Biometrika*, vol. 6, pp. 1–15.

NAGY, P. (1979) *Country Risk. How to Assess, Quantify and Monitor It* (London: Euromoney Publications Ltd).

NIE, N. H., HULL, C. H., JENKINS, J. G. STEINBRENNER, K. and BENT, D. H. (1975) *Statistical Package for the Social Sciences* (London: McGraw-Hill).

ORGANISATION FOR ECONOMIC CO-OPERATION AND DEVELOPMENT (1974) *Debt Problems of Developing Countries*. Mimeograph. Paris.

O'NEILL, T. J. (1980) 'The General Distribution of the Error Rate of a Classification Procedure with Application to Logistic Regression Discrimination', *Journal of the American Statistical Association*, vol. 75, pp. 154–60.

PINCHES, G. E. (1980) 'Factors Influencing Classification Results from Multiple Discriminant Analysis', *Journal of Business Research*, vol. 8, pp. 429–56.

PRESS, S. J. and WILSON, S. (1978) Chosing between Logistic Regression and Discriminant Analysis', *Journal of the American Statistical Association*, vol. 73, pp. 699–705.

ROBINSON, J. N. (1981) 'Is it Possible to Assess Country Risk?' *The Banker*, January, pp. 71–9.

SAINI, K. and BATES, P. (1978) 'Statistical Techniques for Determining Debt-servicing Capacity for Developing Countries: Analytical Review of the Literature and Further Empirical Results', Federal Reserve Bank of New York, Research Paper No. 7818. (An updated and much shortened version of the paper is published as: 'Survey of the Quantitative Approaches to Country Risk Analysis', *Journal of Banking and Finance*, vol. 8 (1984), Spring.)

SARGEN, N. (1977) 'Economic Indicators and Country Risk Appraisal', *Economic Review of the Federal Reserve Bank of San Francisco*, Fall, pp. 19–35.

TAFFLER, R. J. (1981) 'Improving Man's Ability to Use Accounting Information: a Cognitive Synegesis', City University Business School, Working Paper No. 32.

TAFFLER, R. J. (1982) Forecasting Company Failure in the UK Using Discriminant Analysis and Financial Ratio Data', *Journal of the Royal Statistical Society*, Series A, vol. 145, pp. 342–58.

TAFFLER, R. J. (1984) 'Empirical Models for Monitoring of UK Corporations', *Journal of Banking and Finance*, vol. 8, Spring.

THOMPSON, J. K. (1981) 'The Poor Man's Guide to Country Risk', *Euromoney*, July, pp. 182–9.

WRIGHT, W. F. (1980) 'Cognitive Information Processing Biases: Implications for Producers and Users of Financial Information', *Decision Sciences*, vol. 11, pp. 284–98.

Comments on 'Country Risk: A Model for Predicting Debt Servicing Problems in Developing Countries

Roy Batchelor

The chapter by Abassi and Taffler reports heroic acts of econometrics performed on a heroic scale. To the best of my knowledge this study represents, both in terms of methodology and in terms of the range of countries and indicators covered, the state of the art in applying the techniques of corporate bankruptcy and analysis popularised by Altman (1968, 1983) to the analysis and forecasting of sovereign debt rescheduling. Since I am very much in sympathy with the authors observations concerning the need to supplement the (generally biased and over-optimistic) subjective judgements of risk made by individuals, with some more objectively determined measures, it should be taken as read that none of the comments I am about to make in any way absolve practising international bankers from their duty to take seriously the lessons of this chapter. My comments are, in fact, directed specifically at answering questions which a practitioner might have, concerning the analysis presented in the chapter. First, how robust and reliable are the statistical techniques used by the authors? Second, to what extent is the information provided by this type of analysis useful in taking decisions concerning the pricing and distribution of lending?

The authors give one sort of answer to the first question, when they compare predicted reschedulings with actual reschedulings in the out-of-sample period 1979–83. Although less than half of all reschedulings were predicted, their early warning model performed better than the judgemental ratings of the *Institutional Investor*. Presumably, if the model had been updated, so as to incorporate data from 1979–82, say, in predicting the events of 1983, the performance would be better still. While this statistical evidence of reliability is reassuring, I would be happier if there was also evidence of a consistent pattern of economic sense underpinning the model. Discriminant analysis of the kind undertaken in the chapter amounts to 'measurement without theory' par excellence. The fact that certain variables – in this instance, the domestic credit/GDP rate, the inflation rate, per capita new debt and the ratio of existing debt to exports – are correlated with loan performance does not help us answer questions concerning the mechanics of rescheduling and policies to improve that performance. Should we infer that any policy which promises to reduce one or other of these ratios will strengthen the economy and reduce the rescheduling risk? Will the policy really be as efficacious in one country as another? Is rescheduling typically due to economic developments in the borrowing country alone?

If it is true that policies towards debt–service ratios will prevent, and hence are substitutes for, rescheduling, then this is good news for the borrowing country, but rather bad news for the discriminant analysis. On the one hand, it means that countries faced with a particular debt servicing problem have a large range of alternatives to rescheduling – they may restructure the debt, may impose exchange controls, and so on. On the other hand, such economies will not be identified in the discriminant analysis as facing any particular problems in repaying their loans. The use of the rescheduling event as an indicator of distress is, in this sense, a very crude device, and alternative indexes of balance of payments difficulties should, perhaps, be considered.

Regarding the scope of the present study, my feeling is that as researchers on patterns of growth and development have found it useful to distinguish certain types of economy (Chenery and Syrquin, 1975) – large, potentially self-sufficient, units; small open units; 'island' economies, monocultural economies – so it would have been useful in this study to try to develop separate discriminant functions for subgroups of the large set of economies considered. Looking at the set of 'misses' of the early warning model (Table 6), for example, does seem to suggest a certain weakness with regard to small countries. It may be that there would have been so few rescheduling cases within such groups in the pre-1977 period as to leave the analysis with very few degrees of freedom, but the greater number of cases in 1982 and 1983 should make this feasible when the authors update their work.

While the authors have been over ambitious in hoping to find a single theory of rescheduling in all countries, I feel that in framing the theory itself they have been overly restrictive. Although the list of variables considered in the initial factor analysis is large, it none the less covers only half of the rescheduling story. It treats rescheduling as if it were invariably an 'involuntary' decision resulting from some economic failure on the part of the borrower. Now, several reschedulings have reflected a better-than -expected, rather than a averse-than-expected, performance by the borrower, so that rescheduling 'demand' may be voluntary as well as involuntary. Moreover, rescheduling is a joint decision involving not only the borrowing country but also the lending bank. The balance sheet positions of the international banking system, the level of interest rates, and the size of current spreads relative to those obtaining at the time of the initial loan – all these 'supply' factors will in practice determine the extent, timing and terms of a rescheduling.

One problem in integrating such factors into the discriminant analysis is, of course, that they are to some extent endogenous, the bad debts and spreads being themselves a reflection of current rescheduling activity. However, the fact that quantities and prices are determined simultaneously has not inhibited econometric analysis of other, more conventional, markets, and I see no reason why rescheduling and repricing of loans should not similarly be treated as the result of forces of supply and demand.

These remarks all concern the detail of the way in which the discriminant analysis has been conducted. My final comment concerns its interpretation, and indeed the interpretation of any discriminant analysis however well performed. It is simply this. Discriminant analysis at best attaches a measure of 'risk' to each actual and potential borrowing country. This measure may be of a 0–1 kind (rescheduling not probable/probable) or it may be a continuous 'rating' based on the distance of the country in question from the critical rescheduling surface. However, these measures reflect only the risk characteristics of the individual country. From the point of view of the practical banker, however, this is not enough. What matters for the country composition of international lending, and the spreads asked for each loan, is not the overall riskiness of the borrower, but the extent to which the risk is diversifiable. In deciding on which of two equally risky countries should be assigned marginal funds, a bank should prefer that one which is less like its set of existing borrowers, and which will contribute less to the riskiness of the portfolio. In pricing a loan to a particular country, a bank should look not at the intrinsic riskiness of the venture, but at whether this risk can or cannot be hedged by other parts of the loan portfolio. The information necessary for making these decisions relates to the expected covariances between economic performances of all pains of borrowing countries, not (only) the individual country variances. This is not delivered by the discriminant analysis, and this may go some way to explaining why bankers ratings of countries will in general differ from their risks of rescheduling as revealed by such analysis. Consequently I am not sure about how valid it is to assume that countries with low credit ratings in the *Institutional Investor* survey are 'rescheduling cases'. A country could be low-risk but have an economic performance highly correlated with LDCs in general, making it a safe investment for the bank's international portfolio. Conversely, a country might look very fragile, in terms of debt service capacity, but be sufficiently 'different' to attract hedge funds from banks; many monocultural economies fall into this category. In short, we do not get from discriminant analysis the sort of information necessary to engage in effective international portfolio analysis. While the present chapter is, as I have indicated, admirable of its kind, I look forward to extensions which will yield results more immediately relevant to the investment decisions of banks.

References

CHENERY, N. B. and SYRQUIN, M. (1975) *Patterns of Development* (Oxford University Press).

ALTMAN, E. (1968) 'Financial Ratios, Discriminant Analysis and the Prediction of Corporate Bankruptcy' *Journal of Finance*, vol. 23(4), pp. 589–609.

ALTMAN, E. (1983) *Corporate Financial Distress: A Complete Guide to Predicting, Avoiding and Dealing with Bankruptcy* (New York: Wiley).

Index

Abassi, B. 14, 15, 187, 195, 221, 224
adjustment 3, 6, 33–7, 41, 43–61, 69, 75–8
Alchine, A. A. 90, 103
Altman, E. I. 195, 218, 221–4, 227
American Banker 74, 75
Amex Bank 29
amortisation 5, 58, 59, 64, 66
amortisation/debt ratio 192, 193
Andreades, A. 133–4
Anderson, R. B. 57, 60
Angeloni, I. 192, 221
anti-inflationary 24, 34, 60
Argentina 1, 21–5, 29, 41, 72, 73, 147, 158, 216
austerity 24, 25
Avramovic, D. 158, 161, 193, 221

Bagehot, W. 13, 28, 93, 103, 108, 141, 144, 146, 158, 161, 167, 174
Ball, C. A. 202, 221
Bance, N. 221
Banco Ambrosiano 150, 151
Bank America 75
Bank of England 31, 84, 85, 115, 144, 149, 168, 179
Bank of England Act 113, 114
bank run 12, 13, 14, 16, 28, 116, 171, 173–6
Bank for International Settlements (BIS) 51, 61, 73, 147, 148, 150, 156, 159, 181, 210
Banker's Magazine 75, 111
Bankers Trust 75
Bankhaus Herstatt 150
Banking School 113
Barrett, A. G. 193, 209, 222
Barro, R. 109, 111
Batchelor, R. 14, 15, 17, 109, 116, 118, 134, 137, 138, 176, 183, 224
Bates, P. 193, 194, 202, 209–11, 222
Beenstock, M. 12–14, 133, 134, 167, 184, 186
benefits 7, 85, 86, 87, 89, 92, 105, 123
private benefit 7, 85, 105
social benefit 7, 85, 105
Bernanke, B. S. 118, 134
Blanchard, O. J. 176, 183

Blask, J. K. 190, 221
Bloomfield, A. I. 103
Bordo, M. 102, 103
borrowers 6, 11, 33–9, 61, 70, 72–4, 76–9, 122, 155, 226
borrowing countries 2, 6, 34, 38, 43, 58, 61, 62, 70, 76, 130, 131, 142, 157, 158, 225–7
external borrowing 121, 208
Brazil 1, 3–5, 21–9, 38, 42–4, 46, 50, 57–67, 72, 74, 147, 155, 156, 158, 165, 218
Bretton Woods 7, 8, 58, 60, 61, 83, 84, 87, 95, 98, 100, 105, 107, 114, 115, 119, 122, 123, 132, 133
Britain (UK) 28, 31, 70, 73, 83–6, 88, 110, 127, 155, 168
British banks 190
Brittain, W. H. B. 209, 221
Bruner, K. 90, 99, 102, 103
Bundesbank 77
Burns, A. R. 108, 111
Burton, F. N. 189, 221

Capie, F. 183
capital market 12, 13, 14, 24, 58, 170, 176, 187
efficient capital market 168, 169, 174, 176, 181, 184
Cargill, R. F. 144, 145, 161
catastrophe theory 13, 116, 175, 176
central bank 2, 3, 9, 28, 35, 41–4, 52, 66, 71, 73, 88, 93, 94, 96, 98, 100, 114, 119, 123, 127, 129, 130, 136, 139, 143, 149, 152, 155, 168, 179, 182
Chase Manhattan 27, 75, 181
Chenery, N. B. 227
Citibank 27, 77
Citicorp 75
Cline, W. R. 120–2, 134, 139, 192, 221
collateral 11, 44, 127, 130, 158, 159
collective choice 84, 89, 90, 107
commercial banks 2, 4–6, 10, 11, 32–9, 41–4, 47–50, 53–5, 58, 69, 142, 144, 145, 156, 160
commercial bank lending 142, 160
commercial bank loan 120

commodity standard 83, 87, 90, 92
  commodity reserve 95
contagion effect 116, 117, 136
Continental Illinois 75, 136, 165, 168
Cooke, P. W. 161
Cooper, R. H. 107, 111
cost 2, 7–9, 14, 21–4, 33, 34, 38, 42–5,
  55, 72, 83, 84, 86, 87, 89, 90, 92–4,
  123
  information cost 157
  private cost 7, 105
  resource cost 9, 88, 95, 127
  social cost 7, 43, 44, 54, 86, 93, 105,
  178
  transaction cost 42, 89
counter-cyclical flows 156–64
country risk 14, 15, 35, 187–93, 209,
  216, 219, 224
creditors 6, 26–8, 38, 47, 59, 72, 73,
  76–8
  creditor banks 2, 25, 27
  creditor countries 21, 24, 25, 57, 77,
  153, 157
Crockett, A. 133, 134
currency 27, 47, 83, 85–7, 95, 97
  currency school 113, 114
  domestic currency 154
  foreign currency 145, 154

Dale, R. 151, 161
debasement 83
debt 6, 9, 11, 14, 15, 23, 25–9, 31,
  33–6, 40, 41, 45, 52, 53, 59, 62, 64,
  69, 72, 73, 77, 79, 147, 158, 209
  debt problem 1–5, 12, 16, 21, 22, 31
  debt restructuring 158, 225
  debt service 2, 15, 21, 23–5, 34, 35,
  37, 52, 54, 72, 73, 116, 165, 187,
  193, 202, 210, 211, 224
  debt service capacity 209, 218, 227
  debt service ratio (DSR) 147, 148,
  192–5, 209, 225
  external debt 5, 14, 15, 29, 41, 45,
  47, 55, 58–60, 63, 120, 187, 209
debtor 2, 21, 25, 26–8, 37, 38, 42, 43,
  46, 77, 147, 155
  debtor countries 2, 28, 37, 43, 47, 53,
  57, 78, 164
deficit countries 32, 33, 69
deflation 14, 85, 93, 95, 106, 107, 145,
  175, 177
  deflationary pressure 142
deposit insurance 13, 114, 117, 137,
  144, 145, 152, 168, 173, 174

Deutsch Bank 77
devaluation 86, 95, 106
default 11, 13, 14, 26, 41, 42, 74, 93,
  101, 130, 131, 142, 156, 158, 164,
  187, 191, 193, 195
  default probability 191, 192
developing countries 1–6, 16, 21, 29,
  32–4, 37, 41–9, 51–5, 62, 69, 72,
  78, 117, 120, 126, 128, 142, 143,
  147, 148, 156, 160, 187, 195, 224
  non-oil developing countries 147
disbursement 58, 64
disclosure of information 12, 14,
  169–74, 178, 181, 184, 185
discriminant model 15, 188
  discriminant analysis 191–4, 196,
  199, 202, 225–27
displacement 174
diversification 11, 88, 156

early warning model (EWM) 208, 210,
  212, 214–16, 218, 219
Eastern Europe 21, 27, 51, 72, 73
Eaton, J. 133, 134
Economic Commission for Latin
  America (ECLA) 22
Economist, The 148, 158, 161
Economist Intelligence Unit
  (EIU) 210, 211, 220
efficiency 88
Efron, B. 202, 221
equity 2, 27–9, 74, 85
  equity capital 169
euphoria 174, 175
Eurocurrency market 191
Eurocurrency spread 192
Eurodollar market 6, 52, 77
Euromarket 21, 59, 70, 71, 77, 117,
  125–7, 147
  Standing Committee on
  Euromarket 150
Euromoney 15, 41, 190, 191
Evans, P. 103, 104
exchange rate 4, 7, 8, 16, 34, 47, 59,
  66, 84, 85, 87, 98, 120, 123
  exchange control 86, 123, 225
  exchange crisis 4
  fixed exchange rate 7, 8, 85, 86–9,
  91, 94, 95, 101, 105, 109
  flexible (floating) 7, 8, 87–9, 94, 95,
  98, 101, 105, 109, 115, 122
  fluctuating exchange rate 96
expected rates 4

exposure 42, 51, 65, 70, 72, 116, 127, 131, 142, 148, 191
Extended Fund Facility (EFF) 49

Fama, E. 103, 104
Feder, G. 161, 191–4, 199, 211, 214, 221
Federal Reserve (FED) 60, 70, 71, 73, 115, 154, 190
  Federal Reserve Act 114
  Federal Reserve Bank of New York 85
  Federal Reserve Deposit Insurance Corporation (FDIC) 145
fees 25, 26, 39, 78, 93
  service and management fee 191
Fetter, F. W. 162
financial crisis 44, 54, 93, 108, 113–17, 136, 142, 154, 164, 177
  international financial crisis 9, 131
financial externalities 43, 52
financial gearing 174
financial stability 119, 122, 128, 147
  international financial stability 114, 132, 139
financial system 2, 28, 88, 178
  international financial system 2, 6, 9–11, 51, 117, 118, 138
First Interstate 75
Fisher, I 116, 134
Fisk, C. 195, 221
Fitzgerald, D. 10, 136–9
foreign exchange 26, 64, 156
  foreign exchange intervention 109
  foreign exchange reserve 35, 130
fragility 9, 10, 116–18, 122, 123, 136, 137, 139
Frank, C. R. 192, 221
fraud 13, 83, 175
free ride 9, 11, 115, 128, 131, 132, 159, 160
Frenkel, J. A. 133, 134
Franklin National Bank 150
Friedman, B. M. 99, 104
Friedman, M. 7, 87, 95, 97, 103, 104, 108, 117, 134, 173, 174, 183
full employment 83

General Arrangement to Borrow (GAB) 51
General Theory 83
Germany (West) 24, 70, 77
Gersovitz, M. 133, 134
general acceptability 89

General Agreement on Tariffs and Trade (GATT) 87, 127
Glass Steagall Banking Act 114
Goldberg, L. R. 218, 221
gold standard 7, 8, 83–7, 96, 98, 100, 105
  gold convertibility 61, 85, 87
  gold stock 87, 93
Goodman, S. H. 189, 190, 221
Gordon, R. J. 97, 104
government 3, 7–9, 22, 23, 26, 27, 35, 38, 41, 42, 64, 65, 73, 77, 84–90, 92, 93, 94, 101, 108, 158, 160
  government involvement 169
  role of government 96, 107, 168
Gregory, T. E. 106, 111
Gresham's Law 91
Griffith-Jones, S. 10, 11, 12, 141, 142, 162
Grubel, M. 161, 162
Guarantee Loan Fund (GLF) 6, 7, 8
Gruth, W. 158, 162
Guttentag, J. 129, 130, 134, 137, 138, 154, 155, 162

Hardy, G. 219, 222
Harrod, R. 86, 104, 110, 133, 134
hedge finance 116, 117
Heffernan, S. 9, 10, 113, 134, 139, 167
Herring, R. 129, 130, 134, 137, 138, 154, 155, 162
Hicks, J. R. 107, 108, 111
Higgon, R. 110, 111
Hirsch, F. 182, 183
Ho, T. 13, 17, 175, 176, 183
Hughes, M. 162

ICIDI 158, 162
import/reserve ratio 192, 193
indexation 66
industrialised countries 3, 4, 31, 34, 41, 42, 46, 47, 54, 61, 154
inefficient 13, 22, 23
inflation 2, 4, 5, 22–4, 33, 45, 46, 48, 50, 66, 67, 87, 90, 93, 95, 193
Inoue, H. 189, 221
insolvency 73–5, 116, 130, 137, 172, 179
Institute for International Finance (IIF) 128
Institutional Investor 15, 188, 190, 191, 218, 219, 224, 227
  Institutional Investor index 192, 214, 219

interbank market 33, 52, 70, 79, 168, 170, 181
international interbank market 148
interest rate 2–5, 16, 22, 24, 25, 32–4, 37, 41, 47, 48, 53, 54, 59–63, 66, 71, 72, 77, 84, 85, 100, 101, 120, 123, 147
interest rate pegging 98
floating interest rate 143
interest spread 92
international banks 4, 51, 65, 66, 70, 72, 73, 136, 137, 147, 154, 190, 210
international banking system 123, 127
International Borrowing System (IBS) 5, 58, 61, 63–6
International Central Bank (ICB) 2, 9, 10, 16, 17, 28, 113–15, 119, 122, 123, 127, 128, 130–2, 136, 137, 139, 146, 168
International Clearing Union (ICU) 122
international debt 1, 16, 21, 70, 71
international debt crisis 1
international debt problem 116
International Economic Appraisal Service (IEAS) 210, 211, 220
international financial market 3, 46, 48, 51, 52
International Financial Statistics (IFS) 195, 210
international monetary arrangements 84, 101
International Monetary Fund (IMF) 1, 3–6, 12, 23–5, 35, 38, 39, 41–4, 49–54, 57, 58, 61–3, 67, 69, 73–9, 115, 118–23, 131, 132, 134, 145, 156, 159, 162, 165, 167
IMF Article of Agreement 123
IMF quota 25
international monetary system 1, 35
international regime 8, 96
international reserve 5, 59, 147
investment 5, 22, 23, 27, 32, 52, 58–60, 67, 73, 77, 78, 88, 100, 120
irrational 12, 13, 36, 42, 168, 174, 176

jack-knife approach 203, 205
Japan 70, 77
Johnson, H. G. 13, 134
Johnson Matthey 168
Just, R. 192, 193, 194, 221

Keynes, J. M. 7–9, 83, 84, 86, 90, 91,

95, 96, 100, 103–8, 110, 111, 122, 134, 175
Keynesian 84, 175
Kiddy, W. A. 111
Kindleberger, C. P. 133, 134, 141, 142, 153, 162, 174, 183
Korea 23

Lachenbruch, P. A. 196, 197, 203, 205, 222
Lal, D. 158, 162
Langoni, C. G. 3, 41
Larosiere, J. 39
Latin America 216
Latin American countries 1, 21, 22, 24, 51, 58, 62, 72, 73, 156, 165, 218
lender of last resort (LLR) 2, 6–14, 28, 70, 77, 93, 94, 101, 108, 114, 117, 129, 130, 139, 141–54, 164, 167, 168, 173–84
International Lender of Last Resort (ILLR) 10–12, 16, 17, 136, 137, 139, 141–3, 146, 148, 151, 153–8, 160, 164
Libor (London Interbank Offered Rate) 59, 71, 189
less developed countries (LDG) 2–4, 11, 12, 31, 45, 48, 50, 54, 55, 57, 61, 155, 157, 158, 160, 165, 210, 211, 219
lifeboat 14, 179, 180, 182
Lipton, M. 10–12, 141, 155, 162
liquid asset 32, 185
liquidity 3, 12, 35, 41, 43–6, 49, 51, 52, 55, 70, 75, 84, 90, 116, 129, 149, 151, 164, 165, 172
Lira, P. P. 4, 5, 57
loan 2, 22, 24–6, 33, 42, 52, 58, 62–5, 69–74, 78, 93, 121, 130, 156, 177, 191
offshore loans 125
logit analysis 193, 194, 199
Lucas, R. 110

McKinnon, R. 124, 134
McMahon, C. W. 149, 153, 158, 162
McNamara, R. 155, 162
Macmillan Committee 107
Manufacturers Hanover 75
Mascora, A. 101, 104
maturity 25, 32, 39, 71, 72, 77, 79, 188, 192, 193
Mayo, A. L. 193, 209

medium of exchange 7–9, 89, 90, 92, 96, 101, 107, 108
Meltzer, A. H. 1, 2, 6–9, 21, 83, 105, 107–9, 111
Merril, J. 190, 222
Merrill Lynch 27
Mexico 1, 5, 21–4, 29, 34, 35, 41, 44, 51, 58, 62, 65, 72–4, 77, 117, 147, 155, 156, 158, 165, 216
Miller, R. G. 203, 222
Minsky, H. P. 13, 115, 134, 139, 174, 175, 183
monetary arrangements 7, 8, 60, 84, 86, 87–9, 94, 100, 101
monetary authorities 35, 85, 94, 95
monetary policy 15, 25
  international monetary policy 110
monetary regime 97, 98, 101, 102
monetary standard 6, 7, 83, 84, 110
monetary system 83, 84, 88, 92, 95, 101
money growth 8, 25, 95–100, 102, 109, 110
moral hazard 9, 115, 128–30, 132, 142, 155, 159, 178
moratorium 3, 5, 34, 62, 65
Morgan Guaranty 75, 147, 162
Morning Post 106
Morse, J. 61
mismanagement 5, 23, 62
multinational organisations 48, 55

Nagatoni, K. 133, 135
Nagy, P. 190, 222
nominal money 8
Nie, N. H. 222
Nixon, Richard 61, 87
Norman, M. 85

OECD 29, 37
onerous 11, 57
  onerous term 143, 144, 146, 158, 159
oil 1, 2, 5, 6, 16, 21–3, 27, 31, 34, 60, 62, 69, 73, 77, 165
  oil exporter 1, 21, 148, 160
  oil importer 1, 21
  oil price 1, 2, 5, 6, 22, 23, 27, 31, 34, 120, 155, 156, 165
O'Neill, T. J. 202, 222
OPEC 2, 32, 69
  OPEC funds 148
  non-OPEC countries 21, 62
outstanding debt 22, 23, 25, 70, 77
overborrowing 3, 36, 43
overlending 2, 42, 43

panic 12, 13, 16, 17, 28, 93, 144, 170, 171, 173–6
penal rate 158
Phylaktis, K. 12, 164
Pinches, G. E. 197, 202, 204, 222
Poland 21, 25, 29, 41, 73, 74, 158
Ponzi 13, 25, 116, 117, 139
  Ponzi finance 174, 175
pooling of information 128, 132
Press, S. J. 202, 222
Price, L. D. 14, 184
production of money 8, 92, 96
  private production of money 7, 89, 92, 93, 108
  public production of money 7, 89
protectionism 4, 16, 24, 47

Quinn, B. 2, 31

Radner, R. 128, 135
rating index 192
rational 12, 67, 170, 175, 176
  rational assessment 169
  rational expectations 176
  rational society 168, 174, 176, 184
recession 32, 72, 85, 93, 121, 157
recovery 37, 41, 63, 142, 143, 155, 156
recycling 2, 34, 69, 70, 148
Redmond J. 106, 111
Reid, M. 179, 183
repudiation 79
rescheduling 6, 10, 15, 38, 42, 45, 47–50, 53, 69, 73, 75–9, 117, 121, 130–2, 142, 157, 187, 190, 192–6, 209, 211, 213, 214, 216, 219, 224
resources 4, 5, 31, 43, 46, 48, 52, 59, 61
revulsion 175
Rimlinger, F. 195, 221
risk 10, 12, 13, 16, 38, 42, 44, 49, 51–3, 88–94, 101, 102, 147, 226
  credit risk 192
  risk of default 94, 116, 191
  risk premium 189
  risk of rescheduling 208, 225, 227
Robinson, J. N. 190, 222
Rohatyn, F. 158, 162
Romania 21, 158
Ross, K. 191, 192, 214, 221
Russell, A. H. 195, 221

Saini, K. 193, 194, 202, 209–11, 222
Sargen, N. 193, 194, 203, 222
Saunders, A. 13, 17, 117, 135, 175, 176, 183

savings 4, 59, 66, 92
  social saving 93
Sayers, R. S. 167, 183
Schmidt, Wilson 26
Schwartz, A. J. 93, 97, 102, 104, 117,
  134, 164, 166
SDR 59, 120, 128, 167
secondary banking crisis 31
Security Pacific 75
Sharpe, W. F. 183
Short, B. K. 192, 221
Solow, R. M. 170, 174, 177, 183
solvency 3, 35, 73, 74, 154, 164, 177,
  185, 219
Southard, F. A. 119, 135
sovereign 84
  sovereign borrower 57, 187
  sovereign debt 11, 14, 15, 26, 158,
    159, 188, 224
  sovereign insolvency 72
  sovereign lending 34, 117, 139
  sovereign loan 116, 117, 128, 129, 169
  sovereign risk 156, 189
speculative finance 116
Spero, J. E. 162
standard of value 7, 8, 89, 90, 92, 96,
  101
sterling 85, 106, 107
Stiglitz, J. E. 128, 135
Strakosch, Sir Henry 106
Strong, B. 85
supervision 141–3, 157, 159, 160
  international supervision 159
swindling 175
Switzerland 77
syndicated loans 32
  syndicated lending 148
Syrquin, M. 227

Taffler, R. J. 14, 15, 187, 195, 197,
  202, 204, 205, 212, 218, 223, 247
Taylor, H. 158, 162
Thompson, J. K. 190, 223
Time 106
Toronto 41, 42, 49, 51, 62

Toynbee, A. J. 103, 104
transfer of resources 5, 34, 36,
  57–66
treasury 88, 93
Tschoegle, A. E. 202, 221

uncertainty 2, 14, 25, 26, 36, 42, 47,
  48, 54, 60, 83–9, 91–6, 101, 102,
  148, 153, 155–60, 169, 185, 186
underwriting 73
unemployment 85, 86, 106
United States (US) 2, 15, 24, 25, 28,
  47, 51, 57, 59, 61, 63, 73, 85, 87,
  88, 93, 95, 97, 109, 110, 114, 117,
  127, 168, 218
  US banks 190
  US dollar 1–3, 7, 23, 34, 37, 42, 43,
    52, 62, 63, 69, 70, 72, 74, 77, 85,
    87, 106
unit of account 92

velocity growth 8, 95, 98–100, 102
  monetary velocity 97
Venezuela 74, 147
Viner, J. 85, 102, 104

Wallich, H. 148, 163
Watson, M. W. 176, 183
Whitley, A. 158, 163
Williamson, J. 122, 135
Wilson Committee 31
Wilson, S. 202, 222
Wood, G. 8, 9, 104, 183
World Bank 26, 58, 64, 122, 163, 193,
  210
World Bank's Annual Report Statistical
  Annex 58
World Conference on Economic and
  Social Order 57
Wright, W. F. 218, 223

Yugoslavia 21, 27, 72

Zeeman, E. C. 176, 183
Zombanakis, M. 6, 38, 69, 75